THE BIG 50

BOSTON RED SOX

THE BIG 50

BOSTON RED SOX

The Men and Moments that Made the Boston Red Sox

Evan Drellich

Library of Congress Cataloging-in-Publication Data available upon request.

This book is available in quantity at special discounts for your group or organization. For further information, contact:

Triumph Books LLC
814 North Franklin Street
Chicago, Illinois 60610
(312) 337-0747
www.triumphbooks.com

Printed in U.S.A.
ISBN: 978-1-62937-565-6

Design by Andy Hansen
All photos are courtesy of AP Images

For Mary, Linda, and Steve

[Contents]

[Foreword]

I'm not the most visible guy in Boston these days. I love my second life, raising my kids and taking jiujitsu classes. I'm not dying to be in the dugout. I told people when John Farrell was let go that I wouldn't manage the Red Sox for anything less than $1 billion, but I really do miss the city, the fans.

You can't find a better time to arrive in Boston than when I did in 2004. Two rings in my first four years were incredible. I don't think people remember this as much as my dugout fight with Manny Ramirez—for the record, he swung his helmet at me first and hit me on the chin—but the best I ever played was during the 2007 American League Championship Series. People still tell me they think I should have been the AL's Most Valuable Player in 2008, when I finished third in the voting. Some guys are just adamant. They're funny about it, but I'm like, "Dustin Pedroia got it. It's okay. It's all good. We're good."

The circumstances were a little different when I was traded to the Chicago White Sox in 2012. I knew I was being dealt, but I wanted to go to a California team, and two were in the mix. My wife, Julie, was seven-and-a-half months pregnant. I was upset that after 11 years playing with the organization since the day I was drafted—after undergoing multiple surgeries, playing hurt, doing all that stuff—you see the business side. That was tough. I had no connection to the Red Sox for a time. Then you finally get to a point in your life where you realize you're one of many to go through this. And it's all good.

I miss driving down Storrow and just feeling like, *Wow, this is home for me. This is everything.* I miss seeing that Citgo sign and seeing Fenway, just having that guy on the street go, "Hey, Youk, how ya fucking doing?" in a thick accent. Honestly, I get goose bumps just thinking about the energy the city has. People will come up to me when I'm there and just say the nicest things. There was a ton of positive reinforcement with people acknowledging that you gave it your all. That's exactly it: I just wanted to do everything I could to play for that city and win. And we did. In turn, the people saying thank you mean everything to me. It's like, no, thank *you*. There were days that I felt like I was too injured to play, but I knew that the energy from the fans would fuel the adrenaline I needed to go out there.

My call-up in '04 was a whirlwind of emotion and craziness. There was too much going on to really appreciate the history unfolding. The attitude of the guys that year was: well, what does The Curse have to do with us? We're here in the moment. Babe Ruth's curse has nothing to do with us. We're here now. All we got to do is win.

And, quite honestly, I was just trying to survive. You're trying to show them that you're good enough to play at the major league level. You go from being flat broke to getting a paycheck biweekly that was probably double what I made all year in the minors. You're just trying to follow the rules of being a rookie: get the beer, get this, get that, sit here, don't do this, don't do that.

On that team everyone was kind of a veteran. In sports, when veterans are joking with you and making fun of you and teasing you and doing whatever, it's an honor. When they don't talk to you, when they don't tease you, that's when you worry they don't like you. So, I always took it. And I always joke that they made me feel really good while making me feel really bad at times.

Probably the most nervous I ever felt on a baseball field was that year when I came in to replace Bill Mueller against the Anaheim Angels during the American League Division Series. I was a rookie, playing third base at Angel Stadium with the Rally Monkey going, the thunder sticks banging. It was serious. I had never been in that position—or in a major league playoff game. But playing in Boston—even the little I had to that point—helped because that energy didn't faze me.

The hardest thing for me in my career is that I wanted to be an average Joe. But you can't be an average Joe playing for the Boston

Red Sox. This is probably going to sound like the dumbest thing that anyone's ever said, but it's actually the truth: I never wanted to be a superstar off the field; I wanted to be a superstar on the field. But if you're a really good baseball player in Boston, you automatically become a super celebrity. You're a celebrity if you're the guy that gets called up because you're on the Red Sox, and everyone knows every single player on the Red Sox. When you start playing better and you become a name and a focal point, you become a super celebrity because it's just the natural way of things in Boston. But it was cool to live through. Looking back now, I reflect and think, *Man, probably the only thing I wish I would have done different was not care as much about the outside world, like listening to things and hearing the noise.* I did read the papers sometimes because they were in the clubhouse. Even if you didn't, a friend or a parent or a cousin would tell you about a negative story, and then you'd read it.

I was always trying to prove my worth, which is the reason I got where I did. But that attitude was also a negative in a lot of ways because I was always fighting and being combative. Having a chip on your shoulder is a great mentality, but it also can be a detriment off the field. I was always trying to prove my worth in my job and maybe I was always trying to prove my worth outside of my job. That's always a hard dynamic. But it also played well in a city where fans always want you to be the best you can be. Chip-on-your-shoulder guys—like my brother-in-law, Tom Brady; Dustin Pedroia; Trot Nixon—connect well. Trot was a first rounder, but he had that mentality. You need a couple of superstars, but you need those grinders because this city rallies. This city lives on it. Julian Edelman's another example.

I was catching passes for my brother-in-law in California. He said I don't have as good a hands as Gronk, but I'm right there with him. We talk a little bit about Boston. Tommy's become this figure that's larger than life. And because of his personality, he takes it on really well. He's not really an extrovert in a lot of ways where he wants to be going to parties and all that. He's just a football addict who loves the game, loves competing. We'll do little sports back and forth, play ping pong or whatever. I idolize him off the field, the way he handles press conferences. Someone will write a bad story about him, and he takes it on the chin and doesn't say anything. He just goes out and does his job. Baseball's a little tougher when it comes to the press. We talk about baseball vs. football, too. He told me, "I talk on Wednesday and Sunday. I talk twice a week, plus radio on Monday, too." I said, "Man, that's a great thing. Baseball it's like every day."

I think the reason people like me in Boston is just because I played as hard as I could. And I wasn't the sexiest guy on the field. People could relate in a sense, like, wow, he doesn't resemble a superstar or have an Alex Rodriguez-like look or all that. He just looks like a normal dude that goes out here and grinds away every single day. My biggest fans probably were the working class folks. Running down to first base hard every single time is what's going to endear you to the fans in Boston. When you show that, they like that you care—even when you suck. There's a small group of fans who are going to find the negative regardless, but for the most part, I think people loved how I played because they felt like they could oddly relate to me. As I get older and more removed from baseball, I think I appreciate Boston more because the people still appreciate me.

Winning in that Red Sox culture, especially when I was there, was the spotlight of all spotlights. I enjoyed two of the best seasons in franchise history, and they're recollected here. That era of Boston sports brought so much focus and attention to the city. When you're going through it, you're trying to just go out there and play. It was a big deal back then. Years later, I'm glad I had an opportunity to reflect on it in these pages.

—Kevin Youkilis
Boston Red Sox, 2004–12
Three-time All-Star
Two-time World Series champion

THE BIG 50

BOSTON RED SOX

1

2004

Every night Fenway Park is filled with children too young to recall the exorcism. Kids who weren't around when New England danced for the very first time on the corpse of Yankee mystique. Some teens today may be old enough to carry scant memories of the greatest comeback in postseason history, when the Sox—still the only team to scale a 3–0 deficit—trailed the New York Yankees in the 2004 American League Championship Series before winning the pennant. Those teens may even remember first baseman Doug Mientkiewicz squeezing the final out in the World Series for a sweep of the St. Louis Cardinals.

But with each passing year, '04 becomes a memory to fewer and a tale to more. Theo and Tito's discovery of baseball's Excalibur is known to some only through dinner table talk, books, and YouTube. How do you explain the pessimism that once grew like mold across New England, when success has been so abundant this century across all Boston sports? How do you reconstruct the despondence of Red Sox Nation that grew with every loss to the Yankees and every World Series catastrophe? "The thing that sticks in my mind the most is the last out, knowing that we got rid of the burden on every player that passed through the organization," Pedro Martinez said eight years later. "It was a moment of relief for everyone that played the game in Boston. That's probably the biggest one—just getting that last out. I kept thinking about getting that last out, and when [closer Keith Foulke] finally flipped that ball and they called him out, that was it.

"I remember someone telling me, 'My dad passed away last year, and I could die today,' As we were getting off the bus, that person came up to me and said, 'I could die today and I'm at peace. This is all I wanted in my life. I don't want any money. I don't want anything else. All I wanted in my life was to see this trophy coming over.'"

That's extreme and unsurprising but also very indicative of the fanbase's line of thinking. Even in '04 in the immediate aftermath of the bacchanal, there was a sense that nothing else the Red Sox did afterward would matter as much. When nearly a century of unhappiness is attached to one season and one team, how do you cope with the understanding you can never reach that joy again? No, the question isn't new, but about a decade and a half has passed since it first arose in Boston. "Oh my God," Curt Schilling said in 2017. "When you win something like [2004], you always wonder: is the next one gonna take away from this one? We won in '07, [and it] wasn't nearly like '04. We were nine years removed in '13. And I realized after the team won in '13, that there'll never be another 2004."

The bloody sock doesn't lie. Schilling's addition to the group prior to the season was a huge pick-up for Theo Epstein and the Sox as they outmaneuvered the Yankees in an arms race, one that dwarfed the rest of baseball's efforts to stockpile talent. Schilling counted as just another confidence-slinging nut job in a gaggle of them. The '04 Idiots were as talented as they were brash and colorful. With blood seeping into the sock of his injured right ankle, Schilling's performance in Game 6 of the ALCS against the Yankees is one of the most identifiable moments along the craziest ride in Sox history.

A bunch of boring, quiet hitting machines breaking The Curse would have stirred Red Sox Nation. But the eccentricities were almost as outsized as the achievement—and for the better.

It wound up being Martinez's last year with the team before the Hall of Fame ace left via free agency. He was an elder statesman, one who had been on the club since 1998. Martinez pondered...if the team hadn't won the Sox's first title since 1918. "I would have been so disappointed that I came in here with a purpose, and that was the purpose," Martinez said in 2012. "I was called in to build the team around me as the ace of the team. It took me until the last year to actually finally get it, but I could easily say, 'Mission accomplished.' I've actually been to the Green Monster many times...Everybody normally has the history of signing the Green Monster. I refused to until I won it for Boston."

Martinez brought a good luck charm around that was a little out of the ordinary. Nelson De La Rosa, a diminutive actor from the Dominican Republic who has since passed away, was small enough for Martinez to pick up and hoist during champagne celebrations. "It was pretty close to being a perfect match," Kevin Millar said in 2012. "It's hard to do with all the different salaries and egos and stats and everything we create in the world now, fantasy baseball. It was a good match, man. And like I said, we weren't the best players. Believe me, you're not drafting Millar, Mueller, Cabrera, and Bellhorn for your starting infield. It's just the way it was. Keith Foulke throwing 74 mph, dominating the game."

They would throw back shots before games. They would huddle in the same Jacuzzi. Martinez told a story of Millar, Manny Ramirez, and Johnny Damon all taking a dip together. "Can you imagine Jeter, Posada, and Bernie with Mariano jumping in?" Millar asked rhetorically of the Yankees stars of the day.

Epstein, who was in just his second year running the team, found the finishing touches with a young, hungry front office. (Most of those executives, like Theo himself, have moved on. But some core members still remain in Boston like Brian O'Halloran, Raquel Ferreira and Zack Scott. Others, like Jed Hoyer and Amiel Sawdaye, are in top positions elsewhere.) "Whether it was a defense mechanism for survival or just sheer immaturity, we surrounded ourselves. We created this group of like half a dozen, eight of us who were similarly situated in life," Epstein said. "We worked together at the Red Sox for nine months going into it and we just leaned on each other. We worked 80-100 hour weeks, we went out, ate all our meals together, we lived together in spring training, and all we talked about was how to make the Red Sox better."

A member of the Red Sox organization noted before the Chicago Cubs and Cleveland Indians played the World Series in 2016 that they hoped the Cubs—run by Epstein and working on a 108-year

First baseman Doug Mientkiewicz and catcher Jason Varitek jump into closer Keith Foulke's arms after the Red Sox sweep the St. Louis Cardinals in 2004, giving Boston its first World Series title since 1918.

title drought—would lose. They didn't wish ill on Epstein. They simply wanted the story to keep going, the drama to simmer for the betterment of the game.

The Cubs won, and the arc reached its apex. The 2016 Cubs, like the 2004 Red Sox, are Jim and Pam's first kiss in Season 2 of *The Office*. You can have a show and romantic intrigue afterward, but nothing will be as gripping. The Sox won again in 2007 and 2013. For the Red Sox, though, lifetimes came and went prior to '04. Generations passed after the 1918 World Series title. The only way to replicate a climate like 2004's would be time. Mix in the sale of Babe Ruth and just how successful Ruth and the Yankees were as the Sox floundered, and it's hard to imagine a parallel ever existing for this franchise—even a few centuries from now. "I got a call right after the series from Bill Bradley," former Red Sox president Larry Lucchino said. "And he said, 'Larry, I have only one suggestion for you.'"

Bradley, who went to Princeton with Lucchino, played in the NBA and went on to become a U.S. senator. "I said, 'What's that, Bill?'" Lucchino said. "He said, 'Retire. Right now. Retire.' I said, 'No, I'm not going to retire right now.' He said, 'It'll never get this good again.' And so I did not take his advice, thankfully, but I think he meant it quite sincerely.

"There was a woman who said to me after 2004, 'I want to thank you,'" Lucchino said. "'Because of you I have experienced every possible human emotion.' And so I think sort of every possible human emotion came to us in either '03 or '04. And from '02 to '04, we went through every possible human emotion. So the sense of release, relief, and satisfaction was enormous at the end of '04, even though many of us were too sleep deprived to fully appreciate the moment."

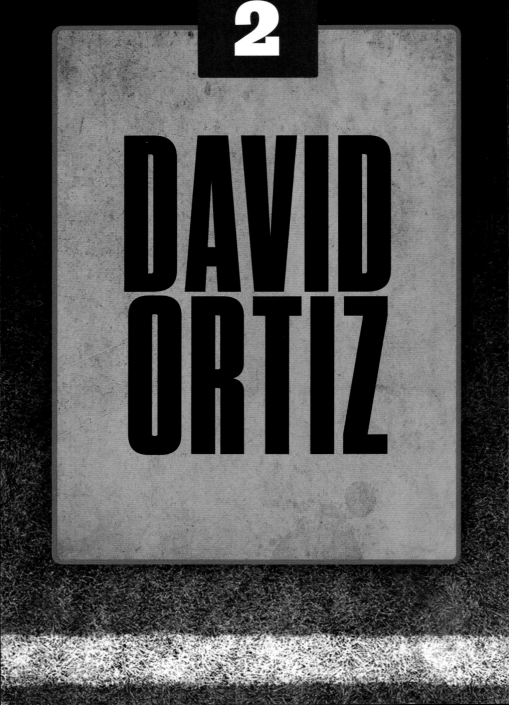

2

DAVID ORTIZ

Had David Ortiz hit 483 of his 541 home runs—plus another 17 in the postseason—as a quiet and shy member of the Red Sox, he would still be beloved. Just not in this way. We wouldn't have bridges and roads in his name. In his final year, gifts would not have lined every road city, and the entire American League All-Star team may not have gathered for his words. He told that group of All-Stars in 2016 that he had come to value passing on lessons in the game more than hitting home runs, even walk-offs. Those game-ending moments are what Ortiz is remembered for more than anything else—that and his stand-alone status as a Sox player who won three rings this century.

Many believe Big Papi will wind up in Cooperstown. He could well get in on the first ballot, too. Ortiz's career .455 average, .576 on-base percentage, and .795 slugging percentage are the best marks in World Series history for anyone with at least 50 plate appearances. But would his candidacy seem so obvious if practically everyone—from media, to the fans, and down to Ortiz's teammates—did not always gravitate to him so?

Even in the world of star athletes, Ortiz became larger than life. When the guy retired, the Sox couldn't give him just the usual alumnus contract. They signed him to a lifetime deal.

Charisma, like many of Ortiz's skills, cannot be taught. Almost always in public, Ortiz appears to be smiling. Faking that kind of consistent happiness wouldn't be easy, particularly in Boston, where the winters are cold, and the talk radio hosts are scathing.

But there were lessons early in Ortiz's life that had helped him in a foreign land, skills beyond the personality with which he was born. Ortiz, a left-handed slugger from the Dominican Republic, signed with the Seattle Mariners for a $10,000 signing bonus in 1992. Whether it was just learning English or something otherwise, most baseball teams did not provide education in the minor leagues at the time Ortiz was coming up in the early-to-mid 1990s. But Ortiz had a head start on some of his teammates. "My parents, I don't know if they knew I was going to be who I am," Ortiz said in 2011. "But they always wanted me to learn."

Back when he was drafted, Ortiz played translator, too. In *Papi: My Story,* Ortiz told of a relationship one of his minor league friends had with a beautiful woman. The only issue is they couldn't speak to one another, so the bilingual Ortiz became a most necessary third wheel.

Ortiz grew up in a Dominican Republic town where the drug trade was particularly rampant, but his parents, Angela Rosa Arias and Americo Enrique Ortiz (or Leo), kept him disciplined. Basketball was his first love, but his father focused on his son's excellent hand-eye coordination and believed he would become a big league ballplayer.

Ortiz's mother, Angela, died in a car crash in 2002. Every time he crossed home plate and pointed to the sky, he was pointing to her. She was always on his mind. "When you are going through celebrations, when you are going through good moments, and I've got all of my family on the field, my dad and my wife and my kids and my sisters, I felt like something was missing," Ortiz said after his last regular-season game when the Red Sox feted him. "I was very close with my mom...Emotion comes through when you start thinking about a member of the family that's no longer around. Every time I talk about my mom, it happens. I think it's pretty normal for all of us. But I got it off my chest, and the celebration continued. I really appreciate how everything went down and how everything has been since Day One."

Day One in Boston happens to tie back to the year Ortiz lost his mother in 2002. That was his final season with the Minnesota Twins, the only other big league team he played for. Minnesota picked him up as a minor leaguer from the Mariners back in a 1996 trade for big league third baseman Dave Hollins. Ortiz, who became known for swings with huge recoil and slow trots around the bases, showed plenty of promise in Minnesota. But the Twins didn't see his full potential. It didn't help that Ortiz clashed with his first big league manager, Tom Kelly.

Minnesota simply let Ortiz walk after the '02 season, releasing him rather than paying him the roughly $2 million he likely would have received in salary arbitration. To that point Ortiz was a career .266 hitter. But he carried an .809 on-base plus slugging percentage (OPS) and had just finished a career-high 20-homer season in '02, a sign of what was to come.

Letting Ortiz become a free agent was a huge blunder. "There's no hiding that one," former Twins general manager Terry Ryan told MLB.com's Rhett Bollinger. "You can put that one in there and lock it down. I'm not running from it. I'm proud of what he's done. Obviously, it was a mistake. The guy has been a great representation of the Boston Red Sox and Major League Baseball for a long time. And it's Boston's gain and Minnesota's loss. And I take full responsibility."

In his first offseason running the Red Sox, Theo Epstein snatched up Ortiz, who also had Pedro Martinez lobbying for him. (Some, though, have said it's been exaggerated over time how much Martinez influenced the decision.) Ortiz didn't receive full playing time immediately, but his greatness started to shine through in 2003 with his first 30-homer season.

Ortiz was the only player to finish in the top five in American League MVP voting every year from 2003 to 2007. But as is the case for many things Red Sox, 2004 is when it all really came together. After Dave Roberts' steal helped tie it in the ninth inning, Ortiz's walk-off homer in the 12th inning of Game 4 of the 2004 American League Championship Series against the New York Yankees put the Sox in position to come back from down three games to none in the series. The next night, Ortiz had a walk-off single in Game 5. He was named the ALCS MVP and then homered in his first at-bat in the World Series sweep of the St. Louis Cardinals.

In the 2007 American League Division Series against the Angels, Ortiz walked six times and homered twice in a three-game sweep. In

2013 he was the World Series MVP after going 11-for-16 with two home runs and eight walks; four of them were intentional. The Sox probably wouldn't have even made the '13 World Series had Ortiz not slugged a game-tying grand slam against the Detroit Tigers in Game 2 of the ALCS. With the Sox down 5–1, Ortiz parked a splitter from Joaquin Benoit in the home bullpen at Fenway Park, as Tigers outfielder Torii Hunter went tumbling over the wall in vain.

Ortiz's health caught up to him. Bad heels and feet kept him in pain at the end of his career, but he went out with an incredible final season, leading the majors in doubles with 48 and in OPS at 1.021 in 2016. "I'm super proud of what I have done," Ortiz said. "I was a big-time underdog. I wasn't somebody who came to the big leagues with this really ridiculous talent. It wasn't that bright at the beginning. But I figured one thing out: if you keep working, don't listen to people because people are always going to have things to say. People are always going to judge you. People are always going to put you down—not everybody, but some people. The reality is that you are the owner of your own future. It's all about how hungry you are. It's all about how good you want to be. It's all about how successful you want to be. That has been my career, and I'm happy and proud of the things that I have done, but that's all I can control."

Ortiz could never fully escape the specter of his inclusion on a positive drug test list from 2003, a list that was supposed to remain private because the tests were administered with the stated intent to only see how many people tested positive. The league and the union were trying to determine whether to institute full-time testing. It was never clear what exactly Ortiz tested positive for, and Rob Manfred, the commissioner when Ortiz retired, seemed to go out of his way in 2016 to cast doubt on whether Ortiz did anything wrong. It will probably never be known what the drug test detected—or if it was a false positive. That lack of clarity is the largest blemish on a legacy that nonetheless stands as perhaps the most important career in Red Sox history.

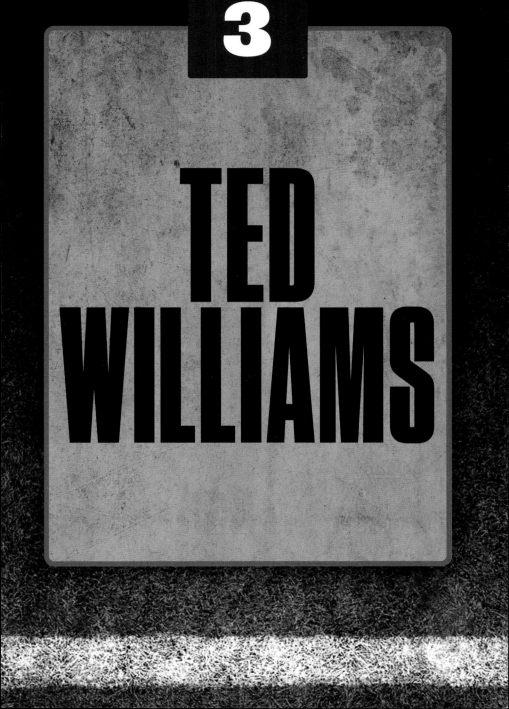

3

TED WILLIAMS

We have all been told by someone our senior—by someone never more sure of anything else—that this player or another set the standard. In a game that occasionally lives more for the past than the present, Ted Williams is separated not only by his superb swing and service to his country, but also how our collective memories have duly lionized him. We must acknowledge the limitations of what we have not personally seen or followed. "The perpetual left fielder of the Red Sox was famous in a time when heroes were constructed with the imagination and with words rather than force-fed and sold through a 21-inch or 56-inch color screen," Leigh Montville wrote in the biography, *Ted Williams*. "The tape measure of the normal did not exist. He did things once, and you saw them once in person or heard them once on the radio or read about them forever. And they grew."

This is no challenge to Williams' standing as the archetypal hitter. It's merely a characterization of how we perceive Teddy Ballgame. The grandeur of any player who came before us is harder to fully comprehend than that of a player we follow now or rooted for as kids. We've seen "the Splendid Splinter" take hacks in video clips over and over. We've heard tales. But for most of us, clips, snippets, tidbits are our only understanding.

Many Hall of Famers prior to the television (and digital) age are accessible only in this manner. Fifty years from now, it'll be easier to fully comprehend David Ortiz's power than it is today to fully appreciate Williams' batting eye because the telecasts in the 21st century are so thorough—and thoroughly available.

In some way The Kid's swing was always a matter of belief. "For virtually all of Ted Williams' 19 big league years, the assembled folk at the ballpark had to report to friends and neighbors what they had seen him do," Montville wrote. "There was no replay. There was no highlights package at 11. How far did the ball go? How mighty was that swing? How mad, exactly, did the Splendid Splinter become?...Word of mouth had to carry the brushfires further."

Yet with Williams the gap between what we fully appreciate and what we do not may be smaller than in the case of any other of his contemporaries or predecessors. Teddy Ballgame's left-handed swing is transcendent, an emblem of mastery easy to comprehend roughly 80 years after his debut in 1939—the same year a major league game was televised for the first time.

For everything that has changed in baseball, the perfection of a swing has not. It is strange but fitting in the context of Red Sox history that one can draw a line from Williams all the way to a young Red Sox fan named Theo Epstein, who will join Williams in Cooperstown for a most different achievement. The resonance of Williams is almost unparalleled. "He was my favorite all-time player," said Epstein, who is far too young to have seen him play during his major league career. "I saw him at one of the Old Timers' Games, saw him take a beautiful cut and swung and missed. You grow up, and there's something so mythical about the guy who wanted to walk down the street and hear people say, 'There's the greatest hitter who ever lived,' and did. Then, the more you read about him and find out about him, the more John Wayne qualities come out. You couldn't read a week's worth of Red Sox coverage in *The Globe* without getting three or four Ted Williams references right. He was sort of the standard by which everything was defined in Red Soxdom. So I just grew up with him as my favorite player. I actually had a Babe Ruth poster in my room when I was really young. But then after understanding [the impact of moving from] Boston to New York the way he did, I took it down and put up a Ted Williams poster."

Still to this day as president of the Chicago Cubs, Epstein has a huge Williams photo hanging in his office. "Him as a rookie, actually on defense kind of jumping up," Epstein said. "Probably it's for a staged baseball card photo, where he's jumping up and trying to make a play with this huge smile on his face. And yeah, I just love it because all the photos you see of him later in his career—after being ground down a little bit by the reality of the games and the media coverage and his own flaws and everything else—you always saw him with his

Ted Williams displays his perfect swing in 1941, the year he hit .406.

head down crossing home plate or focused with a bat in his hands. But you never really saw him smile that much unless he was fishing or doing something else. It's a really cool photo of him with his whole future in front of him, smiling, in front of the Green Monster. It's pretty cool."

The complexity of Williams provides some of his lasting appeal. Or rather the known complexity—the fact that the public was unable to ascertain so much of what makes Williams tick adds to his allure. "It was the center of my heart, hitting a baseball," Williams said in *My Turn At Bat: The Story of My Life* written with John Underwood. "As a kid, I wished it on every falling star: please, let me be the hitter I want to be."

There is permanent allure in a .406 batting average, as Williams famously compiled in 1941 as the last person to eclipse the .400 mark. He was offered a chance by his manager, Joe Cronin, to sit out the final day of the season to preserve the average and instead he went 6-for-8 over the course of the doubleheader. Such a feat—.400—could never happen today. The playing field has leveled with the color barrier broken. Scouting reports are as incisive as they are pervasive. Williams would benefit from those reports and from the improved nutrition and conditioning for the modern game as well. But on balance, he'd lose hits—not gain.

The mark is nonetheless absurd. Williams famously warred with the press and one thing he didn't appreciate was the implication his eyesight was simply given to him. "Sure, I think I had good eyesight, maybe exceptional eyesight, but not *superhuman* eyesight," Williams said in *My Turn At Bat*. "A lot of people have 20–10 vision...[It was because] I was so intense. I saw ducks coming in because I was *intent* on seeing them, I was looking all the time, I was alert for them. And I trained myself from a sandlotter to know that strike zone so I wouldn't be swinging at bad pitches. If as a batter I made a good umpire, it was discipline, not super eyesight."

To hit .344 with a .482 on-base percentage—the all-time record—and a .634 slugging percentage for the course of one's career is even more absurd than batting .406 in a season. Williams never struck out and he still hit for power anyway with 521 home runs. And his age-24 to age-26 seasons (from 1943 to 1945) were given to his country as a Navy pilot. He left baseball again for most of the 1952–53 seasons to fight in Korea as a Marine pilot.

He was forever a patriot and occasionally a jokester and, as Montville chronicled, as erratic and layered as anyone else. That was visible on the field and off. "I have never been regarded especially as a man with great patience. Certainly, as a young player, I had none at all with myself. I was impetuous, I was tempestuous. I blew up. Not acting but *reacting*. I'd get so damned mad, throw bats, kick the columns in the dugout so that sparks flew," he said in *My Turn At Bat*. "I was never able to be dispassionate, to ignore the things people said or wrote or implied. It just wasn't in me. In my heart I don't believe I am any more sensitive to criticism than a lot of athletes, but I am certainly in the upper basket of sensitivity, maybe the top 3 percent. In a crowd of cheers, I could always pick out the solitary boo. I don't mean to say that criticism affected my hitting because the boos always seemed to have the reverse effect."

Williams' childhood in San Diego and his Mexican ancestry on his mother's side were topics that he did not discuss at length. His mother worked for the Salvation Army; his father had a photographic shop, where he worked on passport pictures and the like. Williams loved fishing and malted milk. He was not a good student in school. He certainly was a decent study of pitchers, though. "I don't know how a man wants to be remembered, other than for his achievements," he said in *My Turn At Bat.* "I just haven't thought about it. I believe I am a compassionate man. I believe I'm concerned with people. I don't think I was as concerned or as compassionate in those early days as I am now...I was and am too complex a personality, too much a confusion of boyish enthusiasm and bitter experience to be completely understood by everybody."

PEDRO MARTINEZ

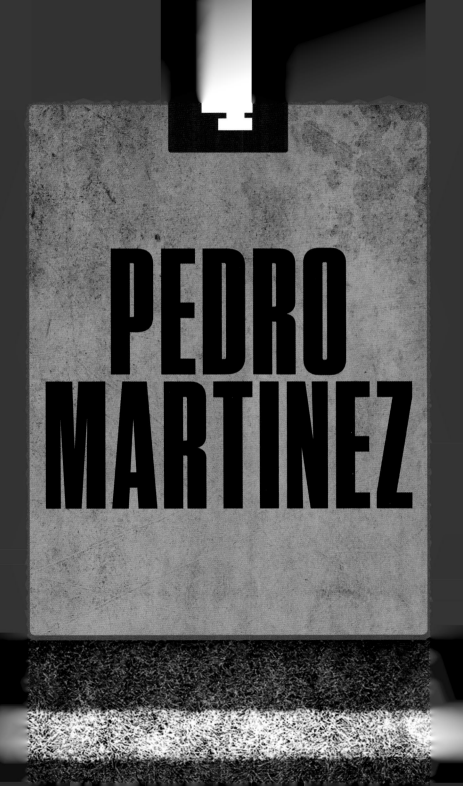

Allow me, your author, to break the fourth wall for this chapter. When I speak of Pedro Martinez, I can still do so through boyhood goggles. When I first became a baseball fan, all I knew were sluggers and demigods. One July night, Pedro slayed them all, and I was hooked. I was just a middle schooler when Pedro was at his peak, and he became my favorite player. He was as compelling to read about as he was to watch. Pedro, the skinny right-hander from the Dominican Republic who once sat under a mango tree with barely enough change to ride the bus, turned my understanding of baseball upside down.

Martinez's power extended beyond the nights where he could strike out 17 Yankees. His gravitas centered on more than the self-assurance required to threaten to wake up a dead Babe Ruth and drill him in the ass. He was my lens to an understanding of what pitching could be, an awakening for a nascent fan. The first All-Star Game I ever watched was in 1999, in the summer before seventh grade. Martinez started that game at Fenway Park. Let me explain why I was even watching it in the first place.

A year earlier, as a 10-year-old in the summer of 1998, I barely knew who Pedro was. Whenever there's a discussion of the steroids era, someone inevitably points out how 'roids revitalized the game, how home runs brought back the fans. I am *that* guy. (So you can thank steroids for this book, then.) I became a baseball fan because of 1998, because of Big Mac and Slammin' Sammy.

When my birthday rolled around in October '98, my late grandfather knew I had just fallen in love with baseball and gave me a framed autograph of Hall of Fame pitcher Carl Hubbell. A lefty for the New York Giants, Hubbell was famous for two things: the unnatural screwball—the rare pitch that requires a great twist of the wrist inward—and for what that screwball did in the 1934 All-Star Game at the Polo Grounds, Hubbell's home park. He struck out five consecutive

American League batters. A murderers' row of Babe Ruth, Lou Gehrig, Jimmie Foxx, Al Simmons, and future Red Sox fixture Joe Cronin. My grandfather was at that game as boy.

Imagine the joy I felt when Hubbell's name flashed on the television screen while Pedro pitched in the 1999 All-Star Game. To begin that night at Fenway Park, Barry Larkin struck out on a hellacious change-up—one that moves like a righty's screwball would. Larry Walker fanned, and so too did Sosa, whose knees buckled meekly on a curve during the at-bat. Unable to catch Pedro's 97 mph heat, Mark McGwire went down to start the second inning to make it four in a row, and Jeff Bagwell K'd later in the second as well.

Pedro didn't K five in a row like Hubbell, but he became the first starter in All-Star Game history to strike out the first four he faced. No one else had even struck out the first three. The strikeout pitches were a swinging change-up (Larkin), looking fastball (Walker), swinging fastball (Sosa), swinging fastball (McGwire), and swinging change-up (Bagwell).

Via Gordon Edes, the Red Sox team historian who was then with *The Boston Globe*, Martinez was asked if he was amazed by his feat that night. "Not really," Martinez said. "That's what makes baseball so interesting. You just never know what will happen. Those guys are some of the best of the world. Anything can happen. That's what makes the game so special."

Martinez's character only enhanced his allure. He has charm and buoyancy combined with a transcendent outlook. "On gameday, first pitch could not come soon enough for me," Martinez said in his memoir, *Pedro*, written with Michael Silverman. "I turned to flowers, my first love, to keep my mind off the clock. In Montreal, I used to walk from my apartment to Crescent Street for lunch at an outdoor restaurant whose balconies were draped with roses and flower boxes. With the sun on my face, I'd sit and gaze at the flowers. In my townhouse in the Jamaica Plain section of Boston, I built a balcony in the back of my unit so I could have space for my garden. On the mornings and early afternoons of my starts, I would dive into my flowerpots and flower beds, clipping dead leaves, weeding and puttering, until it was time to leave for the ballpark."

Such a worldly outlook, which revealed itself during Pedro's playing days in bits and pieces, was catnip for someone of an impressionable age. Martinez inherited his love for flowers from his mother, Leopoldina. "Flowers teach you something," she said in *Pedro*. "They teach you about how to be, how to live inside. The heart of someone is like a flower—a beautiful thing in a person and is an attraction for someone. When Pedro and I found flowers, we would get lost in them."

I believe Martinez's legacy as the greatest pitcher in his prime is safe. Folks can argue Sandy Koufax, and that's fine. I prefer to think of them as complementary. If Koufax has the left arm of God, then Pedro has the right. The cultural importance of both is weighty—Koufax to the Jewish population and Martinez to those of Dominican descent.

The climate of juicing in Pedro's time when mixed with the relatively primitive state of pitching makes for an era that won't be reproduced. Even if hitting spikes to turn-of-the-century levels, today's pitching is better. More home runs were hit in 2017 than in any other season, and 2016 brought the third most. The other two years in the top four—2000 (second) and 1999 (fourth)—were years Pedro won Cy Young awards.

Now, there was considerably more scoring overall in 1999 and 2000 when compared to 2016 and 2017, and it's not like hitters were the only ones using performance-enhancing drugs. The hitting was tremendous. But it's harder to put the ball in play today because high velocity arms and advanced scouting reports are much more prevalent. But if I'm being honest with my childhood self, there are pitchers today who have better pure heat than Pedro, and their breaking balls might move more violently or with later break to boot. (I might dig in on Martinez's change-up; no one has a better change-up.) "Pedro didn't have, I guess, the pure power that some of these guys have," former Sox general manager Theo Epstein said. "He had incredible power to his arsenal, but he didn't, certainly in his Red Sox days, he didn't pitch in the upper 90s. He pitched more in the mid-90s and later in the lower 90s. But you know for sheer perfection of three pitches and the bravado to use them the way he wanted to use them and very artistically and intimidatingly at that, there's probably nobody better. And it didn't last that long. It probably lasted longer than Koufax."

Epstein was the general manager who decided not to bring back Martinez after the 2004 World Series, but Martinez achieved what he set out to do: break The Curse. A Hall of Famer now, Martinez helps out current Red Sox pitchers in spring training and throughout the season. His hold on Red Sox Nation is permanent. When people think of the very best pitcher of all time, many think of Pedro in a Red Sox uniform. I always will.

5

1967

The greatest season in Red Sox history may be one that ended in heartbreak. Isn't that most appropriate for a franchise that for so long was defined by losing? Fifty years later the memory of 1967 hasn't diminished. Time, in fact, seems to have amplified its tale. Those who were around to witness the Impossible Dream are at an age now where childhood memories have been whittled away, but the vignette of shortstop Rico Petrocelli enclosing his hands on a pop-up above his head will be among the last to go. Here's a decent dinner debate: which Red Sox team was more important? The Impossible Dream's ninth-to-first fairy tale—the '67 journey that sprung Red Sox Nation—or the pinnacle of Sox mania in 2004?

It's hard to fathom today what the organization was back in 1967 before Carl Yastrzemski's Triple Crown led a turnaround. It was a sputtering franchise sitting in neutral, if not flying in reverse. But even younger Sox fans, who have known only winning and curse breaking, can appreciate the chicken-and-egg conversation you'll fall into. Because, young reader, if it weren't for the 1967 club, baseball in Boston may have left entirely. Your Idiots would never have come to be. "We were the ones that sparked the fire," 1967 Cy Young winner Jim Lonborg said at Fenway Park in 2017, when the team celebrated its gold anniversary. "And the fire is now Red Sox Nation."

Consider the time period. There was not only peace and love, but also territorial expansion in baseball. The Brooklyn

Dodgers and New York Giants moved west for the 1958 season five years after the former Boston Braves played their first season in Milwaukee. The Sox could have packed their bags, too. "Going back to the '60s when the Red Sox were really doing poorly and all these new ballparks were being built around baseball, [owner] Tom Yawkey was very discouraged for a couple of reasons," late Red Sox historian Dick Bresciani said. "He was trying to rebuild a team, but he thought that he wasn't getting proper support from the state because they had put in the Massachusetts Turnpike about 10 years previously and he wanted an exit [directly to Fenway]. He was quoted a couple of times in the paper, maybe he might have to leave Boston because he couldn't keep competing with teams that were increasing their seating up into the 60,000s, and we were only 33,000-something total at that time. What changed all of his thinking was the miracle pennant of '67. And the fact that the attendance jumped tremendously."

You can thank Yaz and Lonborg and Tony C for keeping the Sox and Fenway Park from disappearing. But the Impossible Dream at the time wasn't a story of baseball economics. At least, that's not what's kept it in the hearts of so many. This was a matter of first love for Baby Boomers and to an extent a perpetual wonder about what could have been.

The Sox fell just short of a championship. St. Louis Cardinals ace Bob Gibson bested them in Game 7 of the World Series. But like the Miracle Mets who would make New York swoon two years later in 1969, no one thought the Sox were supposed to be there to begin with.

Lonborg, the '67 Cy Young winner, suggested he would not have changed the outcome of the World Series. "I don't think some of the magic of this Impossible Dream team would have had the same feeling had we won everything," Lonborg said. "The fact that we got so close and didn't win almost was a better ending than having won it all and then just expecting things to be perfect after that. So, it was bittersweet, but...if I was a writer, I would kind of have written that into the script."

The die-hard Do-Your-Job Patriots fans might find this thinking insane, deeming it a twisted narrative to justify an unfavorable outcome. Others, who may appreciate sports for theater rather than a sense of superiority, should need no convincing that Lonborg is absolutely right. The lack of finality in '67 created a yearning for a winner that grew into a decades-long clamor. The season came out of nowhere, while the '04 team was charged with finishing a job that the 2003 group could not. It'd be hard to call the '04 group a true underdog, but the '67 team was.

A new manager in 1967, Dick Williams, provided a firm voice for a group that went 92–70 after finishing 72–90 the year before and 62–100 two years prior. "When he came into camp, he made a lot of sense," Lonborg said of Williams. "It was all about catching the ball and throwing the ball and making outs, doing it consistently. If you didn't do something properly, you would be talked to in maybe not such a great way. I think sarcasm was one of his defining characteristics. But over time we just realized that you stop making mistakes, and you start doing good plays, and something good's going to happen."

The group assembled by general manager Dick O'Connell was remarkably young. George Scott was 23. So was Mike Andrews, the second baseman. The left side of the infield—Petrocelli and third baseman Joe Foy (who made 106 starts at the hot corner)—were 23 and 24, respectively. Reggie Smith and Tony Conigliaro were just 22 with Yaz being the old man at 27.

But it wasn't until July, when the Sox returned from a road trip with a 10-game win streak and a second-place standing, that they looked at themselves as real contenders. "Up until then I don't think that anyone on the team felt that we had a chance of winning," Yaz said. "And then we had that great road trip...everyone on the team [thought] we were as good as anyone else."

When the Sox landed at Logan Airport, they were mobbed in a way that never could happen today. "That was a weird experience for anybody, and especially when you think about airport travel [today]. You have to go through security," said Lonborg, who was 22–9 with a 3.16 ERA during that season. "The plane just drove down the runway, stopped, and [we] said, 'Nope, we can't stop here, we gotta turn around, and go somewhere else.' It was a big pat on the back, I think, for us to realize that all of sudden we have a following here in Boston and it was special to know that fans were going to come to the ballpark and watch us win ballgames."

Surprises make you change your plans. The prevailing sound throughout Boston became not only Sgt. Pepper's Lonely Hearts Club Band but also the calls of Ken Coleman and Ned Martin.

There was devastation in August, when Conigliaro was hit in his left cheek and eye socket by a pitch from the California Angels' Jack Hamilton. Tony C's career tragically was derailed, but the team was galvanized. The Sox were fortunate they were able to find someone to help replace his production, signing the recently released Ken "Hawk" Harrelson. But it was Yaz who carried the Sox, hitting .417 in the final month of the regular season. "Everything fell into place for me personally the last few weeks of the season," Yaz said. "Because every time I came up, there were men on base. Pitchers couldn't pitch around me, so I had the chance to focus in and hit."

The schedule was perfectly built for drama. The Sox and Minnesota Twins were tied at 91–70 going into the final day of the regular season, playing each other at Fenway. The Detroit Tigers were a half game back and hosting a doubleheader with the Angels. The Tigers needed to win both games to force a playoff. Lonborg delivered the final pitch of a 5–3 victory, and the moment that shortstop Petrocelli clasped the game-ending pop-up over his head in shallow left field is as iconic as Dave Roberts' steal of second base. The Sox didn't have a playoff berth yet, though. They huddled around the rain in the clubhouse, where they heard the Tigers drop the second game after winning the first, securing the Sox's postseason spot. "There's my claim to fame—the last catch," Petrocelli said. "We were all wanting the ball...We were excited about it, and it was a pretty good hitter in Rich Rollins. I think he was a .300 hitter [earlier in his career], so anything could have happened and then he got jammed a little bit, and there was a short pop-up. I had no problems. The high ones could be a problem at the time, but this was no problem. I made sure I squeezed that ball so hard, and that was it. We celebrated. Even if we didn't get into the World Series, it would have been a successful year because coming from ninth place to almost winning it was a big year, was a successful year. So, yeah, it was great from start to finish."

The finish was Gibson's complete game vs. Lonborg in Game 7 of the World Series at Fenway, a 7–2 loss for the Sox. The sting dissipated, but the passion did not. For the first time in roughly two decades, the Sox mattered—and would continue to from that point on. "It's great because it brought the fans back to the ballpark," Yastrzemski said at the 2017 celebration. "How many people showed up for Ted Williams' final game? Ten thousand at the most? How many did we have Opening Day? I don't think it was full. And I know my previous six years, we were lucky to have 10,000 people on a Friday night. So it brought baseball back to New England."

Per Baseball-Reference.com, there were 10,454 at Fenway on September 28, 1960, the date the Splendid Splinter played his last game. On Opening Day of 1967, there were 8,324, and 3,607 showed up for the second game of the season. Opening Day in 1968 at Fenway brought 32,849 people to the park.

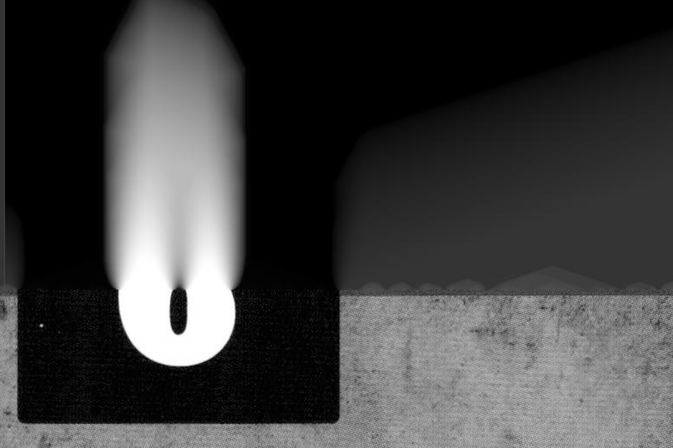

THIS IS OUR F'ING CITY

When the Red Sox at last returned to Fenway Park, the "B Strong" logo that became the symbol of hope and resiliency was painted on the Green Monster. On Saturday, April 20, 2013, the team wore its regular white home uniforms with one variation. The jerseys said "Boston" across the front instead of "Red Sox."

"It means nothing can bring us down," third baseman Will Middlebrooks said at the time. "Everybody is going to pull together and stick together. No event or person or people can bring us down as a city."

The nation was moved. Neil Diamond came in person to lead "Sweet Caroline," the eighth-inning ritual typically performed via recording. "Thank you, Boston!" Diamond said as he took the field ahead of the bottom of the eighth. "What an honor it is for me to be here today. I bring love from the whole country."

Five days had already passed since homemade bombs were detonated near the finish line of the Boston Marathon, a world-class competition held on one of the most festive days in the city. Three people were killed, and at least 264 were injured. Among the dead was an eight-year-old boy, Martin Richard of Dorchester, Massachussetts.

At the time the explosives went off on Monday, April 15, 2013, the Red Sox had just finished a game with the Tampa Bay Rays and were getting ready to leave town for Cleveland. They had just wrapped their traditional Patriots' Day Game, an early start time in front of a sold-out crowd, and their next series was on the road. The Sox thought they'd be playing at Fenway four days later on Friday, April 19. But the manhunt for the bombers put the first game back on hold.

Chillingly, the city was at a halt when the Sox arrived from Cleveland. The players spent most of Friday like many around the city and the world: trying to keep up with the news of the manhunt as the culprits were tracked down. "A lot of TV watching," Sox outfielder Jonny Gomes said. "I didn't really know what to do. We were told to stay inside, so I stayed inside. It was kind of hectic. You didn't know how it was going to happen, where the guy was, what was going on. A lot of emotion. We're not used to it. But it was awesome to see the city together. What they did was just incredible."

Added Middlebrooks: "It was just weird to look out the window and not see any action—any cars or any people...It was like a ghost town with the whole lockdown."

When the Sox came back to the park on Saturday, they wanted to provide a modicum of support to the city through stability and normalcy. "Hopefully today we're able to provide another opportunity for everyone in this city to come together and to show that sign of strength," manager John Farrell said before the game.

A pregame ceremony was planned, and one of Boston's greatest athletes—one of the city's most respected ambassadors—seized the moment. The four-letter word in a five-word phrase David Ortiz used when speaking to the crowd proved more powerful than any four-bagger he ever hit. His most poignant moment on the field may not have been delivered with a bat in hand. "Alright, Alright Boston," Ortiz said while holding a microphone prior to a 4–3 win against the Kansas City Royals. "This jersey that we wear today, it doesn't say Red Sox. It says Boston. We want to thank you Mayor Menino, Governor Patrick, the whole police department for the great job they did this past week. This is our fucking city, and nobody is going to dictate our freedom. Stay strong."

Rarely can a baseball player provide a moment of such empowerment. Boston needed to repossess its city from fear, and for some to a tiny degree, Ortiz helped to that end. The FCC didn't even object to the wording, throwing its weight behind Ortiz's message, which was carried on NESN. After the game Ortiz said the f-word that will never be forgotten was not premeditated. "It just came out," Ortiz said. "It just came out, man. It just came out. If I offended anybody, I apologize, but I feel like this town needs to be pumped. It seems like that was it. Oh, man, it was great. The team has been doing great. The first game—you want to make sure things happen the right way."

During the rest of the season, things happened the right way—all the way through a six-game World Series win against the St. Louis Cardinals. That World Series that—unlike the 2004 and 2007 championships—was finalized at home at Fenway. Roughly a mile from the Boston Marathon's finish line.

The title was transcendent, an emollient. The closest comparable we've seen since the Sox's uplifting 2013 title was the Houston Astros' World Series run in 2017. Hurricane Harvey devastated Houston in August that year, and their baseball team was a welcome distraction and a symbol of a city's resilience. The best team in Major League Baseball surely provided the city that adores it with comfort and normalcy. In the case of the 2013 Red Sox, even those who were most directly impacted may have found an occasional sense of healing. Fans gathered near the Boston Marathon's finish line, a poignant display of "Boston Strong." "I don't think a win-loss record sums up how much we care about this city," Red Sox outfielder Jonny Gomes told me for a MassLive column. "I don't think we put Boston on our back. I think we jumped on their back. They wouldn't let us quit. This World Series isn't icing on the cake. This has turned into a lifetime."

The Red Sox had a lot of newcomers that year, including Gomes, Shane Victorino, David Ross, and Koji Uehara. Patriots' Day ultimately brought the team close to the people here in rapid fashion. For the most part in secret—though some hints were dropped on social media—the Red Sox visited area hospitals and those in need when the team got back to Boston on April 19. "No one prompted them to do anything, but they came up with some thoughts internally," Farrell said. "We couldn't be more proud of the way they responded. They understood their place in this city and what this organization and the Red Sox mean to the people in town. They really felt like they had a chance to help some healing. We didn't know how it was going

David Ortiz delivers his iconic speech, which empowered the city of Boston following the terrorist attacks at the Boston Marathon.

to unfold, but they didn't hold back. They threw themselves in the middle of it and reached out, whether it was tickets they left victims to hospital visits to the number of ways they could acknowledge the first responders. They really understood their place at a moment of need."

At the same time, though, the team's position as healer was a dangerous point to oversell. We have to be measured when assessing the correlation between tragedy and a baseball team's success and then equally as careful assessing the tie between victory and healing. The relevance of the Red Sox winning the World Series to the Boston Marathon attacks seems mutable—even worthy of tempering.

The Sox knew that. Southpaw Craig Breslow was one of the cogs in the bullpen that year and a New England native who has long been respected for his intelligence above all else. He navigated the subject with the deftness of, well, a crafty left-hander. "It's a great story, the success of this team," Breslow said. "I think to point to that tragedy as the impetus to success is probably to belittle the importance of what people have been going through in this city, the loss that people have gone through. Certainly, as representatives of this city, we understand that Fenway Park and the Boston Red Sox offer an avenue where people can clear their minds and focus on something other than what's going on. But again to point to a tragedy like that—of such historic proportions—as the reason for success is probably unfair to those people who suffered losses."

That doesn't mean the Red Sox weren't genuine in their caring, that they didn't feel deeply for this city, or didn't want to win for the city. They did and they should be commended for it. And years later what they did still means a whole f'ing lot to so many.

7

2013

When Koji Uehara struck out the Cardinals' Matt Carpenter on seven pitches for the final out—a splitter got him—the unflappable Red Sox closer pointed to the sky before being lost in a sea of his teammates. The 2013 World Series was the Red Sox's third championship in 10 seasons, a six-game victory in the Fall Classic to cap a season that proved the right plan can hurry along a fantasy—even when you don't quite expect it.

The Red Sox were not supposed to be the best so soon just one year after they finished last, forcing them to jettison the bad apples from the roster. "When the fireworks went off at the presentation of the trophy out there, when the ballpark was filled with smoke, it was completely surreal," manager John Farrell said. "To be in this position, given where we've come from, reflecting back a year ago at this time, there's been a lot that's happened in 13 months."

No curse was broken as in 2004, but Boston's 2013 title carried a circumstance that the 2004 and 2007 championships did not. Sox fans didn't have to stake out the airport to wait for their boys. The World Series trophy was presented at Fenway Park with a packed house spilling over into a euphoric Kenmore Square. It was a celebration for a championship no one believed realistic seven months before.

The last time the Sox celebrated at home was 95 years earlier in the famous 1918 season.

Before the Red Sox grew out all their beards and pounded their chests at second base on every double at Fenway Park, before David Ortiz grabbed the microphone and told everyone just whose city this was in the wake of terror, they were only a team trying to get out of the cellar.

Their manager, Farrell, had mediocre results in two years with the Toronto Blue Jays. General manager Ben Cherington didn't exactly have the instant success that his predecessor, Theo Epstein, did. The Sox won just 69 games in 2012 under Bobby Valentine. The turnaround, though, validated all the moves and personalities. Farrell became the fourth Sox manager—predecessor Terry Francona was the last—to win a title in his first year in Boston. "You can't give Ben Cherington enough credit," Farrell said. "He had a clear-cut vision going back to last August. It started with the trade with the Dodgers [that sent out Carl Crawford and Adrian Gonzalez in 2012]. It freed up a lot of capability to go out and handpick guys that we felt and he felt could embrace everything that is Boston. He hit head-on and he hit spot-on with every guy he brought in here. To think how quickly they came together as a tight-knit unit, this is a team in every sense of the word. It's a team concept. They all bought into it. They love to work. More than anything, there's a will to win that I've never seen before."

Only one other major league team—the Minnesota Twins in 1991—had ever gone from last place to a ring. "When you're around it, you feel it," Cherington said of team chemistry. "It's hard to say it's not valuable. I don't know if any of us know how to engineer it. But when you're around it, you feel the group coming together the way it did. I don't have any doubt it's valuable. I just still don't know how to predict it."

The Game 6 starter, John Lackey, was a poster boy for the improbability of the club. He was a villain in Boston two years before. His arm had been in terrible shape as he tried to gut through a ligament tear in his right elbow. He came back from Tommy John surgery more fit, more focused and became just the seventh pitcher in history to start and win two World Series clinchers in a career. He was the first to do so for two different teams.

Lackey won Game 7 for the Anaheim Angels against the San Francisco Giants in 2002, when he was just a rookie. "This is not even close," Lackey said when asked to compare the two titles. "Honestly, looking back on it, you know what you're playing for when you go into a game like this. I think it almost is better to be young and dumb sometimes when you go into these situations. You know what you're playing for, you know how hard it is to get here. It makes everything especially more special when you get it done. There's definitely more on it."

How did the Sox get there? The easy point of reference is the Los Angeles Dodgers blockbuster trade orchestrated by Cherington. That was a landmark deal in so many ways, and it was indeed a cleansing. But Dustin Pedroia, World Series MVP David Ortiz, Jon Lester, Clay Buchholz, Lackey, and so on and so on—those guys were already on the team. So many key pieces of the 2013 Red Sox were, strangely, key pieces of the 69-win Red Sox from a year earlier.

Heavy lifting was still to come, and Cherington hit on nearly every move he made that offseason, including signing David Ross, signing Uehara, trading for Mike Carp in spring training, even bringing on Quintin Berry late in the year as a pinch-runner. From the veterans on down through the coaching staff, like third-base coach Brian Butterfield, the leadership on the team was phenomenal. "I can't possibly [heap] any more praise upon him," said bench coach Torey Lovullo, now managing the Diamondbacks. "I think where we all kind of benefit, and this entire equation, is having Butter's expertise involved."

Shane Victorino could well have been the best defensive right fielder in the game that year and he arguably was the most valuable player the Red Sox had overall. Victorino, Pedroia, and Jacoby Ellsbury all belong in that conversation. Defensively, Victorino was more definitively Boston's best. Between his arm, his fearlessness, and range in right—he was a second center fielder—he spoiled Red Sox pitchers. He kept crashing into walls even when hamstring and back injuries took him out of the lineup early in the season.

He was playing with a bad thumb, too. "When I hit the barrel of the ball, the bat sits back in the top of my hand," Victorino said. "My finger goes numb once in a while. Like I said, it's all part of it. It is what it is. It's just one of those things. I want to be out there. I want to play with these guys. Look at [Pedroia]. That guy right there motivates me himself. You look at what he's done and all the injuries that he's battled. And I look at it and I say, 'Wow, if this guy keeps doing what he's doing, he's playing almost every single game of the season.'"

Where Victorino grew up, young men aspire to be warriors. "The biggest thing that you can be, for Shane, is the terminology 'warrior,'" his brother Mikey said. "That's how our culture is in Hawaii. Our culture, we're actually warriors. Polynesians are warriors by nature. A warrior will battle through anything and everything."

Then there was Captain America himself—Gomes. Or was it Mr. Clutch? He was a lot of things to the Sox. During one road trip during the 2013 season, a contemplative Gomes discussed the notion of "clutch."

"I think if you were to take a poll of guys: who would you want up with runners in scoring position with two outs in the World Series?" Gomes said, "you'd be surprised who you'd get. You would get maybe a bat-handler, somebody who can shoot the ball the other way, good contact guy. I don't think you would get the big power hitter guy going for a three-run homer."

That description was a little eerie, considering how the Sox's 4–2 win against St. Louis in Game 4 of the World Series played out. Gomes wasn't even in the starting lineup. A late scratch of Victorino (his lower back flared up) brought the bearded ringleader in as the starting left fielder, and when the sixth inning arrived, he lived the very scenario he spoke of. Gomes slugged a tie-breaking, three-run homer with two out in the sixth inning. The swing essentially gave Boston's season new life.

The Sox didn't lose again, and it made for a season of redemption. "We reconnected with our fans," Sox president Larry Lucchino said at the time. "The bloom was off the rose after that 13-month period, September '11 all the way through '12. We had to reboot and reconnect with our fanbase. I think we were successful at doing that, acknowledging the problems we had, making sure they knew how much we wanted to win and how hard we'd work to win."

8

THE CURSE OF THE BAMBINO

It is alternately odd and amusing that some form of witchcraft, a pox or a jinx, has become widely associated with a baseball team. There is, or was, no "curse" of the Red Sox as we know it without one particular author, or maybe two. Dan Shaughnessy's book, *The Curse of the Bambino*, popularized the phrase upon first printing in 1990, and its hold on the fanbase, the media, everyone, is a phenomenon unto itself.

Ask anyone: what did the 2004 Red Sox do? Why they broke The Curse, of course. "The prediction that we would eradicate The Curse of the Bambino, that was sort of [ownership's] Joe Namath moment, if I can be so bold as to call it that," former Red Sox president Larry Lucchino said in 2017.

Many snappy sentences have come and gone in the sports world. Few stick. The genesis of this turn of phrase can be traced not only to 1918, when the Red Sox last won the World Series prior to 2004; and not only to 1920, when Babe Ruth was announced as sold to the New York Yankees; but to a 1986 newspaper article and a couple of folks you haven't heard of.

(Quickly, on the matter of when exactly Ruth was sold: per the Hall of Fame, the date the owners agreed to the Ruth deal was December 26, 1919, as written on the promissory note. The press was informed in the ensuing new year. Not all of the money was paid up front, and some interest meant the purchase price was actually a bit higher.)

A longtime columnist for *The New York Times*, George Vecsey recounted after Game 7 of the '86 World Series all that had gone wrong previously for the Red Sox. His first sentences were not about Bill Buckner or Bruce Hurst or Darryl Strawberry but about Enos Slaughter's mad dash in 1946 and Bucky Dent's home run in 1978. "All the ghosts and demons and curses of the past 68 years continued to haunt the Boston Red Sox last night," Vecsey wrote, "as the New York Mets won the seventh game of the World Series 8–5—with an a cappella chorus of fans chanting the Boston players' names derisively—to bring more gloom to the New England region, which has not enjoyed a World Series victory since 1918...there is no denying that the Boston Red Sox have been playing under a cloud ever since their owner, Harry Frazee, sold off Babe Ruth early in 1920...And that cloud settled over them in this series. All the leads they had, all the chances went down the drain, just as they had in 1946 and 1949 and 1967 and 1975 and 1978."

The column's headline in the paper was "Babe Ruth Curse Strikes Again."

A New York publisher, Meg Blackstone, had heard about The Curse from her grandfather, a Dorchester, Massachusetts, man named Arthur Whitfield Davidson. Blackstone saw an opportunity. "Meg was probably inspired by reading that *New York Times* column," Shaughnessy said in a 2017 interview. "But she sent me a letter in 1988: I would like you to do a book on the bad luck of the Red Sox. And it was kind of unsolicited. She had a summer home in Maine and read my stuff and thought I was the right ticket for that. But the praise was owed to her and her grandfather, and that was the first and only time those words were strung together: The Curse of the Bambino. So that became the title of the book, just kind of this black history of the Red Sox, this narrative of all the bad things that had happened, collected in one place. And as the thing was being written and came out, continuous bad stuff happened, '88, '90, and it kept going up until 2003, kept rewriting and expanding, and...the last version of that book [notes] Theo Epstein buying the book in high school."

The Easter Bunny ain't real. Curses aren't either.

But there were very direct repercussions to Frazee's choice to sell Ruth. Handing off the most famous, if not the greatest, player of all time to the Yankees created a devastation beyond the loss of Ruth's future production. In trading Ruth, Frazee declared the Sox needed more than just one star to compete, when in reality he was pressed for cash. He parted with Ruth for no players in return—just the dough—plus an element that's almost more interesting: a $300,000 mortgage on Fenway Park. Often, we say a team owns another as a figure of speech; this arrangement is about as close as it gets. A theater owner,

Frazee used some of the money to pay debts and finance shows and wound up selling the Sox in the summer of 1923 for $1.25 million. In the fall the Yankees won the World Series for the first time after losing in the series the previous two years.

Colonel Jacob Ruppert was the most famous Yankees owner at the time of the Ruth deal and also the money man. But the idea behind the trade belonged to co-owner Cap Huston. (Huston's full name—Tillinghast L'Hommedieu Huston—is almost too good to be true.)

The Sox won four of the first 15 World Series from 1903 to 1918, but after the sale of Ruth, Boston managed only one American League pennant in a 47-season span from 1920 to 1966. "The immediate impact of Ruth's loss was obvious," Shaughnessy wrote. "And things only got worse when Frazee traded or sold the rest of his high-priced stars, most of them to New York where they were taken care of by Frazee's landlord, Jake Ruppert. [Ed] Barrow's move from Red Sox field manager to Yankees business manager expedited the process and assured that the Yankees would acquire only Boston's best. The Red Sox became like an L.L. Bean catalogue for the Yankees. Every time the Yankees needed to fill a hole, Barrow called Boston, ordered the player he wanted, and had Ruppert write out a check."

Barrow was the manager for the 1918 title team, when Ruth had a 2.22 ERA and hit .300 with a league-leading 11 home runs. In the Bambino's first year with the Yanks, he hit 54 out.

The bad fortune the Sox suffered afterward, decades down the line—86 years this curse went—is coincidental, and you know it. They lost the World Series in seven games in 1946, 1967, 1975, and 1986. But taken all together, it's lurching to find how much went wrong following the trade of one man.

Only the irrational and gullible sorts would presume a man could wear a uniform and have his destiny in a baseball contest preordained by his clothes. Yet—from the ushers to the owners—that's how everyone began to feel. Or, at least, come the 1990s, it's what everyone started to talk about. If you were on the Sox, you were cursed. "I'm starting to hate talking about the Yankees," Pedro Martinez said in frustration in 2001. "The questions are so stupid.

They're wasting my time. It's getting kind of old...I don't believe in damn curses. Wake up the damn Bambino and have me face him. Maybe I'll drill him in the ass, pardon me."

Certainly, the media pushed it along. "We are teammates," Martinez said of Ruth on the eve of his Hall of Fame induction in 2015, when he was to receive a plaque just as Ruth did. "I had the opportunity to go over and look at [Ruth's] statue and I did apologize for the comments I made that day. That was Shaughnessy and Jonny Miller [of WBZ Radio] getting in my face. I said those things because I didn't believe in curses. But I know, especially after that moment, I got to really appreciate how good the Bambino was and how good he was to people in society and for baseball."

9

TONY C

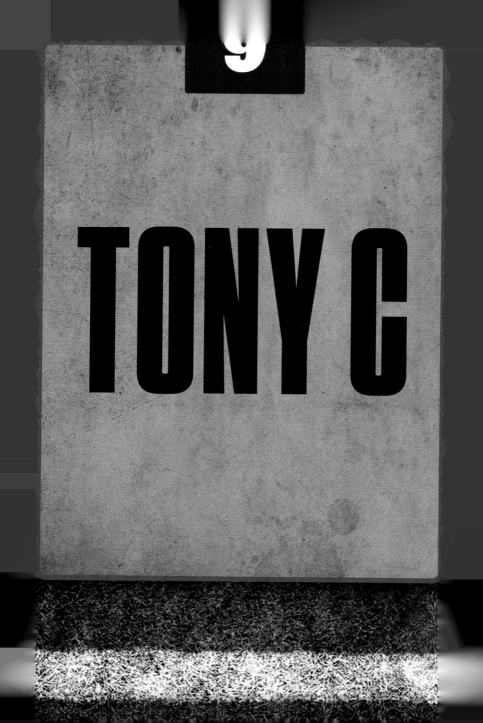

Nearly two decades have passed since Tony Conigliaro's death. Occasionally, when his brother, Billy Conigliaro, signs autographs at Fenway Park, a somewhat uncomfortable situation arises. "They come up and ask me, 'How's Tony doing?'" said Billy, Tony's teammate in the Red Sox outfield in 1969–70. "Sometimes I'll say, 'Not too good.' Sometimes I'll say, 'He's okay.' Sometimes: 'He passed away in 1990.' I don't know what to say. I don't want to make people feel bad."

Billy takes it in stride. People only ask because Tony was a star in so many ways—both as a power hitter and a pop crooner. Few would pause to consider the possibility that such a strong, vibrant man would unexpectedly die young. "They went to college here and they saw him play," Billy said of the fans' well-intended inquiries about Tony. "And they lose track of what really happened."

What really happened to Tony Conigliaro was tragedy. A pitch to the head in 1967 robbed him of his vision in his left eye, derailing his career. At the same time, it created an opportunity to show the resilience that he is remembered for. In February of 1982, seven years after his last game in the majors, Tony suffered a heart attack while riding with Billy to the airport. Billy got him to the hospital as fast as he could, but a lack of oxygen took its toll. Tony died in February 1990 after eight years in a severely disabled state.

Both in life and on the field, we're left to think what could've been.

Conigliaro was a force of nature at the plate, a kid from Revere, Massachusetts, who in

1967 became the fastest to hit 100 home runs in American League history. Through his first four seasons—including his final game of the Impossible Dream '67 season, when he was hit in the eye—Conigliaro had 104 home runs in 494 games. That's the same number of homers Bo Jackson had through that many games and one more than Alex Rodriguez. When right-hander Jack Hamilton's pitch caught Conigliaro, he was a .276 hitter with a .339 on-base percentage and .510 slugging percentage. "If Tony hadn't been hit, I don't think it's really going that far afield to imagine that he was headed to the Hall of Fame," The Sports Museum curator Richard Johnson said. "He was that good a hitter. I saw him play. Wow, he was great. He was the best right-handed power hitter I've ever seen at Fenway Park. And that's a short list that would include Dwight Evans and Manny [Ramirez] along with him."

If you're of a certain age, your greatest association with Tony C might be a steak salad at the restaurant bearing his name near the Burlington Mall or Fenway. But Conigliaro was Mookie Betts. He was Xander Bogaerts. He was better—and he was local.

Conigliaro was born in Revere, Massachusetts, and went to St. Mary's High School in Lynn. He was raised in Revere and eventually moved to the same street as Johnny Pesky in Swampscott. In 2015 a 22-year-old Betts was the youngest Red Sox player to homer on Opening Day since Conigliaro hit one out as a 20-year-old. That was in 1965—half a century before Betts did it. When Betts made that start in '15, he was the youngest Opening Day center fielder for the Sox since Conigliaro was 19 years old in 1964.

Billy and Tony played baseball constantly as kids, but they weren't exactly fans of the hometown team, pining only to play in front of the Green Monster. "We played baseball all the time in the summer on the asphalt down at Suffolk Downs racetrack with a taped up baseball," Billy said. "Nobody told us to play. We just played for the fun of it. We played half ball [like stick ball but with a ball cut in half], Wiffle Ball, any kind of a ball with a broomstick handle. [We] played all day long, then football season we played football. Then in winter we played hockey. But we were always doing this stuff. We weren't hanging out at Fenway Park, thinking about the Red Sox. We just liked to play."

The first pitch Tony Conigliaro saw at Fenway in '64 resulted in a home run over the Green Monster. He finished with 24 homers and a .290 average that rookie year, a season in which he was just a teenager. Over the following winter, he became a bona fide recording artist. His single, "Why Don't They Understand," was distributed by RCA. "He was a character," Billy said. "He wasn't just a baseball player."

Tony was a personality, a stud whose play put him in Fenway's spotlight and whose charisma brought him a spot on *The Merv Griffin Show*. "He was a cocky, typical 6'2", good looking, girls-hanging-all-over-him-type of guy that was great in basketball and great in baseball," Billy said. "There's funny things that happened. I got a million stories."

Billy is one of Tony's two brothers, along with Richie. The latter didn't go pro, but Billy played five seasons in the majors, including three with the Sox. Tony was the standout. "Spring training, for instance," Billy said, "I was trying to make the team and played against the Mets in St. Petersburg, and Tom Seaver was pitching. It was only an exhibition game, but I hit a home run off him way down the left-field line, like one of the longest home runs I ever hit. The next day in the paper it said, 'Tony Conigliaro Homers Off of Seaver.'"

Billy saw the saddest stories firsthand, too. He was there on August 18, 1967, when Tony took the pitch from Hamilton, leaving Tony looking like a spotted dog. His swollen left eye socket was entirely dark. "I've relived it a million times," Billy said. "We talked during the day. He was in a little slump and he mentioned he was going to try to hang in there a little bit longer at bat, not pull out. He always stood close to the plate anyway. And the pitch was—I've said this before—the pitch was definitely thrown at him. I don't think Hamilton wanted to hit him in the head. He could have thrown at his side or his butt, but it went up right in his head, and we just figured he'd jump up, and he'd be fine. We didn't know the helmet flipped off, and [the ball] hit him directly in the temple. So then, what happened after that, it was terrible. Luckily, he didn't die from it...The greatest thing was no one ever expected he'd come back after that."

What Billy hopes remains Tony's legacy is the fact he did return to the big leagues. After missing all of the 1968 season, Tony returned to rip 20 home runs in 1969 and a career-high 36 the next year. That season in 1970 was a turning point. The Sox dealt Tony to the California Angels in October. "Fans were bull, I was bull, everybody was upset, but they still did it," Billy said. "And to this day, I don't know why they did."

Tony didn't make it through the year as a player, hanging 'em up at age 26. "This is the end of Tony C," Tony said after leaving Los Angeles and meeting his family at the airport in Boston. "I've learned that health is more important than money."

Except it wasn't the end. He tried to pitch. Then, at the plate, he started to adjust. One day Tony told Billy to close his left eye. "He threw a ball to me, and it bounced off of my hand, and I dropped it," Billy said. "He said, 'That's kind of what my vision's like.' I said, 'Well, how the hell do you hit like that?' He said, 'Well, I just made an adjustment, and that's all I can say.' His vision was like 20/200...It's amazing to me."

On Opening Day of 1975, Tony was back with the Red Sox, batting cleanup as the designated hitter behind Yaz. Fred Lynn, batting second to begin his Rookie of the Year and MVP winning season, was in center field. "He's starting, and the place went absolutely bonkers when they announced him," Lynn said. "And then he got a base hit. And it was magical. It was really fun to be a part of it. The bad part was that...he wasn't seeing the ball as well as he did when he was younger...[Tony] had to produce, and it just wasn't happening, and I don't think he felt good about it, and then he just kind of walked away from the game. That was the sad part. But the Opening Day, I'll never forget it when they said his name, and, jeez, he was very beloved. The fans just loved that guy."

Billy was driving Tony to the airport when tragedy struck again in the form of a heart attack. "I asked [the doctor] what could have caused that. He said, 'We have no idea,'" Billy said. "'He's strong as can be. We don't know what caused it.' The other problem was the lack of oxygen because by the time I got him there and by the time they got the breathing tube in, it was quite a long time, so that caused

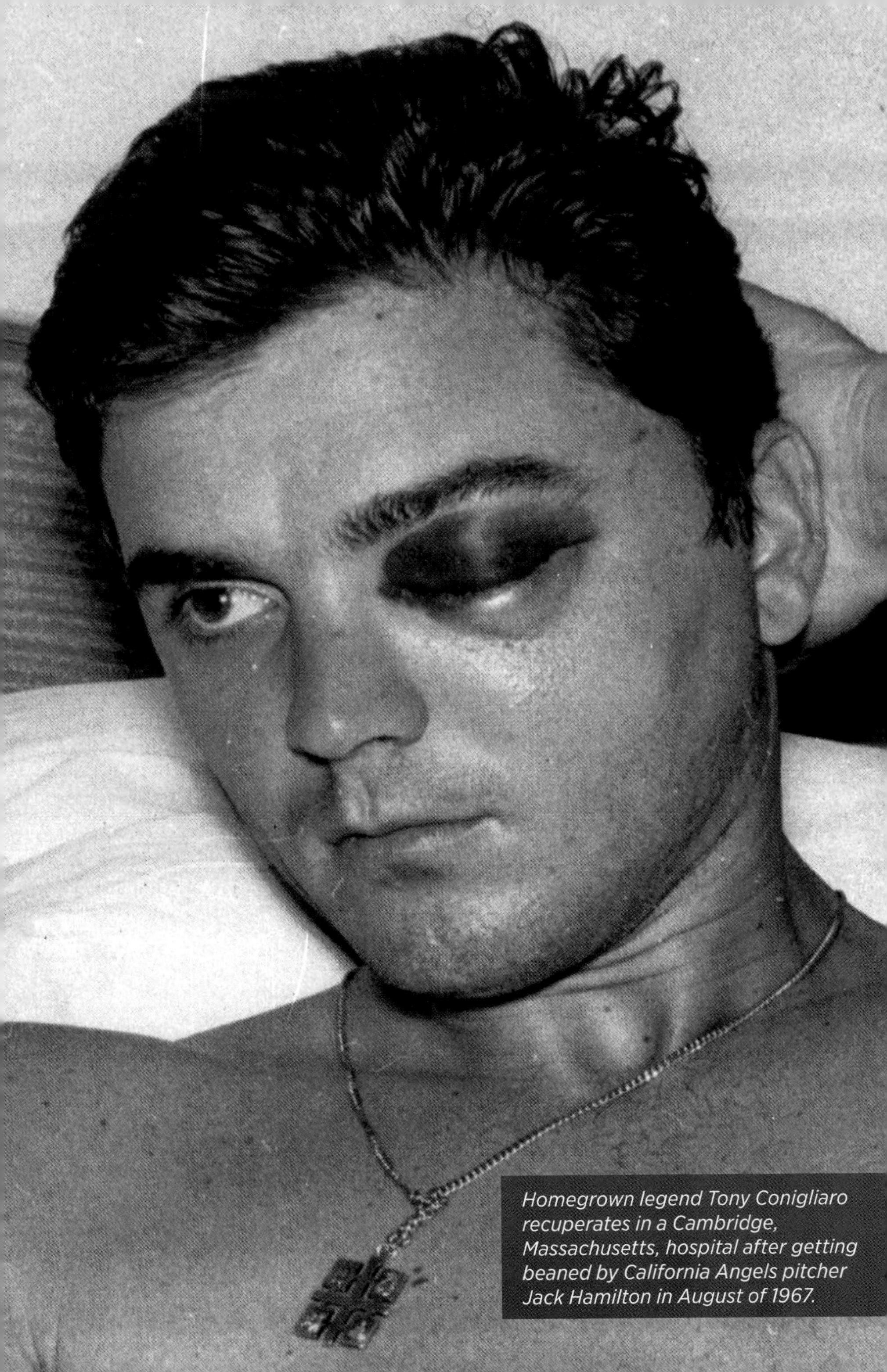

Homegrown legend Tony Conigliaro recuperates in a Cambridge, Massachusetts, hospital after getting beaned by California Angels pitcher Jack Hamilton in August of 1967.

the brain damage. When he passed away [eight years later], I was at Salem Hospital with him, and his pulse rate just kept going slower and slower and slower until it left no pulse."

Kidney failure and pneumonia were the causes of death. A movement amongst fans to retire Tony's number didn't exactly work out, but it actually may have worked out for the better. In 2017 the Red Sox unveiled a glass display on the concourse at Fenway, appropriately near Gate C, commemorating Tony C. "It's amazing they would do that after all those years," Billy said of Sox management. "I never heard of that being done, but we're very, very grateful. It's a lot more meaningful than having his number retired...People can look at and learn about him 'cause obviously that was so long ago when he played. They just hear stories."

Presented to a major leaguer who has overcome adversity through Tony's hallmark traits of spirit and determination, an award today is given annually in Tony's honor at the Boston Baseball Writers dinner.

YAZ

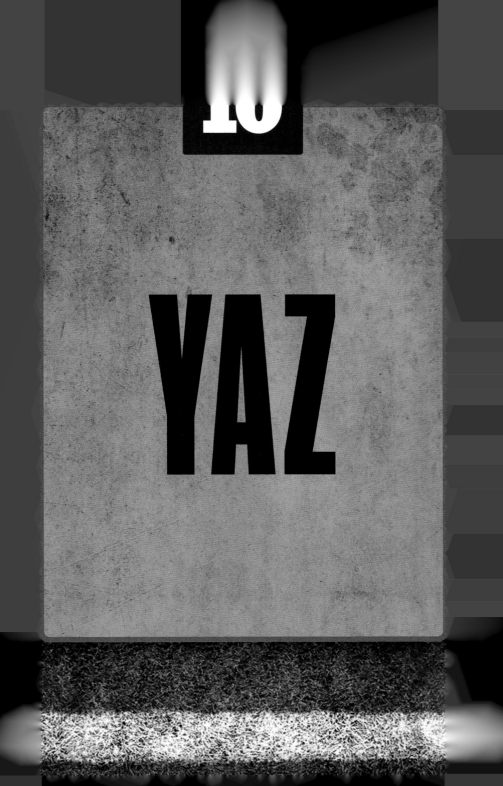

Hawk Harrelson batted right behind Carl Yastrzemski and never could quite figure it out. Why did they keep pitching to Yaz? "I used to ask myself that question a lot when I was on deck," said Harrelson, whose iconic voice had called 33 years of White Sox games. "And then bam, there's a double. Bam, there's a home run. They kept pitching to him, and he just kept beating the shit out of 'em. I mean, it was just that simple. I learned more about hitting behind him, when he won the Triple Crown [in 1967] in the midst of the greatest pennant race of the history of the game—and certainly the history of the Boston Red Sox—than I did from any hitting coach I ever had. Just watching him. And when he came to the plate, they threw the best out there they had against him every time going down that stretch. And he just killed 'em."

Harrelson's best year in Boston was in 1968, and he said he owed it to Yaz. Harrelson became obsessed with No. 8, with being better than the short guy from Long Island who wound up playing 23 years for the Red Sox and only the Red Sox—a team record. Hawk was bigger, stronger, and made it his goal to "stick it up his behind."

Few could. Yaz was not imposing at 5'11". At the time he agreed to a deal with the Red Sox around Thanksgiving in 1958, he weighed about 160 pounds. But he was groomed for greatness by his father, a decent ballplayer whose own career was forsaken to provide for his family as a potato farmer in Bridgehampton, New York. That area today is known as part of the glitzy, wealthy Hamptons. But when Yaz was born in 1939, there was no extravagance. The country was emerging from the Great Depression, and the world was about to enter another great war. Potato farming was a legacy undertaking from the old country, Poland, as explained by Yaz in his autobiography, *Yaz: Baseball, The Wall, and Me*. "My father loved baseball," Yaz wrote. "After the long hours we all put in on the farm, athletics were our relaxation, and we worked hard to relax. All the

Yastrzemskis and Skoniecznys [his mother's family] were on a baseball team run by my dad called the Bridgehampton White Eagles."

Yaz's father could have signed with the Brooklyn Dodgers, but the pay of $75 a month wasn't worth the possibility of giving up the land, a surer meal ticket. "When Dad finally decided that, yes, he would take a chance on making the majors, it was too late," Yaz wrote. "A few years after he had turned down the Dodgers, he hurt his shoulder. When he tried out for them again, he had lost the extra playing edge. He never told me, but I always sensed that he was determined that the hard times, the chance that slipped away, the difficult farm life... none of that was going to happen to me. I was going to get every opportunity to play baseball."

Yaz's story is a New York story. He was a New York Yankees fan—if you can forgive him. But his journey to the majors is representative of any New Englander's. The cold. A small-town life. "Wintertime? Snow? It didn't matter. I cleared a path from the house to the garage," Yaz wrote. "I'd have on a huge parka, put on a pair of big gloves, and I'd go out there for two hours every day in the wintertime."

After dinner he'd head back out to the cold garage for more drills. (And you thought raking was a fall activity.) Yaz got it in his head that he would become the highest paid bonus player ever. It's admirable that Yaz was comfortable admitting this. People knock players for wanting money, but that kind of goal is ultimately representative of wanting to be the best. Plus, who doesn't want some financial security?

If the Yankees in a sense stole Babe Ruth from the Sox, the Sox got a little revenge scooping up Yaz when the Yankees and a whole slew of others were in pursuit. The Yankees have themselves to blame, though. Yaz wanted to be in the Bronx with the short porch in right. Fenway's build for a left-handed hitter was not appealing. He had taken batting practice at Yankee Stadium at the team's invitation, wearing a Yankees uniform and slugging four home runs in 10 pitches. Yaz's father was handling the negotiations and held steady during a meeting a few days later, demanding $100,000. The Yankees offered $60,000. The scout handling the negotiations threw his pencil in the air in exasperation. "Nobody throws a pencil in my house. Get the hell out and never come back!" Yaz remembered his father shouting after jumping out of his chair.

Yaz went away to college briefly at Notre Dame, and a Red Sox scout named Bots Nekola got to know Yaz's father well. They agreed to a $108,000 bonus, plus good money in the minors and tuition. "When Joe Cronin, the general manager of the Red Sox, heard the deal finally was finished, he came over to see what he had bought," Yaz wrote. "Cronin couldn't believe my size—5'11", 160 pounds—and the amount of money I was getting. The first thing he said—and I could never forget it—was: 'We're paying this kind of money for *this* guy?'"

This guy, whose first nickname was actually Yastro, was able to escape the shadow of Ted Williams. When they first met, Williams told Yaz not to let anyone screw with his swing. In their spring training together in 1960, Yaz's locker was right next to Ted's. Williams was moody, Yaz wrote: "Then when he would talk about hitting, I didn't know what the hell he was talking about."

Writers asked if he was learning a lot from Williams, so he gave the only answer he could: of course. The preoccupation with following in Williams' footsteps was more of an outside force at the time. Yaz was equally concerned with proving he belonged alongside the mere mortals. In 1961 the pressure became more real. Williams had retired, and Yaz was to make his debut. The left fielder was succeeding the greatest hitter that ever lived.

Like Williams before him, Yaz became a standard for future generations. "They used to call me little Yaz in the minors because I had my hands up high like he did," said Fred Lynn, who is now often compared to Andrew Benintendi. "I'm not quite as strong as Carl. But there's similar styles. I didn't swing as hard every time as he did. But Carl was a workhorse. He really worked hard at his craft. He would take extra BP. He'd take extra balls off the wall. He was a really good outfielder, by the way. Everybody remembers his hitting, but he could play that wall like nobody else. He was really, really good at it. And I didn't get to play with him a lot in the outfield. As a hitter I used to watch him. Because if he hit in front of me, chances are they'd

Helped by training with a Hungarian Olympic coach, Gene Berde, in the offseason prior, Yaz was the MVP of the Impossible Dream 1967 season. He was on the '75 team, too. Like so many Red Sox greats, Yaz never won a ring. He still got a ring, though. "I asked the Balfour people, who make all those special sports rings, to have [a design] resemble what I thought a World Series ring should look like since I never had one of my own," Yaz wrote. "My retirement ring had 23 stones for 23 years, and I had my stats on one side, the important ones—the 400 homers, the 3,000 hits, the 3,308 games played. I had 20 rings made up and put a different friend's name on each one." One even went to president Ronald Reagan.

On the day of the 50th anniversary of the Impossible Dream, Yaz made a relatively rare appearance at Fenway Park. He's not the constant presence around the stadium that some alumni are. He's still a small-town kid. "What do I think?" He said as he sat down to talk to reporters. "Gone by too quick."

BROOKLINE'S OWN THEO EPSTEIN

After he won the World Series for the third time in his career and ended the anguish of a second fanbase, Theo Epstein walked to the mound in the rain. It was a little after 2:00 AM in Cleveland on November 3, 2016. The Cubs and the city of Chicago were just beginning to appreciate what it meant to win for the first time in 108 years—a similar contemplation to Boston's in 2004, when Epstein was in just his second year as a general manager and the Red Sox won for the first time in 86 years. Identifiable by his strong brow, Epstein stood in the middle of the mound. He was flanked by Jed Hoyer and Jason McLeod, two executives who were with him during the early days in Boston, too. Together, they held the Cubs' "W" flag, the emblem that signifies a Cubs win.

Which mattered more to a kid from Brookline, Massachusetts, who was heartbroken after the 1986 World Series? Engineering the 2004 title in Boston or 2016's with the Cubbies after a total rebuild of the Cubs roster? "It's like two of your children, you know?" Epstein said that night. "You love 'em both. You don't want to compare 'em. Different origins, different personalities, but you treasure both of them. I'm just happy for this organization. It's not about me or comparing to the Red Sox."

When Theo was first elevated to general manager in late November 2002, his inner rock star was drawn out as well—whether he wanted it to be or not. The hoopla preceded him. The Red Sox had just made a run at Billy Beane, the architect of the Moneyball A's. But Beane didn't want to leave Oakland despite a promise of riches in Boston. Entering their second season of Sox ownership, John Henry, Tom Werner, and Larry Lucchino settled for an in-house option, a 28-year-old assistant general manager who went to Yale and then got a law degree from the University of San Diego. "He gets the job, and literally it was that classic overnight thing," said Red Sox president Sam Kennedy, one of Epstein's best friends and his Brookline high school baseball teammate, "where he was a one-word name sports celebrity, and we hadn't done anything yet. It was like John, Tom, and Larry made the call to give him the job, and like all of a sudden, we'd go to Audubon Circle for lunch, and it was like going to lunch with like a rock star."

Epstein and Kennedy both worked under Lucchino in the San Diego Padres organization, and Lucchino brought them with him to Boston. The early years in Boston were a lot of work, a lot of play, and, ultimately, led to an insular existence.

One would think the 2004 title has to be the most special to Epstein. Firsts are always aggrandized. But the actual task of compiling a winner may have been tougher as the years went on. The 2007 team—always overlooked—was fully Epstein's blueprint rather than an altered version of a roster partially built by his predecessor in Boston, Dan Duquette. And the 2016 Cubs were a product of a blank-slate vision Epstein brought to Chicago when he left the Red Sox after nine years as GM.

That's the technical side, though, of building a team. And his obvious impact on the 2004 roster isn't to be dismissed. Epstein is the one who signed David Ortiz ahead of the 2003 season, a move at the time that no one believed was going to lead to a Red Sox Hall of Famer but was nonetheless the product of diligent planning and analysis.

If there is one thing above all that Epstein did not have in 2004, though, it was a heightened sense of what it all meant. Many have heard about people going to visit gravestones after The Curse of the Bambino was broken. Yet, at his age and experience, could Epstein fully comprehend the gravity of the accomplishment? "The biggest difference between the Red Sox experience and the Cubs experience is much better perspective," Epstein said in 2017. "Much more appreciation and much better self-awareness, honestly. At that age...I think it's impossible to see the job from all sides and understand the impact you have on others, both positively and negatively. And that's a big thing in our society today. You can cover a lot of current events right now just by saying, 'hey, the world would be a better place if people better understood their impact on others and/or the impact they can have on others, positively and negatively.' So, when you're 28 going on 22, which is what kind of all of us [in the front office] were, what we were at the time, how we acted—we were all single, didn't have the most well-rounded lives. You don't sort of understand things as they happen. You just do them. It felt like a wild ride from which we never came up for air until kind of the World Series hangover, sometime at the beginning of the 2005 season. But it was just a ride... When you're older, you take a moment to stop, breathe things in, understand how difficult it is, see it through other peoples' eyes. Like the 2016 World Series, I got to see it through my now 9-year-old, then 8-year-old's eyes. And that added so much richness for me in real

Theo Epstein speaks to reporters during his introductory press conference on November 25, 2002, when the 28-year-old became the youngest general manager in baseball history.

SAM KENNEDY

It's not exactly Theo treatment, but the other half of the Brookline Two does get recognized. "Yeah, once in a while at Dunkin' Donuts," Red Sox president Sam Kennedy said. "But very rarely, almost never. Thank God... Growing up here and then having lived here the last 16 years, walking around Fenway, I feel like when I see people, I'll see people from literally middle school, high school, college. I went to school in Connecticut, so there's a lot of Trinity people around. I feel like I know so many people in this town, but I don't think I get recognized by virtue of my position with the Red Sox."

It'll happen more and more. Kennedy, who succeeded Larry Lucchino as Red Sox president, grew up with Theo Epstein. They were famously high school baseball teammates at Brookline High School. Epstein's star has ascended so publicly. Even though Kennedy's visibility isn't as great, he's been a huge part of the Sox's operation. The roster choices belong to president of baseball operations Dave Dombrowski, but Kennedy controls the budget and every facet of the operation.

He and Epstein remain terrific friends. "Larry dubbed us the Brookline Two," Kennedy said. They first worked together for the San Diego Padres under Lucchino. "My Larry tie was Theo," Kennedy explained. "So I was a Yankees intern when [Epstein] was an Orioles intern. And we were friends through high school and we stayed in touch through our internships. In '95 when we graduated, Larry went out and bought the Padres with John Moores and brought Theo with him [from the Orioles]. About, I guess, a year later, I went out sometime in '96. Theo learned from Larry that there was an opening in corporate sales and recommended me to Larry."

Kennedy was working in New York at WFAN, selling radio spots. "Larry hired me to go out there," Kennedy said. "That was the first time we worked together as colleagues, if you will."

Then came the fall of 2001. Lucchino asked Epstein and Kennedy to visit him at his home in California. "[He] said, 'Come on over. Let's have a beer and a talk,'" Kennedy said. "He said, 'Tell me everything you guys know about Boston.' So we told him everything we knew about Boston. We're like, *Holy shit, this could actually happen.* And then he, they, got the team. They were announced as winners."

Kennedy and Epstein were going with him, too. It wasn't the easiest transition, though. For a time the Padres wouldn't let Epstein and Kennedy go. They were under contract. Maybe the Padres should have held their ground.

time through the experience. And in '04, I don't have that. I was riding the wave of everybody else. It was thrilling and incredible, but I didn't have much perspective on it at the time."

Collaboration has always been one of Epstein's hallmarks. But because he was young and hired as Moneyball fever was taking hold, Epstein is often associated with the number-crunching crowd. That's not wrong necessarily, but it is probably overblown. People skills come first. "Really competitive, really bold," said Hoyer, who reunited with Epstein in Chicago as the second in command, "incredible ability to relate to everybody in a different way. He can go give a board presentation and look like he's totally at home and he can sit in a coaches' room and have beers and be totally at home. He can sit down with a player and be totally at home. I think that's incredible skill. And I think that's part of why he's so popular with people sort of across the spectrum. Different people in different areas of baseball. That's a very impressive quality that not a lot of people have."

Epstein's own comportment can create misperception. Hoyer said he's not as buttoned up now in Chicago as he was in his time in Boston. But Epstein can have piercing focus, and his intensity can work to his detriment if a team is, say, going through a rough spell. "Maybe 'cause we were sort of young as a front office, and my sort of resting affect is not like bubbly, happy, I think some people took us as cocky or aloof or some combination thereof or overly serious," Epstein said. "[That] definitely wasn't the case. We were thrilled to be going to Fenway Park every day for work and working with people that we respected and admired. And we had a blast. I mean it was a lot like hanging out with your college buddies every day. But we were trying to get the Red Sox on track. We had our fun, we kind of had our 20s experiences together within the walls of Fenway Park. I didn't like to show that face to the outside because we were really serious about winning. And we always had a lot going on, a lot on our minds and trying to think a couple steps ahead, so we could avoid some of the drama that was always one door away in the Red Sox world."

It came for him eventually. Always does.

The collapse of the 2011 team was the end of Epstein's time in Boston, leaving something of a mess for his assistant GM, Ben

Cherington, to clean up, and Cherington did, winning a World Series in 2013. But nine years and a pair of titles, including the first in 86 years, made Epstein's tenure in Boston overwhelmingly successful. How does Werner look back at Epstein's time? "With great fondness," Werner said in 2017. "I think that he was the right guy for the Red Sox. He was smart, understood the value of analytics...People don't really appreciate the importance of surrounding yourself with other great executives, but the team that he assembled was great. I was disappointed when he left. Bringing a World Series to a great place like the Chicago Cubs, I understand that. I urged him to stay. But he decided to leave, and life goes on. And I felt like that was something that he needed to do. And when an executive wants to leave, it's hard to keep them."

Theo may work in another city for the rest of his life. But everyone will always wonder if Epstein someday wants to come home again, back to Boston and Brookline. Some have speculated he could work in politics, an idea he has publicly shot down. Either way the Red Sox and Boston were a launching pad for one of the most famous executives in the country, no matter the line of work.

Home is where the first ring is. Or so everyone in Boston will always like to believe.

When Epstein and the Cubs visited Boston in April 2017—a month into the first season after the Cubs broke their own curse—the first thing Epstein said he did was drop his bags in his hotel room and take a long run along the Esplanade and through Back Bay. "The city was just shining. It's a special place," Epstein said. "I love Chicago. That's a world-class city. Boston is, too. Every time I come back here, I'm just reminded how lucky I was to grow up here. Everyone out on the streets was in a good mood, the city was looking great, I got an unsolicited high-five because I ran past another jogger going the opposite direction. It was cool. This is the best city in the world to walk around and go for a run in." It is not bad for Duck Boat parades either.

12

PESKY

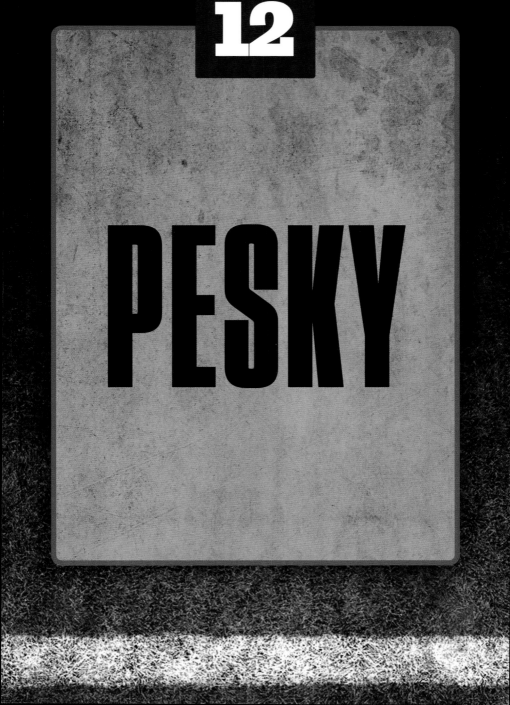

The first home game of the 2004 American League Championship Series for the Red Sox was funereal. The New York Yankees romped to a 19–8 win, putting them in position for a series sweep. As the dirge played prematurely and fans sulked out of Fenway Park, Johnny Pesky, Mr. Red Sox, would not leave. "One thing that comes up that I'll never forget was after Game 3 of the 2004 ALCS," *Boston Herald* columnist Steve Buckley said. "He was out in the streets signing autographs, and then more and more people start coming up to him: 'It's Johnny Pesky!' He says, 'I'll make sure I'll get everybody.' And I was standing there watching it. Finally, somebody produced a beach chair, and he sat down on a chair right on Yawkey Way on Jersey Street there. He was a very popular player, but no one who's alive now remembers him as a player. They just remember him as a happy-go-lucky [guy]...He lived in that same house in Swampscott for years and years."

Pesky had not played a major league game since 1954, but his presence was ubiquitous. He played for three teams in his career from 1942 to 1954 and was with the Sox until a June trade in 1952. But he may as well never have worn another uniform. Pesky was a Sox manager (1963–64 and again in 1980), coach (1975–84), and broadcaster (1969–74). He was a special assistant and an instructor from 1985 on with some varying titles mixed in and a fixture of spring training. "Anytime you see Boston, you remember a legend," Pedro Martinez said in 2012. "One of the few legends that I got to spend time with and actually share a lot of moments—I can say a lot of moments—was Johnny. If you see Boston as a tradition, you have to think about Johnny Pesky and Ted Williams—people like that—Carl Yastrzemski, the history. Everywhere in the city of Boston you seem to have Johnny Pesky. I know that every story about every season that ever started—started with Johnny Pesky in spring training. That was the first face you saw in spring training. Once you get there, you see that old man with the fungo. Everyone will tell you that's Johnny Pesky."

Pesky was born in Portland, Oregon, in February 1919 just after the '18 title run that preceded the great drought. He was 85 years old when he pulled up the chair outside Fenway—not in the least tired of the attention that comes at the center of the Sox universe. He led a lifetime of waiting and endearment. Pesky helped the Sox raise the championship banner in 2005. "When the Red Sox had their long-awaited ring ceremony in April 2005, celebrating the team's first World Series championship since 1918, it was Johnny Pesky who got the loudest ovation at Fenway Park," longtime MLB.com beat writer Ian Browne wrote. "This despite the fact he played his last game for Boston in 1952."

The man, for whom the right-field pole at Fenway Park is named, died in 2012 on a Monday. Bruce Springsteen played at Fenway the following two days. His lighting crew illuminated the pole, and Springsteen acknowledged Pesky during the show. The Sox held a loose policy that they would only retire the numbers of players inducted into Cooperstown. Pesky's No. 6 was made a worthy exception in 2008.

Despite the assumption Pesky's Pole may create for today's youths, Pesky was neither a right fielder nor known for many home runs down the line. He was a shortstop and third baseman primarily and he played some second base as his career wrapped up. He reached 200 hits in each of his first three seasons and had a .313 career average for the Red Sox. The late lefty Mel Parnell, a Sox broadcaster and Pesky's teammate, came up with the name, Pesky's Pole. Pesky hit .321 at Fenway, but it's not like he was banging dingers everywhere. Pesky had just 17 home runs overall in the big leagues, and six of them were at Fenway Park, where the cozy right-field corner is graciously positioned 302 feet away and the aforementioned pole stands. "Mel Parnell started that," Pesky told *The Boston Globe*'s Bob Ryan. "I won a game with a home run down the right-field line against the Athletics. Elmer Valo nearly broke his elbow trying to catch it. But I didn't have any power and I knew it."

A look through box scores shows us this was in 1946. Pesky hit an eighth-inning solo homer to break a 1–1 tie against the Philadelphia

A's, and the Sox won 2–1. The name of this slugger wasn't actually Pesky, though. He was born John Michael Paveskovich, the son of Croatian immigrants. His father was a lumber mill worker. "Pesky was the nickname the kids came up with for me," Pesky said via *The Globe*. Pesky noted that his mother was not happy when he changed his name legally to Pesky in 1947.

Before he was a ballplayer himself, Pesky was a clubhouse attendant in the minor leagues. He was 23 years old when he debuted in the majors. Pesky's rookie year included a .331 average, which put him third in the MVP voting. At year's end a $5,000 bonus came as a kind gesture of owner Tom Yawkey, per Bill Nowlin of SABR. Pesky and Mookie Betts are the only Sox players to have at least 200 hits in a season before turning 24. Pesky is still scattered across Red Sox team records—if not necessarily in a leading position. He's one of three Red Sox shortstops to have a hit streak of at least 26 games. Xander Bogaerts had one of the same length, and Nomar Garciaparra had two such streaks, one ending at 26 as well; the other ended at 30. Fun fact: Pesky and Marty Barrett are the only Red Sox known to have pulled off the hidden-ball trick more than once.

A stint in the Navy, where Pesky met a Lynn, Massachusetts, woman named Ruth Hickey whom he married, cut into the heart of his playing career. He didn't play his sophomore season until 1946—four years after his debut. He led the American League in hits in '46 just as he did in '42 and just as he would do again in '47. Pesky started to decline in his mid-30s and retired after 10 big league seasons. If he hadn't had a chunk of his mid-20s taken away by the war, his statistics (and maybe a Hall of Fame case) could have looked drastically different.

In his post-playing career, rather than in Cooperstown, is where Pesky gained permanence. If you're curious how drastically the manager's position has changed, consider the influences Pesky mentioned when he took over as Sox skipper in 1963. Spencer Abbott was a minor league manager Pesky played for in Portland. "My how he would holler and scream," Pesky said, per a *Fitchburg Sentinel* article from 1963. "He expected every player to be a combination of Ty Cobb and Babe Ruth. He hated to see one of his players as much as smile.

dugout. I'm not going to be that tough, but I've found that a guy has to have a little heel in him to manage well. You can't let 'em run over you. If any member of the Red Sox needs any urging, rest assured that I'll be around to give it him."

Pesky made a mark more as a coach and a broadcaster than a manager. Jim Rice credited Pesky for helping him learn how to play the Green Monster. The anger Dan Duquette stirred in 1997 when he told Pesky he could no longer be in the dugout during games never really subsided, though the rules would prevent Pesky or anyone else in the dugout today unless he were one of the official coaches (i.e. hitting coach, first-base coach, etc.) "He comes back as a broadcaster. That's when he kind of elevated himself because he was this friendly voice on the TV doing games with Ned Martin and Ken Coleman," Buckley said. "Then they made him a coach."

There's no more important coach in Red Sox history. "I just think that his soul was attached to Boston in some way that nobody's ever probably able to describe," Martinez said. "That makes Johnny unique, makes his soul unique. Just like we have the pole, I don't think Pesky will ever go away. If anybody thinks about going away from Johnny, they'll have to look at the pole and right away remember who Johnny was."

13

JIM RICE

When Jim Ed Rice debuted in 1974, the standards he faced as a Red Sox left fielder were Carl Yastrzemski and Ted Williams. Forget the hitting numbers. Among those whose loyalty and service to the Red Sox can be measured in years and exclusivity, Yaz and Ted were benchmarks there, too. All the way around, Rice found his place in history alongside them. Williams spent 19 seasons in Boston and never strayed to another club as a player. Yaz called Fenway home for a record 23 years without playing elsewhere. Rice is third on the list with 16 years for the Sox and only the Sox. It's a tidy lineage of Green Monster guardians. All three made it to the Hall of Fame, including Rice after a particularly long wait. That call came in 2009 in his 15th and final year on the writers' ballot.

When Rice began his career, he easily could have felt the weight of his predecessors' excellence. Yaz was still playing, serving as a teammate and ultimately a great mentor. They don't live far from each other now as retirees. "People say, 'Was it pressure?'" Rice said in 2017. "No, it wasn't pressure. It was just work. It was something that I enjoy doing. I had a good instructor that was willing to work with me, Johnny Pesky. And I had a great manager that I enjoyed being around, he enjoyed being around me [in] Don Zimmer. I had [coach] Eddie Yost, [teammate and coach] Tommy Harper. I had a bunch of great guys that were around me and willing to help me in any way that they could."

Rice was a hitter first and foremost and part of a powerhouse trio of Sox outfielders who patrolled with Fred Lynn and Dwight

Evans. "We complemented each other," Rice said. "I had always known that Dwight was known as a good defensive guy, and Freddy coming out of USC was known for defense and offense, and I was just known for my offense. And so what I had to do was mainly work on my defense to be competitive with those guys as far as being three outstanding outfielders."

Born and raised in South Carolina, Rice, a stellar football player in high school, was the 15th overall draft pick in 1971. Foregoing major football scholarship offers, he ended up hitting 382 home runs with a .298 average, .352 on-base percentage, and .502 slugging percentage in the big leagues. In the middle of an otherworldly three-year stretch during which he hit .320, averaged about 41 home runs per season, and had 200-plus hits in each of the three years, he was the American League MVP in 1978. The 213 hits Rice collected during the '78 season are tied for second most all time in club history for right-handed batters. Rice had four 200-plus hit seasons, which is second in club history (for righty or lefty batters), trailing only Wade Boggs' seven.

In a 20-minute conversation about his career, Rice veered more toward his approach in the field than his approach at the plate—more of what did not come quite as easily, more of what was not so often seen. One day Yaz told Rice to come out with him to left field. They were standing in the dugout at Fenway and started to walk toward the Monster. "By the time [Yaz] hit shortstop, he folds his hands together, looked at the wall, and said, 'Man, I can't teach you anything. You got to go out there and learn on your own,'" Rice said, laughing. "And that was the day that Johnny Pesky [who was a coach then] and I went out there and started working every day...The wall that you have now is not the same wall that we played on. It was more of a tin. You had dead spots. So really, the best advice that he gave me was that you're going to have to learn on your own. I can't teach you because the ball would do different things. I recall we're playing against Milwaukee one day, and Hank Aaron hits the ball out of the ballpark—foul. I ran over there and turned my back, and the ball came back fair. And I said, I'd never do that again, and that was one of the things [Pesky] said: 'I can't teach you about the wind. You have to go out there and learn.'"

Rice said it took him about a week to really feel comfortable. But the work didn't stop. In every ballpark he went to, he always took fly balls and grounders with Pesky's help. One's eyes had to adjust to the glint of the aluminum seats in Minnesota, and you had to stop the ball from finding a drain down the left-field line in Kansas City. For anything hit to his left, Rice knew center fielder Lynn was there. Their relationship may have been deferential in these moments, but a real competitiveness existed between their friendship. They were known as the Gold Dust Twins.

Rice was sitting at home watching soap operas when he learned he was going into the Hall. The last player to make it in his final year on the ballot before Rice was Ralph Kiner of the Pittsburgh Pirates in 1975, the year Rice was runner-up in the Rookie of the Year race to Lynn. It could be called a race at least until Game No. 155 on September 21. The Detroit Tigers' Vern Ruhle broke Rice's left hand with an errant inside pitch, taking Rice out of the Rookie of the Year race and, more importantly, out of the lineup for the postseason. "Vern Ruhle didn't try to hit me," Rice said. "I tried to get out of the way. I couldn't get out of the way and I went as far as I could have. Of course, I really felt, and I still feel like, that if I had played in the World Series, we definitely would have won." The World Series went seven games against the Cincinnati Reds, and the Red Sox lost without Rice. The wait for a Sox ring lasted another 39 years, perhaps, because of one errant pitch.

In discussing his Hall of Fame wait, Rice started down an interesting path. It's not unreasonable to wonder if his numbers could have been even better in those terrific late 1970s seasons or throughout his career if the style of baseball was different back then. "You got to give yourself up, hit the ball to the right side, advance the runner to third base," Rice said. "And if we didn't—Yaz did it, Rico [Petrocelli] did it. If I didn't do it, Don Zimmer, Ed Yost will say, 'Hey kid, you didn't get the job done.' And Yaz will come and say, 'Hey you didn't get the job done.' Those are some of the things I learned before I got to the big leagues. I had a pretty tough coach in high school. I had a great American Legion coach."

Rice's combination of power and contact remains extraordinarily rare. At his zenith in '78, he had a .315 average and 46 home runs and 126 strikeouts in a whopping 163 games—including the one-game playoff the Sox lost to the New York Yankees. There are only three other players to have at least 210 hits and 45 home runs in a single season: Joe DiMaggio, Lou Gehrig, and Jimmie Foxx. Gehrig did it three times; the others accomplished it once. Rice is the only one to do so after 1937. "The thing that really got me at the time is that my numbers never changed," Rice said of the Hall. "The numbers stayed the same, and all of a sudden they say, 'Hey, we're looking at this guy for the last time. This guy put up some good numbers.'"

14

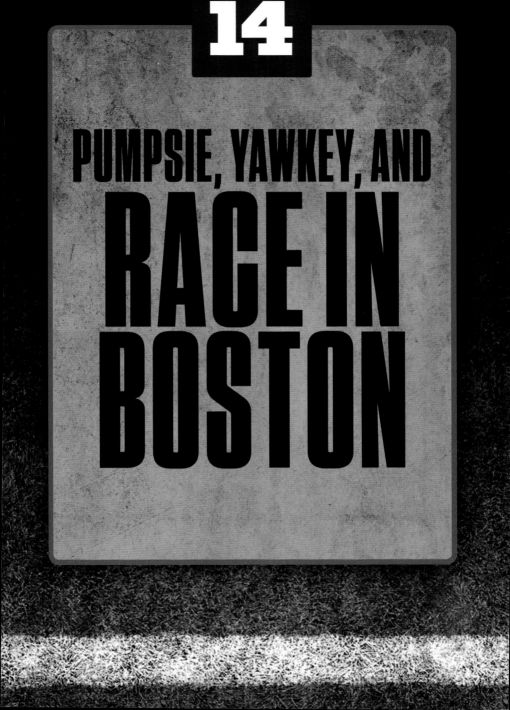

PUMPSIE, YAWKEY, AND RACE IN BOSTON

Race in Boston—both as it pertains to the city generally and the legacy of its baseball team—will remain a never-ending conversation. To say 2017 produced a fever pitch in dialogue would be inaccurate. But, empirically, the volume reached a greater decibel than it had in the years immediately preceding. And there was probably an amplification locally because the epicenter of the topic was attention-grabbing for those who may not normally be concerned with race relations. Fenway Park, as well as a street adjacent to it, Yawkey Way, drew anyone loosely following the Red Sox or simply Boston happenings into a conversation as uncomfortable as it is necessary.

The history of race relations in Boston cannot be duly summarized here—for either the baseball team or the town it represents. Infamously, the Sox were the last major league team to integrate. Pumpsie Green, a black infielder, played his first game for the team in 1959, a dozen years after Jackie Robinson broke the color barrier for the Brooklyn Dodgers. Tom Yawkey, the longtime owner of the Sox, was believed by Robinson to be "one of the worst bigots in baseball," as Robinson wrote in 1967. Robinson tried out for the Red Sox under Yawkey in 1945 and Robinson felt it was a farce from the get-go. "Robinson himself was satisfied with his performance, although by the time he left Fenway he was smoldering about what he felt to be a humiliating charade," Howard Bryant wrote in the seminal book, *Shut Out: A Story of Race and Baseball in Boston*.

Yawkey's many enduring philanthropic endeavors are not to be discounted, but at the same time, they are also immaterial to his approach to minority players in his time as Red Sox owner. A decade and a half into his own time running the team, John Henry publicly stated he wanted to remove the former owner's name from the street that serves as part of the Fenway experience during games. "The Red Sox don't control the naming or renaming of streets," Henry told the

Boston Herald's Michael Silverman in August of 2017. "But for me, personally, the street name has always been a consistent reminder that it is our job to ensure the Red Sox are not just multicultural but stand for as many of the right things in our community as we can—particularly in our African American community and in the Dominican community that has embraced us so fully. The Red Sox Foundation and other organizations the Sox created such as Home Base have accomplished a lot over the last 15 years, but I am still haunted by what went on here a long time before we arrived."

The city as a whole has long dealt with a reputation for racism, a reputation that should never be suggested to define every single person in the city or its surrounding towns. But it is a reputation that nonetheless persists and was not born out of thin air. Whether the modern-day perception of the city is fair—or commensurate with the actual conditions of the present—has been debated hotly.

A multi-part series by *The Boston Globe* in 2017—a newspaper owned by Henry—sought to examine the city's race relations in a deeper way than a mere recounting of individual anecdotes, which is what many radio and personal arguments can devolve into. *Here is what I have personally seen confirmed, and here is what I have not personally seen, and around we go.* The collective experience is much harder to define, and *The Globe* made an attempt to do so. "A national survey commissioned by *The Globe* this fall found that among eight major cities black people ranked Boston as least welcoming to people of color," *The Globe*'s investigative team wrote. "More than half—54 percent—rated Boston as unwelcoming. The reputation is real and pervasive—but, most important, is it deserved?...All told, the findings were troubling. The reasons are complex."

The Globe series was produced after Baltimore Orioles outfielder Adam Jones said he was called the n-word at Fenway Park on May 1, 2017. A couple of days later, the Red Sox banned an unnamed fan for life, following a separate racist interaction in the stands. Overall, the Sox under Henry have taken significant strides to improve race relations and repair the Sox's reputation, an arena where the team cannot please and (has not pleased) everyone. "I'm here to send a message loud and clear that the behavior, the language, the treatment of others that you've heard about and read about is not acceptable. It's not acceptable to the Red Sox," team president Sam Kennedy said in announcing the ban of the fan. "Yesterday I think I was angered, frustrated. And today I feel more a sense of sadness, just deep remorse that these things happen in our society. But it's the reality of the world that we live in."

After Jones went public with his experience, New York Yankees pitcher CC Sabathia was blunt in his assessment of the treatment of black players at Fenway. "It's happened to me—not surprising," the Yankees left-hander said, via *Newsday*. "It's bad. You get called names—the n-word, all kind of stuff—when you go to Boston...I'm glad that he spoke up. It's disgusting."

Asked if he heard similar accounts from other black players, Sabathia said: "There's 62 of us, and we all know: when you go to Boston, expect it...I've never had it anywhere else except there...Even shagging in the outfield before the game, sometimes you get it."

In September of 2017, after Henry had made his intentions to change Yawkey Way known but before *The Globe* story ran, a group of white people unfurled a banner down the Green Monster mid-game that read: "Racism is as American as baseball." Three held the banner; two documented the event. "There were originally about eight people involved who had this idea, and those eight people come from various organizing groups in the Boston area," one group member, who would only comment anonymously, said by phone, "mostly groups that affiliate with racial justice causes. And the banner came in response to the racist comments at the beginning of the season at Fenway [that Adam Jones spoke of]. But overall, we saw, we see Boston continually priding itself as a kind of liberal, not racist city, and are reminded also constantly that it's actually an extremely segregated city."

Experiences and perspectives, naturally, vary. "I look at the lack of black players. You got to realize one thing: I grew up in South Carolina. I was from the South during that time...with the rebel flag and everything else," said Hall of Famer Jim Rice, a black outfielder who spent his entire career with the Red Sox, in a 2017 interview. "It wasn't anything changing from South Carolina to being in Boston. To me it's like when I came to Boston, it seemed like everyone was confused.

Because you had the blacks on one side, you had Italians on one side, you had the Jewish on one side, you had the Irish on one side. Being in South Carolina, it was just black and white. So it was more confusing up here than down there when you really think about it."

Race and racism in the South is its own topic. But the culture also has long been tied to an outgoing attitude, a greater willingness to engage strangers. "Being from the South, we didn't really see color. We saw color, but we didn't see color," Rice said. "We spoke. And I found myself speaking to someone on the street [in Boston], and the first thing the person said, 'You're not from here.' I said no. He said, 'We don't speak here.' You just keep walking. It was tough to think that people carry that mentality. But you dealt with it. That was it.

"And everyone saying well, man, the Boston Red Sox are racist, [the] Red Sox were the last team to have a black. I mean, like, man, I didn't have anything to do with it. So you're telling me that I'm offered a job, I'm offered to show my skills, and because they only had one black player, I should say no because you only had one black player? I mean, you think about it. I think two years I played I was the only black player. But no one would look at that. I still had a job I had to go out and perform."

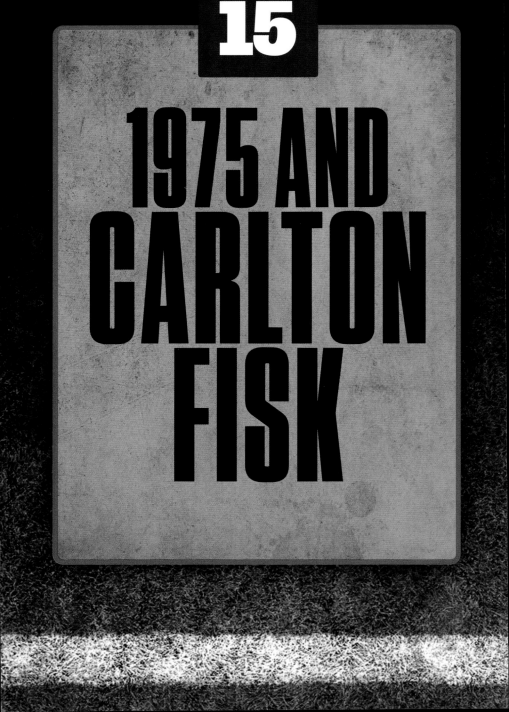

15

1975 AND CARLTON FISK

Before waving it fair, you have to go back a year. The Red Sox were up seven games in the American League East when they woke up on August 24, 1974, with a five-game win streak in their sails and a likely division title laid out in front of them. They went 14–24 down the stretch and lost 20 of their last 32 games. By September 4, they were tied for first place but never again held first place alone. Naturally, the Sox finished as many games out—seven—as they once led.

There was a, well...gold lining. Jim Rice was called up in August '74, and Fred Lynn was called up in September, representing the major league debuts for the Gold Dust Twins, who would form the great triumvirate with Dwight Evans in right field. The outfielders were thrown into the mix with some of the older guard: '67 vets like Carl Yastrzemski, who was at first base rather than in the outfield, and Rico Petrocelli was at third base as opposed to shortstop.

There was no collapse in '75.

A catcher named Carlton Fisk hit a career-high .331, the same mark as Lynn that season. The fourth overall draft pick in 1967, Fisk was born in Vermont and grew up in New Hampshire, attending both Keene State College and the University of New Hampshire. He played for two teams in his 24-year, all Sox career: Red first, then White. But one year, '75, and one swing will always swing back to him. "Gigantic personality, big old type A," Lynn said. "Pudge was definitely the leader on the field. Because he's the catcher, he sees things. He's in charge of the staff. Every time he spoke..." Lynn then made a loud groaning sound to imitate Fisk, "probably being on the farm I think in New Hampshire, he had to yell at people all the time, yell just to be heard. He was just a bigger-than-life guy, personality-wise. He's obviously a really fine defensive catcher and he could hit, too, and he was my first roommate."

He wasn't exactly punctual. "I don't think they had clocks where he lived," Lynn said. "Because he was always late...That's the only negative thing I could say about him. He's just a wonderful guy and a great friend."

Tony Conigliaro was back for Opening Day of 1975, completing the long road of recovery after being hit in the left eye, though he wasn't his old self and played just 21 games.

Rice and Lynn took over the Rookie of the Year race, and the whole season may have hinged on the broken left hand Rice suffered late in the year. Lynn won both the ROY and American League MVP. Lynn ripped 21 homers, one shy of Rice's team high. "Everybody had a bad taste in their mouth from '74," Lynn said. "And we had a collection of young players, Jimmy Rice and myself. Dwight Evans had been there like a year or so. [Designated hitter Cecil] Cooper had just come up, [shortstop] Rick Burleson who'd just come up, [catcher] Timmy Blackwell—there's a lot of guys that were young. Really the nucleus of the club was pretty doggone young, basically under 25. So no one knew what to expect from us. But, yeah, I wasn't the lone wolf as a rookie. There was a bunch of us, so it was easier."

The 1967 Impossible Dream team may be the most romanticized season in Sox history, on that side of 2004 anyway. But '75 grabbed a hold of peoples' hearts as well, including *The Boston Globe* columnist Dan Shaughnessy. "It's hard for me to separate how old I was," Shaughnessy said. "It was like an F. Scott Fitzgerald [ideal], just a time of like, sweet glow about the whole thing. It didn't appear to be compromised. It was just the right mesh of everything. I was an eighth grader when the '67 season started, and the team sucked every year. But in '75 I had been a writer, and that team, they had this horrible collapse in '74 and kind of a bad one in '72. There was just this notion that they would fuck up."

Carlton Fisk attempts to wave fair the ball he hit for a walk-off home run in the 12th inning of Game 6 of the 1975 World Series.

Led by Bill "Spaceman" Lee (260 innings), Luis "El Tiante" Tiant (also 260), and Rick Wise (255⅓ innings), the pitching staff was riotous and effective. "The Lynn-Rice thing, they were our age so that kind of helped," Shaughnessy said. "Luis was irresistible, and the fans just—it was unqualified love. It was almost like a college town type of thing. And they felt worthy. Bill Lee was hilarious, he was smart, just had all these characters to kind of work to it. We probably were whatever the inverse of jaded is: just overly enamored...Even the bad stuff that happened, it turned into being funny. There was never any kind of a negative edge to it or cynicism."

The Sox went 95–65. They pulled into first place in late June and held steady, never seeing their lead dwindle to below three and a half games before winning the AL East. El Tiante outdueled Jim Palmer in September. "The expectations started to grow as we started to play well," Lynn said. "We got the attention of the league and everybody else when May rolls around and we're jelling as a team. And then, June, now we're fighting for a top spot. It happened pretty quickly."

The Sox swept the Oakland A's in the first round of the playoffs to make the World Series, where the Big Red Machine waited with Johnny Bench, Pete Rose, and Joe Morgan (the Hall of Fame second baseman, not the manager). They won a whopping 108 games.

Game 6 of the '75 World Series was at Fenway Park. Boston trailed in the series three games to two when Fisk batted to begin the 12th inning of a game tied at 6. Already there had been heroics: pinch-hitter Bernie Carbo hit a three-run homer in the eighth inning to knot up the score. In the midnight hour, Fisk hit one of the most famous home runs in history—remembered both for its setting and its reaction.

Pat Darcy's second pitch of the night was a fastball that Fisk yanked toward the Green Monster—or, he feared, the grandstand. Like a man possessed, Fisk started hopping up the first-base line, waving both his arms at the baseball, which acquiesced to the future Hall of Famer by staying fair and banging off the foul pole for a walk-off homer that forced Game 7. Dick Stockton's call was just as iconic: "There it goes. It's a long drive. If it stays fair—home run."

The television shot taken by Louis Gerard for NBC that captured the moment stands out nearly as much as the actual act. As Doug Wilson chronicled for *The Globe* in 2015, one of Gerard's shots was blocked, so the decision was made in the moment to stay on Fisk, who rewarded everyone with a frenzied plea directly to a ball. The moment was made for joyous mimicry, the comparison for any theatrics a batter undertakes off the bat, particularly in a moment of fair/foul uncertainty.

It was nice while it lasted, but a familiar outcome loomed.

The ties that bind the '67, '75, and '86 seasons together go beyond just a World Series loss. Naturally, they were all excruciating, drawn-out experiences that put the team and the fans so close to the prize before stomping on hearts like wine grapes. All those World Series went seven games, none of them working out in the Sox's favor. "I have three games or so that could really stand out," Lynn said, reflecting on his career. "I lost every one of them, and one of them's Game 7 of the World Series. It was really a magical time for this city and to come so close to winning...I was used to winning. I won at the amateur level, won the Triple A World Series, too. That's the first time I had gotten to a championship game and lost. So that really kind of put a damper on the whole season for me. It was a big hole. It still is, it really is to this day in my resume. I didn't win a championship, and that was as close as I got. I didn't think that was going to happen. I think all of us collectively thought that with the talent that we had in that room that we would be knocking on the door every year. Sooner or later, we'd get it done. But it didn't happen with the playoff system that it was then. If it was the playoff system now, where you could be a wild-card, I think we would have won a World Series before 2004, but that's not the way it was though. Losing that series was very painful."

16

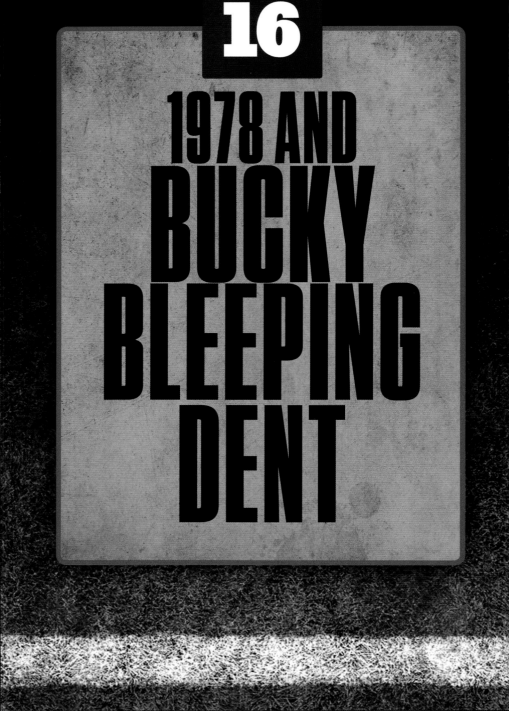

1978 AND BUCKY BLEEPING DENT

For decades Red Sox fans were mired in a state of schadenfreude. Bonds were built on dramatic defeats. When you believe it is your birthright to watch a team lose, in a small way, you've actually been conditioned to enjoy losing. (Please reach out to your therapists for more.)

As readily as you'd recall the wallpaper and the Yankee Candle burning when Johnny Damon hit the grand slam in Game 7 of the 2004 American League Championship Series, you'd compare notes with a friend on precisely where you stood when the worst came to pass.

For those who lived it, Bucky Bleeping Dent is high on that list. He was Aaron Boone before Aaron Boone. Dent, a light-hitting shortstop, became a reference point for every Red Sox killer that follows. Plenty of players on the 1978 Sox had been to the World Series just three years earlier, losing in seven games to the Cincinnati Reds. But the sting was different in '78. There was no World Series build-up. Game No. 163 in '78 was a winner-take-all contest for the American League East. The ride simply ended. "You don't have too much chance to think about it," Luis Tiant said. "Everybody goes in the clubhouse. We cried. Everybody cries. I don't care—Yaz, myself, everybody, it was a bad day for us. Maybe it was the worst day in baseball for me. That day—that was a bad day."

Most know Dent hit a home run for the Yankees in 1978 and that he wasn't expected to. Some of the specifics of the dagger may be cloudier, and that's unsurprising because Dent was otherwise unremarkable. A 5'9" shortstop, Dent had hit just four home runs entering October 2, 1978. He was batting ninth. But the seventh-inning shot off Sox right-hander Mike Torrez went over the Green Monster to torpedo a season. The Sox led 2–0 in the seventh inning when Dent's go-ahead homer came on a 2–1 pitch down the middle with two on and two out. The Sox lost 5–4 with the decisive run scoring on Reggie Jackson's eighth-inning solo shot.

(Dent didn't stop there. He actually went on to become the World Series MVP for the Yankees, going 10-for-24 in a six-game Fall Classic against the Los Angeles Dodgers. And a year earlier in '77, Torrez was with the Yankees and won both his starts in the World Series, which was also won by New York over Los Angeles in six.)

The whole game encapsulated so much of the Sox's plight. Naturally, the Yankees, the defending World Series champs who were headed to their third straight World Series, were the antagonists. There was no wild-card back then, a shame considering this was a match-up of two teams that won 99 games of their first 162. A coin toss gave the Red Sox home-field advantage. This team was historically good—59–22 heading into the final game—playing near Kenmore Square. As of 2017 the Sox's 59 wins at home had them tied for the eighth most home wins in the majors from 1950 on.

The Yankees, of course, wanted to be in the Bronx. Badly. In Bill Madden's book on Yankees owner George Steinbrenner, we learn how irate Steinbrenner was when he heard the Yankees lost the coin toss. "Heads?" Steinbrenner yelled at Yankees team president Al Rosen on the phone. "You imbecile! How in the hell could you call heads when any dummy knows tails comes up 70 percent of the time? I can't believe it!"

Of course, playing at Fenway wasn't enough. Ron Guidry, who finished 25–3 with a 1.74 ERA, was on the mound for New York and would eventually be named the league's Cy Young winner. In the ill-fated seventh, the Yanks had runners on first and second after back-to-back two-out singles off Torrez, the starter. Dent fouled the second pitch of the at-bat off his left ankle, bringing out the trainer and evening the count at one. He was given a new bat and choked up on it like a Little Leaguer. The next pitch was piped. Left fielder Carl Yastrzemski moved to his right, hoping for a chance at a carom off the

Monster. His knees buckled as the ball cleared the wall, looking a little like he had just been shot. The Sox let it slip away—both that day and earlier in the season.

Boston was up seven games in the division to start September. The lead was 10 games entering play July 9. And inside their final game, they were ahead early, too. Yastrzemski's solo home run in the second inning staked the Sox to a 1–0 advantage. Jim Rice's single in the sixth made it 2–0.

Like many famed moments, everything else that could have gone differently in a game becomes secondary for many. Dent was the difference, they say. Not for Fred Lynn, the center fielder who nearly doubled the Sox's lead to 4–0 in the sixth. "I look at that game differently than everybody else because I see it through different eyes," Lynn said. "So when Dent hits the home run, yeah, that hurt us. But what hurt us more was [Yankees right fielder] Lou Piniella making two defensive plays that he's not supposed to be able to make. To be honest one of 'em, I was hitting. We're facing Guidry, and Yaz had hit a homer early, and we had two guys on, and there were two outs, and I came up. I hit a rocket down the right field corner...Piniella ran it down, lunging, snow cone catch. So that saved two runs right there. And that might have knocked Guidry out of the game. And if we get into that middle relief corps, the game's over. We're up 4–0 and we knock him out, it's over. So that saved two runs right there, kept Guidry in the game."

Piniella was a step away from the warning track when he caught the rocket off Lynn's bat, a curveball inside that Lynn had turned on. That wasn't Piniella's only contribution.

The Yankees wound up with one more run in the seventh and another in the eighth after the Dent homer for a 5–2 lead. Yaz and Lynn had RBI singles in the eighth to cut the deficit to one, facing Hall of Famer Goose Gossage, the only reliever the Yanks used. In the ninth inning, Rick Burleson drew a one-out walk. Jerry Remy, the next batter, lined a pitch to right field. Piniella lost the ball in the sun, and it bounced in front of him—but he somehow kept the ball from getting by him. That kept Burleson at second base. If Burleson gets to third with less than one out, the Sox have a much better chance of tying.

"And Rice hits a long fly ball, the next hitter, which would have tied the game," Lynn said, "[Piniella] saved three runs basically. I think about it all the time. In fact, I asked Lou when he was managing Seattle and I was working at ESPN. I said, 'Why were you over there? You know I don't pull him. You should have never been there.'

"He said, 'Well, Ron had thrown a lot of innings.' And he didn't think his breaking ball was that good that day. So he played me more to pull, which was really good thinking. Not exactly what you want to hear from your outfielders. They see things that sometimes managers don't see because they're in the heart of the game, and that was a really good play, really smart play. And that play beat us more than Bucky Dent, doesn't bother me though!" Lynn added sarcastically.

Rice won the MVP that season, hitting 46 home runs. Dennis Eckersley had a 2.99 ERA, went 20–8, and finished fourth in the Cy Young voting in his first year in Boston. This was one hell of a Red Sox team.

After the game Steinbrenner walked into the Red Sox clubhouse and told Sox manager Don Zimmer, "It's too bad that the best two teams in baseball had to play this game," which Dave O'Hara chronicled for the Associated Press at the time. Dent said afterward he didn't see the ball leave. "I just heard the fans. I've been struggling and I can't believe it."

Somehow, Red Sox fans could.

17

FENWAY PARK

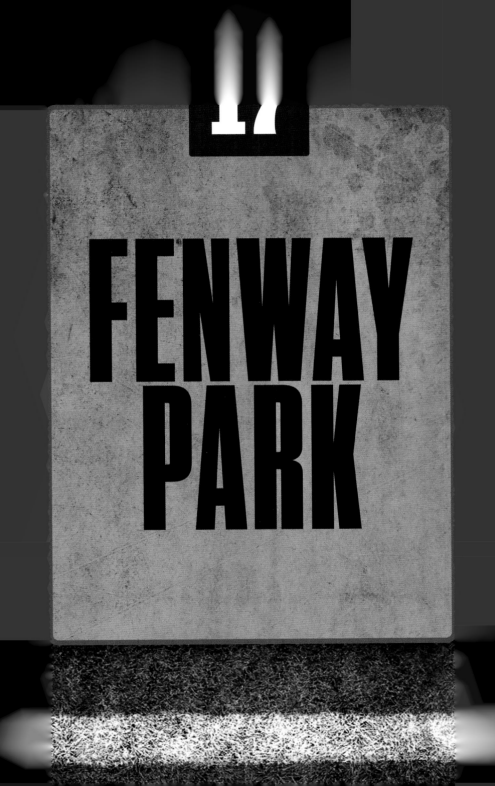

The time I find Fenway Park most pleasant is when it's most still—long before and after games or on an off day. If you want a glimpse for yourself, there's public access via paid tours.

The soft Dartmouth green of the Monster and the other walls, the flow of compressed navy seats, and the view of downtown Boston beyond right field form near-meditative grounds. You don't have to think about the stars that once played at Fenway and all the sport-specific history to appreciate the joint. Yes, Babe Ruth pitched on that mound. The frenzy of a walk-off home run over the Green Monster is neat. But if you briefly consider Fenway Park as just that—as a park, as a green space—you may find a different enjoyment.

At the end of the 2017 season, an Uber driver told me something surprising. He didn't like Fenway Park. Or—at the risk of mischaracterizing his point—he found it uncomfortable and hoped the Red Sox would eventually build a new stadium. He was an older fellow, a little on the heavier side, too. Indeed, Fenway can be cramped. But the magnetism of nostalgia seems to outweigh the need for creature comforts. (But perhaps this is only true for those who are too young to know what they're nostalgic for.)

Red Sox ownership would rightly point out the stadium's comforts have been upgraded immensely during their tenure, which began in 2002. Through the first decade of the John Henry, Tom Werner, Larry Lucchino era, in a stretch that runs through the 2010–11 offseason, they directed about $285 million in club money to a stadium constructed in 1912. "Our intention was to preserve and protect Fenway Park, which was more than just making a decision to stay at Fenway," Werner said in a 2017 interview. "It was to try to improve the fan experience at Fenway, which covers lots of decisions, including creating more and interesting seats, such as the Green Monster seats. But it included amenities and creating a hospitality level that we thought was better than the [since-removed] .406 Club."

The history of Fenway is as well documented as Ted Williams' swing. What may be more compelling to consider is the future. Was my Uber driver on to something? Is there any juice left to squeeze out of this lemon, or is there an inevitability to a move in the ensuing decades? They saved Fenway, but such a resurrection may itself have an expiration date.

"The conversation doesn't come up for several reasons," Red Sox president Sam Kennedy said. "One, we think the ballpark really works well given our geographic location, the proximity to public transportation, and being right in the city. Two, the $325 million-plus investment [overall] into renovating the old house, sort of the huge amount of capital, private money that has been poured in by John and Tom and their partners."

So, no, they're not going to pave paradise. But they might build on the parking lot. "We see a huge opportunity for the next 15 years to continue to create value and enhance the overall experience at Fenway with development in the neighborhood," Kennedy said. "One of the things that John and Tom have driven over the last 15 years has been the desire to acquire and control real estate parcels in and around Fenway Park. So we've been quietly and strategically acquiring parcels that are all currently surface parking lots or structured parking lots around the ballparks. And so now we're in the mode of: okay, we've dealt with 425,000 square feet that is Fenway Park itself. Given that it's 200-plus years old, we're going to continue to need to invest each and every year at Fenway. But not at a clip of $30, $50 million a year the way we did in the old days. So, we're going to turn our attention to neighborhood opportunities and redevelopment that would hopefully enhance the overall experience—not too dissimilar to the Petco Park setup [in San Diego] or the St. Louis Ballpark Village. There's lots of ways to continue to create value for the neighborhood and the fans and the ownership through development, so I think those factors will cause us to stay here for at least the rest of John and Tom's ownership of the club, which I anticipate being a lot longer."

When the Sox were up for sale most recently, not every group involved would have kept Fenway. The decision by Henry's group to do so was in part owed to nostalgia, but it had more to do with strategic long-term thinking. Put another way: it's about money. It just so happens that the most financially prudent choice might have also been the smartest from a marketing and enjoyment standpoint as well. Upgrading an old park is cheaper than building anew and also brings less of a headache. Lucchino and Kennedy worked together on Petco Park in San Diego for the Padres, and the project was sued constantly. Construction at one point halted.

Lucchino is credited with helping to usher in this exalted era of the modern stadium with Camden Yards in Baltimore, the Orioles' eminently pleasant, comfortable park. Longtime baseball executive Janet Marie Smith, who has degrees in architecture and in urban planning, was central to the Camden Yards project and Fenway's renovation as well. "These older ballparks [were] not forced by a multitude of code and marketing initiatives that spread us all out and put in cross aisles for vendors and separated every seat category," Smith said in a 2013 interview, "and inches which turn into feet, which turn into complete other levels, [and] reduces the intimacy. And at the end of the day, it is the intimacy that really adds energy to the parks in a way that you almost never find in the new parks because they're simply more spread out."

When Fenway Park opened, it was a single-deck grandstand design around the infield and down the right-field line. Center field had bleachers, but there was no seating in left field. There was a 10-foot fence in left field on an embankment, an incline known as "Duffy's Cliff" and named after Duffy Lewis, the starting left fielder for the team in the park's inaugural 1912 season. (He's a Red Sox Hall of Famer.)

The Green Monster, as it's known today, didn't really take shape until Tom Yawkey bought the team in February 1933. A large construction project in 1934, which had to be redone in part because of a tremendous fire, included the removal of Duffy's Cliff and addition of a 37-foot concrete wall in its place, along with a slew of other changes. In 1936 a 23-foot screen was put in place above the wall—it had to catch all those Nomar home runs—and a screen remained in place until the Sox installed the Green Monster seats ahead of the 2003 season.

"I love the irregularity and the intimacy of the place," Lucchino said in a 2017 interview. "I love the fact that you could look at certain parts of the ballpark and see vividly historic moments. I like the simple feel of seats being as close and as low as they are and the grandstand being pushed forward because of the columns. There's something inherently desirable about watching baseball from that perspective, with the intimacy. And I love the fact that it was broadly accepted as everybody's ballpark. I remember reading, when I first got here, a book on ballparks by Curt Smith, former White House speech writer... He said Yankee Stadium may be baseball's most historic ballpark... Wrigley Field is perhaps its prettiest. But unquestionably, Fenway Park was the most beloved. And that was all I needed. We proceeded to repeat that phrase over and over because I think it is true."

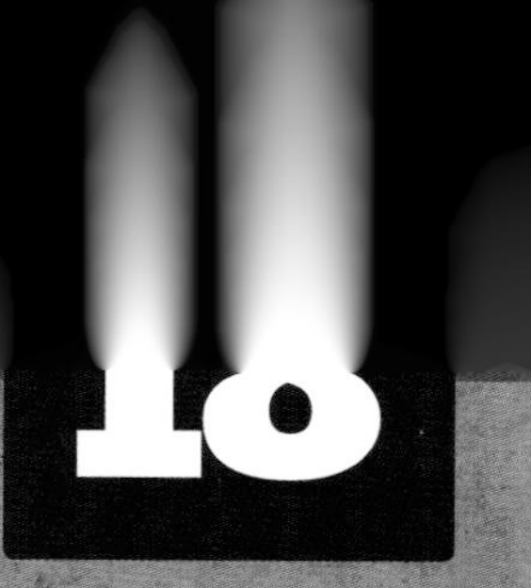

10

MANNY BEING MANNY

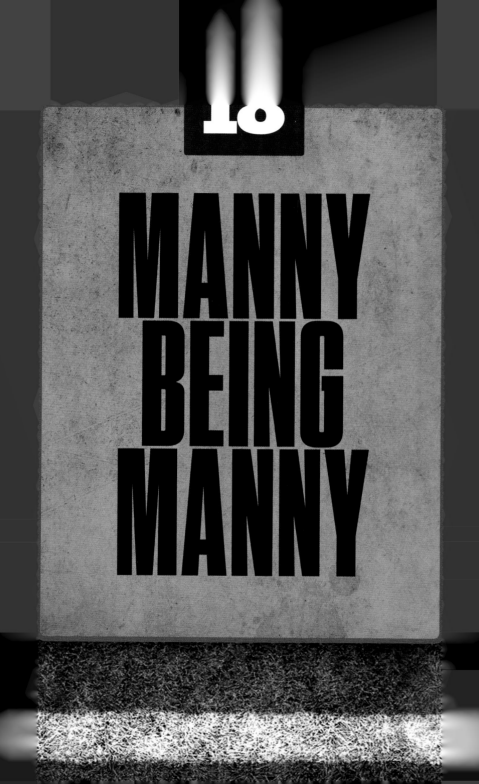

"Manny being Manny" took on a life of its own for both the fans, who adored one of the sweetest swings of a generation, and the player himself. Maybe it's fitting Manny Ramirez spent his teenage years in enemy territory—New York City. As much as Boston loved the right-handed slugger, he was duly hated at times as well. He was dominant on the field, but flighty off of it—the kind to make a plan for lunch with David Ortiz and then never show up because he was at the field. He did much worse, too. For many, there was an overall acceptance of (or at least resignation to) the enigmatic, one-word persona: Manny.

Ramirez hit .412 (7-for-17) with one homer in the 2004 World Series sweep of the St. Louis Cardinals, earning him the MVP award for the Fall Classic that broke The Curse. That's on top of the .308 average and American League-best 43 homers he put up in the regular season.

That year he and Ortiz became the first AL teammates to bat .300 with at least 30 homers and 100 RBIs since 1931.

The next year, during a mound meeting at Fenway Park, Ramirez disappeared into the Green Monster...so he could relieve himself. Back in 1993 with the Cleveland Indians, Manny's first career hit was a ground-rule double to left field. He went into a home-run trot and approached third base before walking out of his daydream and back toward second.

There were 555 validated trots that followed in his regular-season career, and 274 of them came in a Red Sox uniform. His time in Boston, from 2001 to

2008, stamped him as one of the most important signings in franchise history. Look, when you hit like Manny, you're probably not distracted as often as people think. "It was a little bit more complicated than people made it out to be at the time," former Red Sox assistant general manager Jed Hoyer said of Ramirez's reputation, "because we did see a guy that was exceptionally hard working. That made it hard to get your head around. I would go work out early in the morning before work, and it'd be me and Manny at the gym at Fenway... because he would go in really early and work out and go back home and go to sleep. People really didn't see that. People saw the baggy uniform and didn't see the fact that this guy was in ridiculous shape. People saw the dumb stuff he did, but they didn't see the fact that he was as intelligent or as thoughtful a hitter as there was. I just think the complexity of him sometimes got lost. And believe me, there were plenty of unbelievably frustrating moments that were lived through. Honestly, I almost lose track of all of them."

Ramirez would have a two or three-week period where he couldn't be reached. The Sox, including his teammates, would be frustrated. (Red Sox manager Alex Cora, who played with Ramirez from 2005 to 2008, was one of the few who could more readily get through to Ramirez.) "Those things happened," Hoyer continued. "You can't wipe them away. But at the same time, I always felt it was a little bit more complicated because we also saw some of the other stuff. And let's face it: he was incredible. The guy was an incredible, incredible hitter. And the biggest competitive advantage we had in those years is we had David and Manny hitting back to back the whole time...it made the lineup impossible to pitch to."

Former GM Dan Duquette inked Ramirez to an eight-year, $160 million deal after the 2000 season. Ramirez had an incredible 165 RBIs in his second-to-last season before coming to Boston, a figure no one's bested since before the second World War. In 2001, his first season in Boston, he reached base in the team's first 23 games and was April's AL Player of the Month.

Through all the antics and disconnected gazes, Ramirez could absolutely mash. Such a compact, short swing shouldn't belong to a man so large. Beauty isn't usually part of the lexicon for most right-

The always eccentric, often flighty Manny Ramirez emerges from the Green Monster prior to the Red Sox's game in August of 2005.

handed swings, but it is here. He was a dude in the postseason, too. Ramirez is one of three players with hits in 17 consecutive postseason games, the big league record.

His hands were absurdly quick. Few can turn on a 96 mph fastball on the inner half of the plate as Ramirez did in Game 2 of the American League Division Series in 2007. Ramirez decimated a thigh-high pitch that looked like it was already in the catcher's mitt, crushing a walk-off well over the Green Monster. It was a precise and instantaneous knockout blow, geometric excellence. The swing connected just as a boxer's uppercut to the chin would.

Ramirez's 29 playoff home runs are a major league record. It's seven more than the next closest on the list, Bernie Williams. But when it comes to those moonshots, you do have to wonder. Would Ramirez have hit all 29...well, before we finish this thought, let's first acknowledge what a shame it is that we have to wonder at all. But we do: how much of Ramirez's excellence was owed to performance-enhancing drug use? He brought the question on himself via multiple positive tests for PEDs in his time in the majors. Unlike many others there's no speculation with Ramirez. He used. He was caught in both 2009 and 2011 (after he left the Sox) in addition to also reportedly testing positive in 2003 (while he was with the Sox), when the league was doing initial trials that were supposed to remain anonymous. Such a thick dossier may well keep him out of the Hall of Fame.

In a 2014 interview with Ken Rosenthal, Ramirez said PED use turned out to have a silver lining. "I use myself as an example to my son who is in college, playing baseball: 'Look what Daddy went through because Daddy didn't do things right,'" Ramirez told Rosenthal. "When you do things right, you don't have to look back. You always look forward. Sometimes we get caught up in the moment. We start hanging out with the wrong people. But everything in life happens for a reason, so you can appreciate what you are."

The PED usage didn't amount to the darkest moments of Ramirez's career. In 2008 he shoved Red Sox traveling secretary Jack McCormick to the ground over a ticket request that was put in too late. Three years later Ramirez was arrested and charged with domestic violence in Florida. His wife told authorities Ramirez slapped

I want you to forgive me because it was my fault,'" Ramirez said. "I behaved bad here with everybody. I want you to forgive me. He said, 'Manny, thank you, I was waiting for that.'"

He said in 2014 that religion had taken a more central role in his life. "When I went to jail with that problem with my wife, they didn't let me see my kids for maybe two or three months," Ramirez said. "One day, I wake up and I look myself in the mirror and I said I needed a change. So I started going to bible studies and I saw that it was good, so I kept going, and God helped me to change my life."

Ramirez's time in Boston was nearly cut very short. In the 2003–04 offseason, the Red Sox were ready to trade Ramirez to the Texas Rangers as part of the package to land Alex Rodriguez. They held on to Ramirez instead until the trade deadline in 2008, when things started to sour. Such is the course of life in Boston. Ramirez and Kevin Youkilis had a famous dugout altercation less than two months before Ramirez was dealt. "I realize that I behaved bad in Boston, and the fans—they were great," Ramirez said during that '14 visit. "I also really realize that I behaved bad and I apologize for that. I'm a new man."

Many have proclaimed as much; fewer have proven it. In an ideal world, Ramirez would be remembered primarily for such a gorgeous swing and for his quirks. But said quirks were coupled with deep flaws, mistakes that complicate the legacy of both the ballplayer and the human being. Amazingly, Ramirez was still playing baseball in 2017 in a Japanese league, but not in Nippon Professional Baseball, the most competitive league that feeds some of its top talent into the major leagues. You can question Ramirez's integrity as a ballplayer, but the fact he has continued to play so long suggests a man who, at his core, still loves the game.

19

2003

There's a Boston quick-trigger reaction, and then there's insanity. One move didn't drop the axe. Manager Grady Little was on his way out in 2003—regardless of one pitching change. He was never going to be the new Red Sox regime's guy, and leaving Pedro Martinez in too long during Game 7 of the American League Championship Series against the New York Yankees didn't change that. (Could a World Series win have stayed the execution? Probably, but the overall fit wouldn't have changed.) "Look, my life is about that moment," Little told *Sports Illustrated* in 2013, 10 years after the Sox lost the pennant on an 11th inning home run from Aaron Boone. "My life is about people judging me on one game when I managed about three thousand. Shoot, I made a decision. The results were bad that day, but I made those same decisions to get us there."

Little was an old-school guy at a time when the battle lines were just starting to being drawn between old and new. The Sox were new and hip and trying desperately to look like anything but the muse for Mystique and Aura, Yankee Stadium's most famous patrons. General manager Theo Epstein, not yet 30, had just completed his first year on the job in '03, and the Yankees-Sox rivalry was approaching its apex. The whole country was either swept up in the mania or swept up in despising a Northeast media frenzy and megateams with whom others in the league just couldn't compete.

Little had a sound appreciation for the moment going into his final night as skipper. "It's been incredible, alright," Little said ahead of Game 7. "A lot of us that are involved in the ballclubs right now, I think in the dugout, it's a little bit different than the fans' perspective of the whole thing. We are down there trying to focus in on each particular game and trying to win that particular game. It's like the series we played against the Oakland A's [in the first round]; a lot of people have told me since then that it was a great series, a classic series in postseason play, but it's something that we never realize in the dugout. Probably the feeling for fans in the New York area and the Boston area, all of the Red Sox fans, all of the Yankee fans all over the country, they are getting a big thrill out of this and they are anxious for this game to get started tonight just as we are."

The 95–67 campaign was the last full year for Nomar Garciaparra in Boston and David Ortiz's first season mashing alongside Manny Ramirez. "Cowboy Up" was the slogan, a mentality that Kevin Millar hammered home of forgetting the past. Bill Mueller won the batting title with a .326 average that year. John Burkett and Casey Fossum combined for 44 starts behind the top trio of Pedro Martinez, Tim Wakefield, and Derek Lowe—a group upgraded with one Curt Schilling that winter.

They were painfully close without him.

A five-game American League Division Series with the A's, a series of actual Sox success inside a year highlighted for down-to-the-wire failure, gave a sense it really could be the Sox's year. Really! That Oakland team won 96 games. Boston started the series down two games to none, embarking on a comeback punctuated by one of the absolute filthiest pitches you'll ever see. The Sox were ahead 4–3 in Game 5 with lefty Terrence Long coming up to pinch hit against the righty Lowe in the ninth inning. The bags were full, there were two down. Lowe reflexively stuck out his rear end as Lowe's signature two-seamer looked to be headed straight for his hip. Instead, with his typical screwball-like movement and arm-side run, the pitch jumped right back over the plate with a 1–2 count.

The intense disappointment of the next round's match-up with the Yankees precipitated considerable amounts of change. The '03 Sox season is baseball's version of the *Empire Strikes Back*, the entertaining but gloomy stage setter for Red Sox heroics to follow.

The loudest this author has ever heard a stadium in person was when chants of "Pe-dro, Pe-dro" rained down on Martinez in the eighth inning of the ALCS as a 5–2 Sox lead with five outs to go slowly dissipated in front of 56,279 in the Bronx. Derek Jeter started the rally with an opposite-field double over right fielder Trot Nixon's head on an elevated 0–2 fastball. Switch-hitter Bernie Williams stroked an RBI single to center field, taking an outside corner fastball the other way for a sweet piece of hitting and a run. Hideki Matsui, a left-handed hitter, represented the tying run, and Pedro already had 115 tosses. The Sox were up 5–3. In today's game Martinez would have never stayed in for another toss, and left-hander Alan Embree would have been brought on instead.

A mound meeting with Little out there kept Martinez on the mound. He was ahead on Matsui 0–2 before a line drive down the right-field line, a 93 mph fastball that the lefty Matsui turned on, went for a ground-rule double and put the tying runs in scoring position—still with just one out. Still in the game, Martinez put a 95 mph fastball on the inside corner to Jorge Posada, who blooped a game-tying single. That was pitch No. 123. (Maybe Pedro should have just kept throwing curveballs like Houston Astros pitcher Lance McCullers in 2017.) "Pedro Martinez has been our man all year long and in situations like that he's the one we want on the mound over anybody we can bring in out of that bullpen," Little said immediately afterward. "He had enough left in his tank to finish off Posada. He made some good pitches to him, squeezed his ball out over the infield, and there's nothing we can do about it now. Pedro wanted to stay in there. He wanted to get the job done just as he has many times for us all season long and he's the man we all wanted on the mound."

Little's not wrong on this front: Martinez made some good pitches. But Embree would have been a better match-up for Matsui. (And if we're being real: Little would have been killed by fans and media if he gave Pedro an earlier hook, and the bullpen coughed up the lead, too.)

The almost infallible Mariano Rivera took over from there, outlasting Boston's Tim Wakefield, who gave up Boone's walk-off on a knuckleball that knuckled to the very middle of the plate in the 11th. Boone crushed it down the left-field line. "And so a new generation of

New Englanders has learned the risk of rooting for the Red Sox," Dan Shaughnessy wrote for *The Boston Globe* the next day.

Boone, a third baseman who became the Yankees' new manager after the 2017 season, had never played outside of Cincinnati before that season. He went from the Midwest to permanent Big Apple lore. "It's kind of a crapshoot a little bit, trying to square that thing up sometimes," Boone said of Wake's floater. "I considered taking a pitch leading off the inning there but just decided to get a good pitch to hit. And, you know, he got one up there, and I finally ran into one...I guess it was my time."

Wakefield, 37 at that point, could have been wrecked mentally. Many Red Sox wept.

"I think we beat them. I don't think they beat themselves," Yanks manager Joe Torre said. "I know the Red Sox fans are going to be very proud of this ballclub this year. They were the toughest team in the eight years I've been managing this team, and Grady Little should be congratulated. I know he probably doesn't want to hear it right now, but this ballclub believed in themselves, they never thought they would ever go away. I mean, the series against Oakland—the Red Sox fans, I know they are going to be proud. There are the handful of people up there that will be the wah, wah, wah, stuff like that. But most of those people are pretty damned proud of their ballclub."

Who was Torre kidding? He, Boone, and the Yankees had just overseen another funeral for the Red Sox, the annual rite.

20

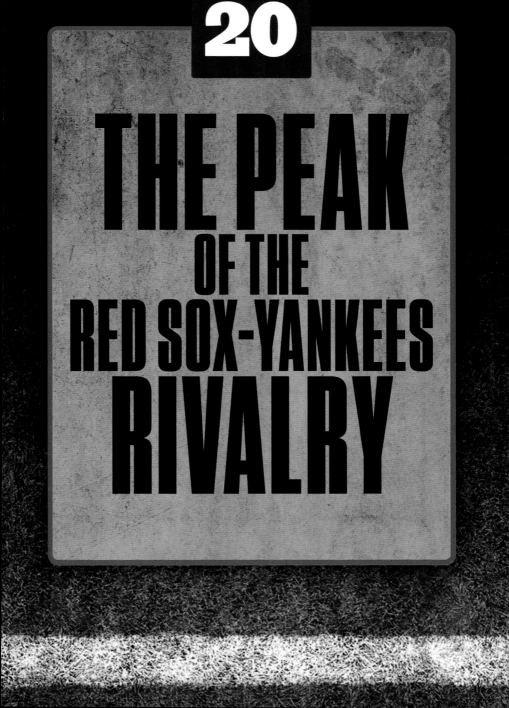

THE PEAK OF THE RED SOX-YANKEES RIVALRY

Even in 2017, the easiest way to introduce former Red Sox president Larry Lucchino was a catchphrase from 15 years earlier. "You may remember him as the guy who called the New York Yankees 'the evil empire.' That will be paragraph two of his obituary," Lucchino said, recalling how he had been introduced at an event days prior to a 2017 interview. "So yeah, it still stays with me. It was a spontaneous, not preplanned comment. I said it to Murray Chass of *The New York Times*, and he had a greater sense of its enduring nature than I did. I was just venting, and he thought that was a vivid image, shall we say."

Chass' story ran on Christmas of 2002 after the Yankees signed Cuban pitcher Jose Contreras, who ended up being a bust relative to the hype and dollars, spending more years and having more success with the Chicago White Sox than anyone else. But the frenzy for the free agent was all-consuming. The Sox and Yanks were in an overall arms race ahead of the impending clashes of 2003 and 2004. The Yankees' pockets at that time appeared limitless, and baseball's rules weren't strong enough to deter owner George Steinbrenner from diving deeper and deeper. "The evil empire extends its tentacles even into Latin America," Lucchino told Chass once the Yanks had their man.

It was, unintentionally, a piece of brilliant marketing. Boston was already an underdog: a smaller city with a smaller but still sizable payroll and zero World Series rings to count since 1918. But with Lucchino's phrasing, George Lucas' dark side of the force was introduced—not by those paid dramatists in the press box but by upper management. It was *Star Wars* on a diamond. The competition was coursing from barstools in Brockton all the way through mansions in Newton. "We were always the underdog," Red Sox chairman Tom Werner said in 2017. "The rivalry was historic, and Larry's coining of the Yankees being the evil empire was obviously good for the competition."

For such a famed rivalry, it reached its pinnacle at the turn of the century with consecutive meetings in the American League Championship Series that went seven games, plus brawls on the field, and monstrous efforts to one-up each other away from it. Colorful personalities, constant media coverage, and ruthless behavior. During the Contreras negotiations, then-Sox general manager Theo Epstein bought up hotel rooms where Contreras was staying to try to keep others away. No access, no competition, right? "The next day Epstein returned to Contreras' room to officially seal the deal," *Sports Illustrated*'s Tom Verducci wrote. "That's when he saw two shadowy figures moving in and out of the room. They were with the Yankees and dispatched there with one assignment from owner George Steinbrenner: come back with Contreras or you're fired. They offered $32 million to sign Contreras and keep their jobs. A bit later, Contreras asked to see Epstein. He was crying."

Contreras told Epstein it wasn't personal. There was simply better offer. The next winter (in 2003) the Sox were negotiating in person with Curt Schilling. That was the famous Thanksgiving courtship at Schilling's Arizona home. The Yankees were dying for a chance at Schilling, too. In this pursit the Sox headed them off.

Then, within weeks Hoyer and Epstein were also wooing Alex Rodriguez at a hotel. Both Schilling and A-Rod had no-trade clauses to waive. A-Rod would have come to Boston, too, but the Yanks got him because they could handle his gigantic contract when the Red Sox couldn't. The Sox had to settle for just Schilling.

But the whole process was something of an offseason acid trip. The Sox brass reflected on the surreal proceedings, as they flew back to Boston after netting Schilling—but not A-Rod. Assistant to the general manager Jed Hoyer recalled: "I remember Theo and I sitting there, like *Ugh, that's something we'll never experience again*. A, thank God we got that done. Can you imagine being on this plane if we haven't signed him? And then the second thought was: *Wow, we'll never have that happen again*. We were in this guy's [Schilling's] house for three days negotiating without an agent. And then three weeks later, we're with A-Rod alone in a hotel room. That does not happen. It hasn't happened to me since, right? And it happened twice in like a three-week period."

Whether the Red Sox and Yankees birthed the greatest rivalry in the history of the sport is a little more complex and ultimately subjective. It's certainly the most prominent. But talk to some old Brooklyn Dodgers and New York Giants fans about how much they hated one another's clubs (and the Yankees, too). Giants-Dodgers carried over to California. It's not like the Chicago Cubs and St. Louis Cardinals are simpatico. The Houston Astros and Texas Rangers fans are damn feisty these days, but baseball isn't king in Texas.

Certainly, Sox-Yanks has had the most global reach of any baseball pairing. Connecticut-based ESPN, it's safe to say, played a role, and the players started to harbor the same territorial mentality as the fans. When Rodriguez tried to slap away a tag from Bronson Arroyo during the '04 ALCS, the Sox were livid. This was after Jason Varitek and A-Rod had already squared off near home plate in the regular season. "We could take the thing with A-Rod and 'Tek and let it go as a normal brawl or whatever," Pedro Martinez said in 2012. "But the second one was like, 'No, you're not doing that to us. Not anymore.' So we decided to just go after them with bad intentions. I remember we held a meeting, and we set it clear...We were ready to fight, kick, and scratch and do whatever it takes."

One way or another, the baseball world moved along I-95 in the early aughts. Those who didn't care about the Sox and Yanks started to care either because of interest in a David and Goliath story or because of disgust of the media's obsession of it. But there was so much talent on hand. These were virtual All-Star teams. "All the emotions, all the adrenaline, all the competition, competing against the Yankees has been outstanding through the years," David Ortiz said in his final days as a player. "I have competed against so many great players coming out of the Yankees. There's a lot of intensity. And there has been some players that once you go and play and compete against the Yankees and you don't see them there any more, it's like, hmm...you know it kind of hits you a little [that they're gone]."

People need to stop looking for Manny and Pedro and Jeter and A-Rod to walk back through that door. Accept the new characters and let their stories unfold. Their tales are worth your time. In 2017 the Yankees accused the Red Sox of stealing signs with an electronic device in the dugout. It was a classic poke in the eye. The day the news broke, the Sox flat-out accused the Yankees of leaking the story to the press. "The Yankees decided they wanted to give it to *The [Times]* today for whatever reason," Sox president of baseball operations Dave Dombrowski said.

To be clear: one of the game's most well-respected executives accused the game's jewel franchise of a mild form of sabotage. Commissioner Rob Manfred happened to be visiting Fenway Park that day. Manfred seemed bemused. "I do believe that this is a charged situation from a competitive perspective," Manfred said. "When you have the kind of rivalry that the Yankees and the Red Sox have, I guess it's not shocking you could have charges and counter charges like this. We will conduct a thorough investigation of the charges on both sides."

The Sox turned around and accused the Yankees of wrongdoing, which was cleared. In the end the Sox were fined. Dombrowski hasn't bought up any hotel rooms yet. But the single most important thread in Red Sox history—their juxtaposition to the Yankees—has new life. Mookie Betts and Aaron Judge and Chris Sale and Giancarlo Stanton have assured us of that.

21

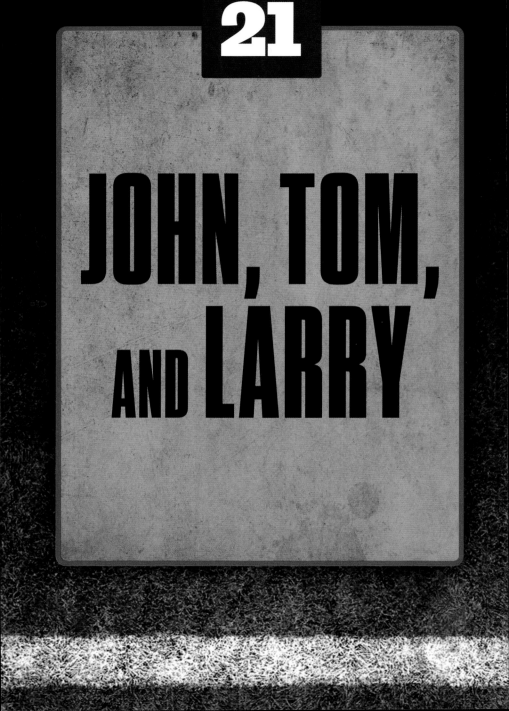

JOHN, TOM, AND LARRY

Red Sox fans and the Boston media are accomplished complainers. Occasionally, its ownership group deserves a reprieve from the cynicism. Three championships speak for themselves. The revitalization of Fenway Park and the growth of the Red Sox Foundation are essential, too. But nothing really works, no legacy is cemented without winning and competitiveness and their requisite investments. When it comes to the Red Sox experience, John, Tom, and Larry have been excellent custodians.

Principal owner John Henry, chairman Tom Werner, and former president Larry Lucchino agreed in December 2001 to buy the team from the Yawkey family and their trustees for a then-record $700 million. "We set out to do a few things in our introductory press conference," Werner said in a 2017 interview. "They covered being successful on the field and bringing multiple World Series back to Boston, which I think people thought had an element of hubris to it since they hadn't won one in 84 years. We believed that we could not only win one—but more than one."

You may not like every choice the group, which does extend beyond those three, has made. You may feel the involvement in Liverpool soccer is a distraction. But a parade came quickly. How? Well, for one thing, experience didn't hurt. Henry had been an owner of the Florida Marlins, Werner was a San Diego Padres owner, and Larry Lucchino was president of the Padres and Baltimore Orioles. "If we had made rookie mistakes, we already had made them," Werner said.

Connections help. Consider: Lucchino brought youngsters Sam Kennedy, his gregarious successor as president, and Theo Epstein with him from the Padres. Those connections resulted from a wealth of baseball experience. "It was an intense auction-like atmosphere into the end of 2001. And I still think it was more like roulette than rational selection," Lucchino said in a 2017 interview. "But I'm glad the selection was us because we were the one group that didn't need training wheels or to learn on the job. With me, John, and Tom, we had, I don't know, 35, 40 years of baseball operational and ownership experience. I think that was often overlooked as people see the cycle that was initiated when we got here."

This group won't be in place forever. And it may not be until its eventual exit that people remember what the alternative can look like. Some of you are old enough to remember when winning and competitiveness were not birthrights across the traditional four major Boston teams.

The top two forward-facing Sox figures, Henry and Werner, don't offer anything near, say, George Steinbrenner-like bombast. Lucchino—still in the ownership group—was the media bulldog. Henry is a soft-spoken guy who coincidentally owns a megaphone in *The Boston Globe*. His younger days as a college dropout and guitarist—ahead of incredible success trading commodities futures—are reason to believe if he did put himself out there more often, he'd be a fascinating listen.

Werner, a Hollywood executive, isn't exactly a thunderous presence in the media, but he did run for commissioner and is a little more willing to mix it up. "I can only speak for myself: the club is what's most important, and the relationship the club has with its fans," Werner said. "The appropriate place for owners to be is in the background. Some owners buy sports franchises to embellish their own legacy. But for us, it's always in service to the Boston Red Sox. We know at some point there will be another group or another owner who will buy the Boston Red Sox, and I'm proud of the fact that what we've done is improve the stature of the club, of its fans, and to leave it in a better place than where we bought it."

There's no indication that the time when another group comes in will be soon. The owners directly said otherwise prior to the 2017 season. And their passion for the Red Sox was displayed in how the group came together. "[Werner] was responsible for me coming here," Lucchino said. "He asked me if I would consider joining up with him in his effort with [minority owner] Les Otten to buy the Red Sox, and, of course, I said something like, 'the Red Sox, that's baseball mecca, that's Fenway Park, that's special. And I was a baseball executive, so it was the easiest thing to do, although the task of acquiring it was not easy. But throwing myself into the process was easy at Tom's invitation. And then I was the one who encouraged John Henry to be involved in our deal because he was talking to me about perhaps going with him to Anaheim or some other team he was trying to buy. I said, 'John, I can't really ride these horses at the same time. I'm going to stick with Tom and the Red Sox.' And then about a week later, he called me—and I remember vividly because I was at the Yale-Brown football game; it was at halftime. He called and said, 'You think there's room for me in Boston?'

"I said, 'Room for you? You're just what the doctor ordered! You're a baseball guy. It's already been approved, and you love the game and you got deep pockets. You're perfect.' So for a long time we called him Investor 11 to try to keep his name out of the press."

The Red Sox are indeed a business as well as a de facto public trust. Werner and Henry have made grand profits on the Sox. Good for them. The altruism of sports ownership is hard to completely evaluate because the books are never disclosed publicly—at least not intentionally. (Some teams' financial documents were leaked in the past.) What percentage is actually reinvested and given back? Who knows?

We do know this: relative to their peers across baseball, the Sox owners have shown a continued willingness to outspend most anyone across the board. The Sox are a model for philanthropy in sports. But it's not just expenditure. Kennedy and Epstein said there was a philosophical change when Henry and Co. took over, challenging all departments to reimagine themselves. "They worked really well together in their own way and they had a great vision for when they

THE THEO AND LARRY SHOW

The relationship between former Red Sox president Larry Lucchino and former Red Sox general manager Theo Epstein is layered and compelling. "There are so many different sagas to that opera," Lucchino said. "It was operatic and Shakespearean."

Mentorship and cooperation gave way to rough waters. They had tremendous success together—and also enough conflict that Epstein briefly resigned from his post during contract negotiations in the fall of 2005. That's when Epstein snuck out of Fenway Park in a gorilla suit. "There were some abrasions certainly and some disagreements," Lucchino said in a 2017 interview. "But out of that dynamic came something very good and insightful, youthful. I don't know, maybe it's creative dissonance or it's dialectic...whatever word you want to use to describe the collaboration. It was very definitely a collaboration that had its good moments and its less good moments. But I have enormous respect for the gifts he brought. I was willing to take the chance."

Epstein was hired in November 2002. The move was risky: he was only 28 years old. But within two seasons, they were on top of the world. "I was invited to a dinner at the White House that [Yale alum] George W. Bush was having," Lucchino said. "He was not my president. I'm a lifetime Democrat. I've always liked him and had a good relationship with him, so I looked forward to seeing him that night. As he walked in...for this informal dinner, he yelled across the room, said, 'Hey, Lucchino, I hear you hired a 28-year-old GM, better be good!' I said, 'Mr. President, he went to Yale.' He said, 'Strike 2!'

bought the team. They had a vision for the potential of the Red Sox and they realized it," Epstein said in a 2017 interview. "Larry's great at building an overall business organization and hiring great people and setting an incredible standard for hard work and sort of doggedness and intelligence and he rubbed off on everyone in the organization.

"John, brilliant guy...a great processor of information and decision maker and he was really warm to me through really my entire time at the Red Sox, supporting me in a lot of important ways. And Tom, Tom did brilliant things with NESN and was involved in a large part of the organization kind of behind the scenes. Such a reasonable, good

"I think people were surprised [at the hire], but I knew Theo pretty well and I knew his gifts and his drive," Lucchino continued. "I thought that we could do some good things together, and we did. And toward the end, I think he wanted to move on. People evolve in their careers and I probably need to be constantly reminded of that."

There was always a fascination with their relationship, though. Distribution of credit was always an interesting topic in their shared time. One thing's for sure: Epstein would have handled that 2005 walkout differently now. "The people who know how baseball decisions were made and how we built a baseball operations department...and shaped its impact on the organization were the ones pulling all-nighters in the offices of Fenway Park in the baseball operations basement," Epstein said. "That's my reality. And I also felt like I had a lot of autonomy, like it was never a power struggle at all. Whatever differences we had were sort of differences in like, values and organizational: what we stand for as an organization, how we handle things like credit and blame, and whether we'd operate with humility, whether we cared about optics and things of that nature. And so I would have handled it much, much differently now than I did then. I made a huge mistake by failing to realize I could have simply just kept showing up to work. I didn't need to walk away. I didn't need to walk away to fix those things. I could have just said, 'Well, I'm just going to keep showing up to work because I don't want this to be a big story. I don't want this to be a big deal and I don't really wanna leave.'

"But at the time, in all my absolutism and sort of youthful extremism, I saw it as black and white, but really there were so many shades of gray involved."

natured guy, who put out a lot of fires and was a big part of the vision that ended up becoming a reality."

What may be most difficult to parse—as this ownership group approaches two decades—is a distribution of blame and credit, of responsibility and power. Things did appear messy at times. Most who have been married would say that's only natural. How exactly were decisions—both the good ones and the bad ones—made? The reality is a lot of choices are hard to reduce to simplistic terms. "We were all involved in everything," Werner said. "It might be a misperception that I was like just doing the TV [work with NESN]. We were involved in all of the decisions and creating what we thought was a great environment for both players and executives to work."

There, of course, are other individuals involved besides the biggest names. That's always been true. "We were a very inclusive organization," Lucchino said. "We did try to include a variety of people, including assistant general managers, including people from the business side. So the dynamic was not restricted to just us. But there was a role that each of us played, and I thought that maybe one of the overlooked elements of this era of Red Sox history was how well [we worked] despite the perception from outside reporters that there was constant bickering and disagreement and all of that.

"You don't achieve the kind of on-field, off-field success that we had unless everybody in the organization is kind of pulling in the right direction and making a variety of contributions. So I just don't think you can do that under the circumstances that were suggested: the sort of dramatic bickering, disagreement, sometimes overplayed. You have to make thousands of decisions every year. There's going to be a bunch of things you disagree with...That's good. Last thing you want to do is work with somebody who agrees with you on the 436,000 decisions that you have to make this year."

1986

More than 30 years later, 1986 still seems like a slightly touchy subject. Just slightly. And I'll hedge right away: I speak of an undertone I detected in a few voices. Maybe they'd deny it to the rafters. None of those Red Sox are still grieving over the World Series loss to the New York Mets. Not often, anyway. But decades of discussion, privately and publicly, have to whittle down one's patience. The plain disappointment of losing probably doesn't ever fully dissipate either—nor would you really expect it to. The lingering thoughts have a tinge of deflection and rationalization mixed with reality. "People don't talk about that anymore," Calvin Schiraldi said by phone in 2017 when asked about Game 6. "It's over and done with. I think if the Red Sox hadn't won in '04 or whatever and after that, yeah, they'd probably still be talking about it. But since they won...it's gone. It's history."

Part of an outstanding 1986 lineup, Jim Rice hit .324 with 20 home runs and 110 RBIs that season, which featured a transcendent and arduous postseason. "The difference [between] right now is that you had to win the eastern division or western division," Rice said. "You didn't have a wild-card like you have now. And so I think it was much tougher then than it is now."

Specific to that year's postseason, it really was an accomplishment to make it to the Fall Classic. The Sox won an epic seven-game American League Championship Series with the California Angels just to get there. The history of '86 does deserve to be more than just a remembrance of one moment, and many Red Sox fans do have a more holistic, reasonable approach. We can view it through many prisms—even inside a two-game span.

When the ball went through Bill Buckner's legs in the 10th inning of Game 6 at the Mets' Shea Stadium, the game was already tied at 5. A 5–3 Red Sox lead to begin the bottom of the inning was already blown. Schiraldi was on the mound to start the frame and gave

Bill Buckner leaves the field after committing his infamous error in Game 6 of the 1986 World Series.

THE DRAMATIC 1986 ALCS

The strangest part about the 1986 postseason is how much seemed to be going in the Red Sox's favor. The seven-game American League Championship Series the Boston Red Sox won over the California Angels would be better remembered if they had finished the job against the New York Mets. But the battle for the pennant was an all-time classic. Games 4 and 5 both went 11 innings in Anaheim. "[We] set out in spring training of '86 and we were picked to finish fifth in our division and sort of after May 1 we caught fire and started winning and developing," Wade Boggs said. "[We] made the trade for Dave Henderson and Spike Owen, and the team started evolving and playing well together. And then, wow, they've got a chance to make the playoffs...and then play California, and we're down [three games to one] to California, and Reggie [Jackson] takes off his glasses and hugs [Angels manager] Gene Mauch. And then, uh oh, here comes Dave Henderson."

It was Game 5. Henderson's two-run homer in the top of the ninth inning off the Angels' Donnie Moore—on a low and away splitter—briefly gave the Sox the lead. The Angels tied it again, and a Henderson sac fly in the 11th—also off Moore—proved the difference in a 7–6 victory. "And then next thing you know, we're going back to

up three straight hits after retiring the first two batters he faced. One run scored while he was still on the mound. Then Schiraldi's replacement, Bob Stanley, threw a wild pitch that knotted it up at 5. That's when Mookie Wilson dribbled a baseball wound with yarns of sadness underneath Buckner's glove, as the first baseman shuffled toward the foul line. "I was the bullpen coach when the Mets upended us in the World Series," former Sox manager Joe Morgan said. "They call down to the bullpen, said, 'Hey, get Stanley up. He's gotta pitch the bottom half of the inning.' So then [Dave] Henderson hit a home run [to start the top of the 10th, and we scored another run, so] they called back down and said, 'sit Stanley down. We're going to keep Schiraldi in the game.' Well, as it unfolded, Stanley was pitching terrific all the last couple months. He was unhittable

Boston and next thing you know we're going to the World Series," Boggs said. "There was probably a little cockiness when we won the first two and went back to Boston that it was over and sort of counted our chickens before they hatched—and no pun intended."

Well played, Chicken Man.

"But it was a wake-up call when we got back to Boston," Boggs said. "And then going back to New York, we had a 3–2 lead and just sort of how Game 6 unfolded and letting the lead get away, but the biggest thing was we had the lead in Game 7 and let it get away, too. So, it was just one of those things. Somebody's gotta win, somebody's gotta lose. And it was an exciting World Series, and I was just really happy to be a part of it."

Tragically, Moore, the Angels pitcher who gave up the homer to Henderson, later killed himself. The blown Game 5 may have been disproportionately linked to his death. "Yet the truth was that there were much worse demons haunting Donnie Moore and probably always had been," wrote Kevin Baker in a 2011 story for *The Atlantic*. "Donnie and his wife, Tonya, had been together since they were high school sweethearts, all right, but this was not a romance...Something had been lost, all right, but it wasn't a ballgame, and it didn't happen in a moment."

down there, and if they hadn't changed their mind, I think we would have won that game."

Stanley, Schiraldi, whatever. No matter how the Sox might have lost, there was still a Game 7, a finale in which Boston led 3–0, going into the bottom of the sixth. So, Buckner didn't singlehandedly flub a Fall Classic. Not even close. "When you're talking about '86 with the ball going through Bill Buckner's legs, I didn't fault Bill," Rice said. "I mean, it could have happened to anyone. I think any time that you play a sport, there's going to be a winner, and there's going to be a loser...If you're a loser, you look forward to doing better the following year. You can't control that. It's part of the game."

A perverse flip side exists for '86 and the other seasons of oh-so-close: '75, '67. What's the reward without the strife? The build-up to

2004 was predicated on losing—and losing in acutely cruel fashion. Maybe we don't have Theo Epstein, the driven Red Sox fan who became the Boy Who Could, if he's not heartbroken as a boy in Brookline, Massachusetts, in 1986. "I don't know. I mean, the same way if I hadn't had a certain teacher one year, maybe my life wouldn't end up in the same way," Epstein said. "You just don't know. We're all products of our experiences. Certainly, like if the Red Sox had won that instead, all of our childhoods would have been a little different and maybe my ambitions would have been as well. Who knows?"

What for a time (maybe for all time) seemed perpetual pessimism in Boston was well and alive in '86. Epstein remembers a math teacher who asked the class if they thought the Sox still had a chance ahead of Game 7. Most students said yes. The teacher told them they were naive. "It was just another example of youthful innocence and naiveté clashing with the cynicism of real world New England experience, right?" Epstein said. "The only people who thought the Red Sox had a chance in Game 7 were those probably 12 years old and younger, and everyone with some perspective and some understanding of history and human psychology thought that they were doomed. I walked into math class all excited about watching the Red Sox win in Game 7 and walked out scratching my head about why maybe grown-ups were so pessimistic. The next night I understood why, I guess."

Wade Boggs hit .357 in 1986. Rice was next on the team in average. "Besides the fact that Wade was frickin' phenomenal that year, Marty [Barrett] had a frickin' ridiculous playoff and World Series," Schiraldi said. "Bruce [Hurst] was unbelievable in the playoffs. For me, put it this way: for me, the World Series was anticlimactic because of the ALCS and because I don't know if that was the last year, but you had four people in the playoffs. Now you've got what: eight, 10, whatever the hell it is. And so, you have four teams in the playoffs. The ALCS and the NLCS to me were the most important series because they got you to the World Series. You get to the World Series, and it's a media circus...it's not that the game is not important. The game itself is anticlimactic, I guess, because of all the crap beforehand. There's more media on the field than there are players, and, I mean, trying to be able to walk through the media to go out for BP is ridiculous."

The Sox entered the World Series as clear underdogs, which is also forgotten with time. The Mets won 108 games in the regular season, and the Sox won 95. The series may have simply worked out how it should have. "I don't know if we necessarily thought we were the better team," Schiraldi said. "I thought we played better. They had a lot more pressure on them than we did. And circumstances just didn't work out for us. The best team doesn't always win, and the team playing the best doesn't always win."

23

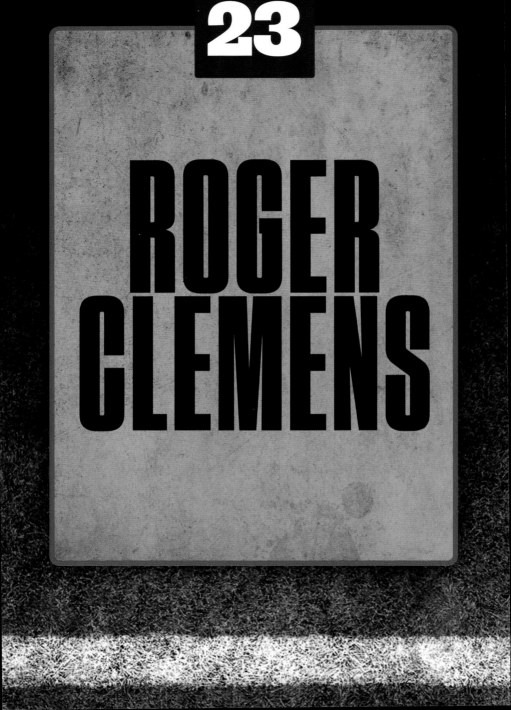

ROGER CLEMENS

Roger Clemens' career was long enough that some may know him from his time with the New York Yankees and Houston Astros but carry little to no appreciation for his greatness in Boston. Clemens always made news in his 13 years with the Red Sox. As was the case in his later years, those headlines weren't always owed to excellent pitching. Today, Clemens waits to see if he can cut through the red tape wrapped around his Hall of Fame candidacy, to see if the members of the Baseball Writers' Association of America will look past the stigma of performance-enhancing drug accusations and a related perjury trial, though he was acquitted from the latter. But the Rocket had many iterations in a 24-year major league career, one that began in the Hub with an overpowering fastball/slider combination in 1984.

Clemens was just 21 years old when he debuted. His signature splitter wasn't yet in use, and no one was pointing fingers about PEDs. Like Nolan Ryan before him and Josh Beckett after him, Clemens is stitched into a classic baseball and American trope: the Texas boy who could sling it or—in the parlance these days—"shove."

"He has the real good fastball. It got on you in a hurry," said Joe Morgan, one of Clemens' old Sox managers. "In the early days, he had an unhittable slider. Nobody ever hit his good slider, I mean, nobody."

Clemens' 1,332 strikeouts at Fenway Park remain the most in club history. No one has matched his three Cy Young awards in a Sox uniform. And no one's matched his seven Cy Young awards in a career either. Speaking of Young: Clemens' 192 regular-season wins with the Sox have him and Young tied for the most all time. If Clemens does make the Hall, a Red Sox hat would make a lot of sense for his plaque, considering he made 382 starts for the Sox, which amounts to more than half his regular-season career total of 707. "Every time I'm in this town, they've been nothing but great and thankful for the effort and what I tried to do when I was here," Clemens said at Fenway Park in 2012. "I know how I went about my work and what I tried to do here. We came close so many times...I got to pitch in a place where, when I drove into the ballpark from Framingham, people were coming from all over New England, and they cared. That's all I was excited about: people cared, and they showed up to watch you work."

Clemens was the 19th overall pick in the 1983 draft out of the University of Texas. This was a time before everyone—not just the hardcore fans—knew all the hot prospects, before the farm system became part of the purview for bar discussions. "His inconsistency worries some scouts," went one *Chicago Tribune* story previewing the draft. The quick scouting report on Clemens said: "Fastball moves better than 90 mph, and a team gambling on quick mound help will grab him."

But he ended up throwing harder than 90 mph. Clemens' first Cy Young award—as well as the highest win total (24) of his career—came in 1986. He also won the American League MVP award typically given to position players. He's one of just 10 players all time to win both an MVP and CY Young in the same season. (Hank Aaron didn't like it and said so publicly. Clemens responded by saying he wished Aaron was still playing so he could crack Aaron's head open—just one of Roger's many fine moments.)

In the first month of '86, Clemens established himself as the game's preeminent strikeout pitcher. On April 29 at Fenway against the Seattle Mariners, he fanned 20, setting a major league record for Ks in a game. "This has to be the most awesome piece of pitching I've seen," manager John McNamara said that night. According to Glenn Stout and Richard Johnson's *Red Sox Century*, just two of the 138 pitches Clemens threw were pulled by hitters. He threw 97 strikes, and

Fenway exploded when word of his strikeout record flashed on the scoreboard.

There was a lot more excellence to follow. He won his second Cy Young in 1987 and another in 1991. In Clemens' third-to-last regular-season start with the Red Sox, he matched his 1986 feat, striking out another 20 on September 18, 1996. That game against the Detroit Tigers was something of a parting gift. Clemens became a free agent that offseason and went to the Toronto Blue Jays. The Sox didn't re-sign Clemens because they felt—as Sox general manager Dan Duquette famously stated at the time—Clemens was in the twilight of his career. He would turn 34 in the 1997 season.

Clemens went on to dominate in Canada. After his 20th win in '97, he said: "Not bad for the twilight."

"It's just a constant reminder my agents give me when I go out there," Clemens said. "We have a good time with it."

In Boston, Clemens' relationship with the fans and media didn't always match his on-field success. He had, well, baggage. In a 1988 interview with Mike Lynch of WCVB, Clemens lamented having to carry his own luggage, a moment of disconnect from his blue-collar fans. A few months later, Clemens tried to set the record straight—but failed—in another interview with the same station. "[He] only succeeded in getting himself into deeper hot water when he threatened that 'somebody's going to get hurt, and it's not going to be me' if any reporters wrote or said anything bad about his wife or family," E.M. Swift wrote in *Sports Illustrated* in 1989. "No one knew what on earth he was referring to—there had not been any derogatory reporting on members of the Clemens family—but cartoons of Clemens strangling reporters began appearing in the papers."

In 1990 Clemens was ejected from...wait for it...a playoff game. Home-plate umpire Terry Cooney threw Clemens out for cursing at him during the second inning of Game 4 of the American League Championship Series against the Oakland A's. Clemens denied he was cursing at Cooney. The Sox lost the game 3–1 at the hands of ace Dave Stewart and were swept. With or without Clemens, they needed more hitting that day.

In 1992 Clemens aired out *Boston Herald* columnist George Kimball for a story that mentioned Clemens refusing to give an autograph. Clemens didn't address the column right away, waiting about a month before ridiculing Kimball in front of others. Clemens even tossed a hamburger bun at him—or some sort of enriched bread product. "Contrary to common lore, it wasn't a hamburger bun. It was a hard roll for sandwiches, more the consistency of a sub roll," Kimball wrote in a 2007 email to Tony Massarotti, who was with the *Herald* then. And through the soap opera, the first half of one of the greatest pitching careers ever was on display at Fenway. Clemens finally got a ring when he left Boston. To the dismay of Sox fans everywhere, Clemens won it with the Yankees in 2000.

A dozen years later, Clemens said he didn't have any regrets about his time with the Sox. "Not really. I experienced playoff baseball," Clemens said. "I'm surprised that a lot of the older guys I meet never had the opportunity to experience the playoffs and the finality of that. When the leaves change up here and the weather gets such, those are the things I'll carry with me all the time. I learned how to pitch here in Boston. I learned how to pitch inside. There's an art to it, like I tell people. I talked about that with Pedey [Pedro Martinez] last night. He said it was hard for him to learn to pitch inside. I said I would take a 17-inch plate and make it a 24-inch plate."

These days, Clemens' name surfaces most often when it's debated whether he should or will be inducted into the Hall of Fame. "It's not going to change me as a person or as a man, how I go about my life, how I treat other people," Clemens said in 2013. "Whatever floats your boat, go for it."

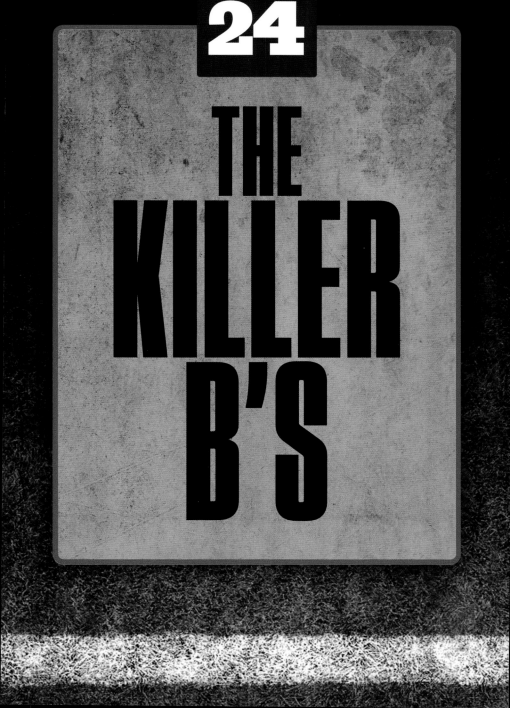

24

THE KILLER B'S

The Red Sox Killer B's—right fielder Mookie Betts, center fielder Jackie Bradley Jr., shortstop Xander Bogaerts, and the latest addition, left fielder Andrew Benintendi—demand your appreciation while they're here. They deserve extra appreciation, in fact, for both their individual talents and the collective they form as half the lineup.

Win. Dance. Repeat. The phrase and accompanying smooth moves are owed to the youthful outfield and their creative celebration after every win. The trio gets together, someone pulls off "the Carlton" or leaps like they're skiing, and the other two drop to a knee and pretend to be rolling camera. It's a fan favorite, an emblem of the modern-day Sox.

Benintendi and Betts are both compact, smaller players but tremendous multi-sport athletes. An excellent bowler who happens to play baseball, Betts' range is absurd, gliding as he makes catches others would never even be in reach of. Benintendi's left-handed swing is the prettiest the Sox have had in a while. He's a quiet kid, a quiet that's sometimes mistaken for arrogance. "I'll keep to myself," Benintendi said. "I don't want to step on any toes or anything like that, especially last year coming up and not knowing anybody, so I just go about my business and keep to myself."

Too hard on himself sometimes, Bogaerts might have the ability to outhit them both at a premium position. He can definitely out-talk them, speaking four languages—English, Spanish, Dutch, and Papiamento—as an Aruba native. Bradley's cannon and catches in center field are absurd, though he can be a streaky hitter. When he's torrid, he's a joy at the plate. A down-to-earth guy, Bradley loves to be a tourist in every road city. He also has a menu item named after him at a Chick-fil-A near the University of South Carolina, his alma mater. "If you go in there and say you want a JBJ special, they will know exactly which one that you're talking about," Bradley said in

2013. "The No. 3, which is the spicy chicken sandwich with a fry, and I usually get a fruit punch Hi-C."

Enjoy these kids.

When it comes to prospects and young stars, there's always a feeling something better and better is ahead. Not in terms of someone else taking their job necessarily but in terms of their own career arc. If someone is young, certainly below 25, we assume they're bound to improve every year. Some do improve, some don't, and others require a step backward first. Fans and media get caught up, if not obsessed, talking about the future. *Boom, home run, Betts. Wow, just think what awaits!* More often, we should talk about the here and now. We run the risk of losing how great—or maybe just plain old good—some players are in the moment. A 24-year-old may already have reached his ceiling statistically (if not in wisdom). Growth may come as a teammate, or in plate discipline, rather than home-run totals.

Either way, a trajectory along a straight line is rare, particularly when someone is already a super high-level contributor. You can only get so good, and scouting reports are constantly updating. As one executive put it in 2017: if players developed in a linear fashion, he wouldn't have a job. Consider that once the youths arrive in the big leagues, they're often more polished than they were decades earlier. The sport has gotten younger in part because teams figured out young players are the cheapest players. "There's so much young talent in the game," Houston Astros ace Dallas Keuchel said. "The days of being 35 to 39 [years old] and playing in the big leagues are very slim now. And teams would rather pay the big league minimum to a 21-year-old than $7 million or $10 million to a crusty vet."

College players arrive in the majors as quick as a flick of Mookie's wrists. Top college programs serve as finishing schools. "Sometimes you got guys, they come from college and they don't get 1,500 at-bats in the minor leagues," manager Alex Cora said. "It's college, a few at-bats in the big leagues. And it's different in the clubhouse compared to when I played earlier. It's a lot different, and you got to adjust."

Benintendi, the most recent addition to the B's, had 657 plate appearances in the minors after the Red Sox drafted him No. 5

overall in 2015. He was 22 years and 27 days old when he debuted in 2016. That '16 year was so special all around. David Ortiz's good-bye coincided with an unbelievable season from Betts in right field, when he was second in the MVP voting behind the best all-around player in the game, Mike Trout. Betts, Bradley, and Bogaerts were All-Stars, as was Ortiz. "We're at a pretty unique time I think in Red Sox history, when you consider how young this team is," John Farrell said heading into the 2017 season, his last as manager.

He was right. But everyone might have expected a little too much. The conversation around Betts is one that became unfair. Because he was lotted in with Trout in '16, there was an assumption he would be that same player—a tick or two away from Trout—going forward. Betts slid back a little bit in 2017 from an .897 on-base plus slugging percentage (OPS) to an .807 OPS. His average dipped from .318 to .264, and his home runs dipped from 31 to 24. Still excellent numbers. He was still, per FanGraphs' defense rating, the third best defender in all of baseball and the best in the outfield in '17, patrolling Fenway's spacious right field.

But because he set the bar so high before and because he was in his age 24 season in 2017, everyone just assumed he'd keep climbing. The story shouldn't have become about regression. It should have been about how special his 2016 was and how good he remained in 2017. (It didn't help that management lacked the offensive additions to comfortably pick up the slack in the power department.)

Bogaerts battled injuries in 2017, playing through them at a time of need for the Sox. The most candid of the group, he didn't deny the team was pressing when the Sox fell behind in the American League Division Series two games to none. Losing Ortiz wasn't easy for the kids nor anyone else in the lineup. "We can't score 10 runs like last year's offense," Bogaerts said.

The Sox then nearly pushed the ALDS to five games but lost in four to the Houston Astros. Whatever the Killer B's become (and you can throw in young third baseman Rafael Devers, too), you can guarantee they won't be together forever. That's another reason to savor their shared moments. Baseball doesn't have a salary cap, but teams treat the luxury tax threshold like one sometimes, as the Red

Sox did in 2017. Baseball as an entity wants parity. It wants turnover and something other than a concentration of all the best players in a handful of markets. Eventually, one of the B's will leave via free agency or be traded. But maybe one or two will sign a long-term deal and spend their whole career at the Fens.

It's remarkable that all of these guys are here together simultaneously in the first place. The front office, particularly former general manager Ben Cherington, deserves a lot of credit for protecting the group from trades. Folks across the player development staff—from farm director Ben Crockett on down to the scouts—all had a hand.

The outfield is so good that it has drawn comparisons to the Fred Lynn, Dwight Evans, and Jim Rice era. "It's the first time that any group has been compared to us," Lynn said in 2017. "They have a long way to go as far as matching the hitting. I don't know if that's going to happen, but defensively, for me, because I'm a defender first—I mean that's the responsibility of the center fielder—it's really nice to see not only Jackie play really well in center, and he can throw, but it's nice to see these guys as a unit play really well. I can't think of an outfield that's playing in baseball today that runs as well and throws as well as these guys do. Now, if they can all start to hit with some power, get a little pop as well, they'll be formidable. But right now they really, really play a solid defense, which is really fun to watch for me."

25

BROADCASTERS

Those calling the game—and in particular those who have mastered how to simultaneously entertain—easily become more familiar than some of the players. Maybe the balance of attention would have been a little different had the 2015 Red Sox been an entertaining club. Maybe the story wouldn't have lingered for so long. But Don Orsillo's unexpected departure from the Red Sox's telecast on NESN would always have become the story for some length of time.

The fact the public cared so much when Orsillo was replaced by Dave O'Brien, accomplished and well regarded in his own right, is a reflection of Orsillo's excellence and how thoroughly he permeated New England and beyond from 2001 to 2015. "I understand it has created some controversy," Red Sox chairman Tom Werner wrote to *Boston Herald* columnist Steve Buckley in 2015. "And I also understand that Don is a great broadcaster, but we felt that starting next year, it was worth going in a different direction reenergizing the broadcast. And when the opportunity presented itself to bring Dave O'Brien to NESN, we just felt after a great deal of thought and consideration that was the right decision to make."

The drama of Orsillo's departure was as captivating as any other Red Sox divorce in recent history. Fans loved him, and the public didn't want to say good-bye to an amiable man who created a seamless coupling with Jerry Remy. The duo would go off on hilarious tangents, and it was Orsillo's ability to let himself go—to be natural, to react as anyone would when a fan throws a slice of pizza at another fan—that endeared him to most. "What was that that came flying in?" Remy asked after a 2007 incident down the left-field line at Fenway, when one fan catapulted a slice of pizza off another's shoulder. "I thought he rolled in the mud before he came to the game, but no, that's not correct, he got hit with some type of sub sandwich or something."

Pizza. It was pizza. "He's the Pepsi Fan of the Game until he gets thrown out," Orsillo, who was unable to contain himself heading into a commercial break, said of the hurler. When they returned to air, Orsillo was still losing it, audibly bursting at the seams. "Sauce first!" Orsillo said, barely getting any words out. "I wonder about the thought process, though."

The list of Sox voices throughout the years carries clout. Remy, now O'Brien's present partner on NESN, was first diagnosed with lung cancer in 2008 and has dealt with relapses that bring out tremendous fan support for the former Sox second baseman. Restaurants in his name opened in 2010, including one right near Fenway, which is now Tony C's.

Joe Castiglione has been heard calling the Sox on the radio since 1983. These days he's on WEEI with partner Tim Neverett. "Can you believe it?" Castiglione asked when the 2004 Red Sox recorded the final out of the World Series. That phrase also became the title of his book.

The prep work for any broadcaster worth their salt is tremendous. "When the ball is put in play, you have to be ready to capitalize on the action," Castiglione wrote. "Don't get caught in the middle of a story or the middle of a sentence by the pitcher delivering the pitch. Any comment you're making should stop when the pitch is made. Ultimately, that's how you are judged: by how you describe the action. When you sit down to write that paragraph, you have to write the sentences one at a time. But all the action on the field happens at the same time. You have to be prepared to describe it all...On the radio *nothing happens until you describe it*."

The night the Sox swept the St. Louis Cardinals and won their first title in 86 years, Castiglione did not overlook the lineage of broadcasters, the stewardship of the chair. "As the Red Sox were celebrating on the field, I wanted to pay tribute to Ned Martin, who [at that time] had broadcast more Red Sox games than anybody else: 32 years on radio and television," Castiglione wrote. "Ned never got to announce a Red Sox world championship. I said, 'Ned would have said, 'Pandemonium on the field.'"

"Pandemonium on the field," was Martin's call on WHDH when Rico Petrocelli secured the pop-up at shortstop in 1967 on the final day of the Impossible Dream season. Martin and Ken Coleman, a Quincy, Massachusetts, native, made music together. The latter was Castiglione's mentor. Martin, Coleman, and Mel Parnell were a trio in '67.

Martin was an erudite man, an expert on Hemingway who had a love for language as well as sport. "Active verbs are really helpful. It isn't an awful thing to have a vocabulary and use it," Martin remarked

SWEET SOUNDS

Ken Coleman served as narrator on a vinyl album that's still in many an attic from the Impossible Dream season. "It was John Connelly, a onetime *Boston Herald* copy boy and news writer for the original WHDH-TV in Boston, who created the clever poetry recited by the late Ken Coleman in the classic record album *The Impossible Dream: The Story of the 1967 Boston Red Sox*," Steve Buckley wrote in the *Herald*. "Connelly crafted prose we all remember so well from 'This is really a love story, an affair twixt a town and a team,' to the sobering lines, telling of the August beaning of Tony Conigliaro.

"Produced by Fleetwood Records of Revere, the album was a companion piece to a television special, also written by Connelly, that aired on WHDH, which was then Channel 5 in Boston. While the TV special [included as a bonus in the new DVD *Impossible to Forget*] is painfully dated and does not hold up well for the modern-day viewing public, the record album is like a piece of classic rock that indeed stands the test of time. Borrowing melodies from the Broadway show *The Man of La Mancha*, which, of course, is where the real 'Impossible Dream' came from, the record album is a clever blend of play-by-play highlights from the '67 season, Ken Coleman's crisp narration, and the words of Connelly."

in 1992, per *The Boston Globe* story relayed in a Society of American Baseball Research biography by Bob LeMoine.

As champagne flowed in 2004, Castiglione didn't forget Coleman. "Later, I paid tribute to Ken Coleman," Castiglione wrote. "As he had done so many times, I finally pulled the Bart Giamatti quote out of my pocket and read: 'It breaks your heart. It's designed to break your heart.' That's how we ended the broadcast."

Giamatti, commissioner of baseball for less than a year when he died in 1989, was a huge Red Sox fan from South Hadley, Massachusetts, who authored an essay that began with those famous words about heartbreak. Coleman read that quote to the Fenway Park crowd on the night Giamatti died.

Coleman, Martin, and Curt Gowdy were inducted into the Sox Hall of Fame in 2000. Gowdy was with the Sox from 1951 to 1965 en route to one of the most decorated careers in broadcasting, which included 13 Emmy awards, 16 World Series, nine Super Bowls, and eight Olympics. In 1969 he became the first sportscaster to win a Peabody award. "It was the greatest spot in the American League," Gowdy told *The New York Times* in 2003 of the old broadcasting booth at Fenway Park. "You could reach out and just about touch the players. It was the happiest 15 years of my life here in Boston."

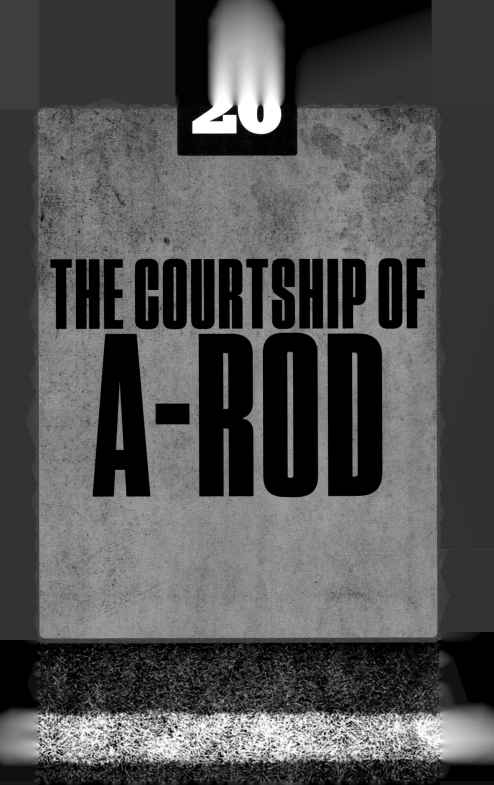

THE COURTSHIP OF A-ROD

Look at the difference a few dollars can make. Through the Alex Rodriguez near-miss and the Giancarlo Stanton flirtation—and a lot of moments in between—the question occassionally comes up: why can't the Red Sox afford *the* big star? The Red Sox charge big prices. A day at Fenway Park can be marvelous and marvelously expensive. So what has occasionally stopped John Henry and Co. from landing the biggest name? It is, ultimately, pragmatism and profitability. (And there's nothing wrong with profitability.)

Indeed, when the Texas Rangers were looking to trade A-Rod after the 2003 season, the only matter that kept him from Boston proved to be money. He had seven years and $179 million left on what was then the mother of all mega-contracts—a 10-year, $252 million contract the Rangers gave him. He wound up being worth every penny performance-wise. Upon turning just 28, A-Rod was a .308 hitter with 345 home runs.

The five-tool shortstop from Miami, who would later date Madonna and Jennifer Lopez, was dying for the big stage and relevance to get out of Texas and join the storyline that dominated all others in those days: Red Sox-Yankees. And Rodriguez was willing to sacrifice a lot of money to make it happen—$28 million off his contract to come to Boston.

There was some other compensation coming back to him. As *The Boston Globe*'s Gordon Edes chronicled: "The Sox were offering Rodriguez the opportunity to become a free agent after two years and every year thereafter, whereas his existing contract allowed him to opt out of the last three years, in which he was due to be paid $27 million a year. They also offered him a signing bonus up front, as well as marketing rights to the Red Sox logo much like the deal Cal Ripken had when he was playing for the Baltimore Orioles."

But concerned about the precedent, the players union wouldn't allow it. And the Sox didn't want to take on the full deal, so they backed off. Former Red Sox president Larry Lucchino called the decision a rational examination. Rational, however, did not describe most fan or media reactions to any of the A-Rod frenzy. The entire process was surreal. "At the time it was very emotional and it was a very big decision in my life," Rodriguez said the next year.

There were so many threads to follow. Manny Ramirez was part of the proposed trade to Texas for A-Rod. Nomar Garciaparra, who wanted a contract to stay in Boston and had grown increasingly disillusioned, called into WEEI to complain about the fact the Red Sox negotiated with A-Rod for 72 hours with the league's permission. A-Rod and Nomar happened to play the same position. Nomar wound up being traded in 2004, but he could have been traded that winter had the A-Rod deal gone through. The talks with Rangers owner Tom Hicks brought friction too, as media leaks perceived to be coming from Hicks' camp irked the Red Sox. "During the negotiations the futures of five All-Star players were in limbo," Edes wrote in 2003, "as another trade, one in which the Red Sox would have sent Nomar Garciaparra and relief pitcher Scott Williamson to the Chicago White Sox for outfielder Magglio Ordonez was kept on hold, a no-go if Ramirez and Rodriguez did not switch teams."

In the end, naturally, George Steinbrenner's New York Yankees swooped in, picked up A-Rod from the Rangers in a deal centered around Alfonso Soriano, and poked the Red Sox right in the eye. "That was the absolute peak of that rivalry in my opinion," former Red Sox exec Jed Hoyer said. "I look back on it. Think about '03 and '04. We played 24 or 25 games against them both years. Right—it's incredible. You have two rivals playing back-to-back Game 7s [in the American League Championship Series]. That's crazy. And it was just like this one-upmanship."

A huge star who could have helped the Red Sox, who wound up with the opportunistic Yankees? The parallels ahead of the 2018 season, when the Yankees landed Stanton from the Miami Marlins in a package for Starlin Castro, were obvious. The difference was the Sox did not come nearly as close to landing Stanton as they did A-Rod. Somewhere in either his own files or the Red Sox's, Hoyer said there's a signed contract from A-Rod that the union never allowed to be executed.

With Stanton there was never a certainty that he would waive his full no-trade clause to come to Boston, rendering a lot of the talk moot. But the money kept the Sox at bay as 10 years and $295 million remained on Stanton's contract, though it'd be less if he opted out in the middle of the deal. The Sox were already in big on David Price, who was playing out a $217 million contract, and on the hook for money owed to the likes of Pablo Sandoval and Rusney Castillo.

Would it have really killed the Red Sox to pony up for Stanton? What about A-Rod all those years ago? Ultimately, ownership wants to make money and wants to run an organization responsibly. That's how it should be. "Only horrible organizations keep spending and spending and spending," said one executive who was around for the A-Rod courtship. There's always a budget. The first year Theo Epstein's group was in place heading into the '03 season, the Sox actually trimmed payroll a bit. When they signed David Ortiz and Kevin Millar, those signings were at a relatively small cost. Could the Sox have technically afforded A-Rod? Sure—if the threshold to meet for affordability is simply keeping the doors open. But success as a franchise has a lot to do with bang for one's buck and what you squeeze out of payroll.

To bring it back to the original question: the Sox could not have afforded A-Rod in keeping with goals of making their desired profit and also creating the organizational structure and long-term plan they wanted. Despite how routinely the Sox and Yanks were understandably slotted together, they were still operating in different tiers of financial planning. The same was true with Stanton. The Sox already had a lot of money tied up. There are only so many big contracts a team is willing to take on. That's particularly true in today's world of parity, where exceeding the luxury tax threshold for three consecutive years adds up to some steep deterrents.

The what-if game around A-Rod's career in Boston is still a neat one, if not a little sadistic. Of course, the first year he got to the Yankees, the Red Sox broke The Curse. The Sox won two World Series before Rodriguez won the only one of his career in 2009. With A-Rod still on the Yankees in 2013, the Red Sox won yet another title. That makes it 3–1 Sox.

In Game 6 of the 2004 American League Championship Series, Rodriguez was running up the first-base line and slapped the ball out of Red Sox pitcher Bronson Arroyo's glove, one of many embarrassing moments for Rodriguez. There was no love lost for A-Rod at Fenway Park.

Arroyo happened to be on the mound during the 2004 regular season, when Rodriguez took a pitch off the elbow. Infuriated, Rodriguez and catcher Jason Varitek went at each other in a brawl at Fenway. Rodriguez was clearly cursing out Varitek, daring him to hit him, and Varitek hit him in the face.

Rodriguez wound up embroiled in a performance-enhancing drug scandal that became its own drama, as he fought a suspension from the league in a nasty public display. The Red Sox might have dodged a bullet then. They might have been better off without A-Rod. But that's hard to fully accept, considering they missed out on a player who hit 696 career home runs.

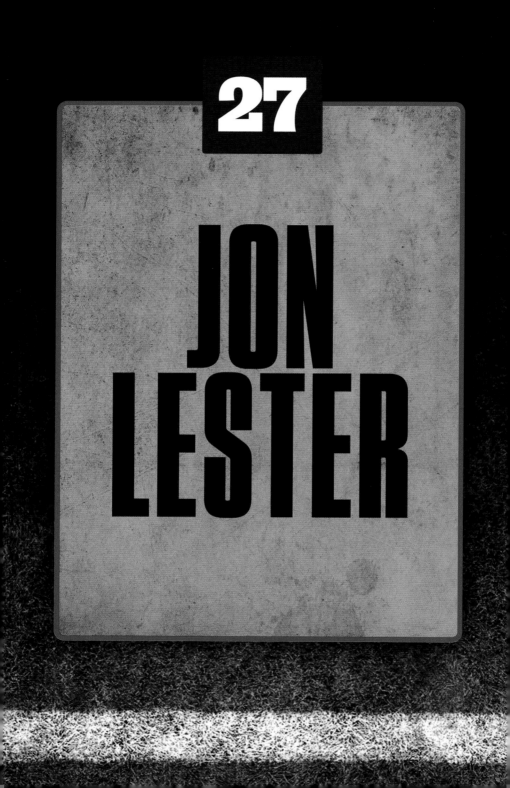

27

JON LESTER

Jon Lester is the one who got away, the lover who deserved better. The Red Sox should have backed up the Brinks truck—put a ring on it, if you will—when they had the chance.

When the world champion Chicago Cubs visited Fenway Park in April 2017, a match-up of two jewel franchises doubled as a reunion. Theo Epstein was back home. John Lackey and Lester returned, too, and all of them were on top of the world once again. Powered by Lester's pitching, Theo's Cubs ended a 108-year title drought in 2016—a bonanza that paralleled Boston's curse-breaking joy a dozen years before.

Sox fans didn't want Lester gone. The din of regret over letting him walk was particularly loud during that return trip to Fenway. Lester was thriving, and his high-priced replacement in Boston, David Price, was hurt at the time and far from a fan favorite.

Lester was aware fans were pining for a do-over. "You play first and foremost for yourself and family, but then you play for the fans as well as the organization," Lester said in the visitor's dugout at Fenway. "When you have that support, we've been through a lot here—the ups and downs, a few really large downs, and a couple really good ups—I feel like these fans are a part of my family, a part of me and who I am, not only as a baseball player but as a person...It's nice to hear that fans on that side miss us, miss me being in a Red Sox uniform."

A 2002 second-round draft pick out of high school in Washington state, Lester's big-game ability and overall comfort in the

Boston market are qualities the Sox may appreciate these days more than ever. The Sox loved Lester's sturdy 6'4" frame and excellent makeup in addition to his stuff coming out of high school. They felt fortunate, too, that he slid in the draft all the way to No. 57 overall. He got good money there, $1 million even, and in turn made good on that investment. He went 110–63 in nine seasons with the Sox from 2006 until the middle of the 2014 season.

Reliability may have been Lester's greatest strength. In five of six seasons from 2008 to 2013, Lester cracked 200 innings. Even the greatest challenge of his life—cancer—barely slowed him down.

Lester was 22 years old and just a rookie in 2006. He debuted on June 10 and made his last start that year on August 23 during a West Coast trip. He went five innings that day, a barrier he was having trouble cracking in recent starts. Lester had been dealing with back pain, too. There was some thought that a minor car accident in August caused it, but Lester was in pain even before that. When the team's road trip moved on to Seattle—close to home for Lester—he went to see his Uncle Paul, a doctor. Jon arrived at the hospital early in the morning, as Dan Shaughnessy recounted in the book, *Francona*. Lester didn't leave until late in the afternoon, after he had been told he had one of two things: testicular cancer or lymphoma. The diagnosis proved to be the latter, a rare form of non-Hodgkin's lymphoma called anaplastic large cell lymphoma.

Fortunately, it was treatable.

Mike Lowell, who was diagnosed with testicular cancer in 1999, was one of Lester's teammates at the time. Lowell told MLB.com: "I don't know what's in store for him. The feelings I can understand because it's a time where he's going to want to be with his family."

Lester went into treatment but stayed in close touch with manager Terry Francona, who was the first person Lester called when he got the wonderful news: after three months of chemotherapy, Lester was cancer-free. With youth and resolve on his side, Lester returned to a major league mound less than a year later, throwing six innings of two-run ball on July 23, 2007, against the Cleveland Indians. "This isn't even about baseball," rotation-mate Curt Schilling said that day, via the Associated Press. "It just doesn't get any better the way a guy like that comes back to us. It's about family. The big thing is he's a great human being, and that makes it an even better story. That wasn't your run-of-the-mill DL stint."

Lester is a relatively low-key guy who rarely gets riled up. Later that year, he reflected on his winter of recovery. "Don't feel sorry for yourself, don't sit at home and think about it," he said. "For the most part, I had a pretty normal offseason. I went fishing and went hunting and did things that I like to do within reason. I just tried to do that and keep my mind off of the other stuff and tried to be as normal as I could."

As the Red Sox trounced the Colorado Rockies in the World Series that year, Lester got the ball in Game 4 for his first career postseason start. He tossed five and two-thirds shutout innings at Coors Field, leading the way to a 4–3 victory and the second Red Sox World Series title in four years.

The story wrote itself. But once Lester was on the mound, a sense of competition took over rather than the inspiring comeback narrative—at least for the pitcher. "I don't know what he's gone through," Francona said ahead of Lester's Game 4 start. "We were proud of Jon before this. What he went through was a very difficult winter I'm sure for [him] and his family. He handled it with grace, a lot of dignity, a lot of perseverance, and because of that, some really neat medical people, the fact that we're even talking about baseball is really awesome. I think before Jon picked up a ball this year it was already a successful year...It makes for a wonderful story that people want to write about, which I understand, but it's about him being better than the Rockies, and I think he has a very good understanding of that, especially for a younger guy."

Lester's stuff really returned in full in 2008 as his strength improved. On May 19 he threw a no-hitter against the Kansas City Royals at Fenway. Smiling, with his arms raised but not fully extended just before an embrace of catcher Jason Varitek, it may be his most famous moment in Boston. He sealed the 18th no-hitter in team history with a strikeout of Alberto Callaspo. (That no-hitter was the fourth Varitek caught, giving the backstop a major league record now shared by Carlos Ruiz.)

Come 2011, like other Red Sox pitchers, Lester looked bad when the chicken-and-beer collapse spiraled out of control. On the field, a 4.82 ERA in 2012 was the low point of his Sox career. But Lester rebounded to post a 3.75 ERA in the 2013 championship campaign, including a measly 1.56 ERA in five playoff starts spanning 33⅓ innings.

By then the clock was ticking. Lester and his agents talked to the Sox about a long-term deal, but they never could finalize one, hitting an impasse going into his walk year of 2014. One Sox offer reportedly was for about $70 million over four years. Lester was dealt to the Oakland A's at the '14 trade deadline for Yoenis Cespedes, a move tantamount to a dare from the Red Sox to Lester: go ahead, sign with someone else during free agency. He did just that, taking $155 million over six years from the Cubs after posting a 2.46 ERA between Oakland and Boston. Ortiz said that Lester called him crying in the offseason when he was debating where to go. "He was like me in that he had the city and the organization in his blood," David Ortiz said in his book, *Papi*. "At times it seemed that when the Red Sox knew that about you, they'd try to take advantage with some 'hometown discount' that didn't measure up to what you deserved."

In 2017 back at Fenway, Lester wasn't hiding from his choice or his former city. "I looked forward to it," he said of his return. "I saw it [on the calendar], and first thing, my wife and mom and dad were like, 'Hey, we're coming to that one.'...I don't want to shy away from coming back here just because I didn't [decide] to come back and went to a different team. That's kind of being, I guess, a coward."

Lester was many things to the Red Sox, but he was anything but a coward.

20

NOMAR

All these years later when you think back to Nomar Garciaparra fever and the way a shortstop with a neurotic, fidgeting batting stance and quite the schnoz sat at the center of Boston sports, it's still a shame. It's a small injustice that he wasn't there to see it through. The Sox traded Garciaparra at the July trade deadline in 2004, three months before breaking The Curse.

"We were like .500," Kevin Millar said in 2014. "We couldn't get hot, and it was one of those years. Then all of a sudden, it was like they traded Ted Williams. Nomar Garciaparra was the closest guy in our generation, right? Two batting titles, where you say, 'What the hell is going... ?'"

Garciaparra got a ring, of course. But after the Sox made him the 12th overall draft pick in 1994 and he played nearly 1,000 games for them in nine major league seasons, there was a tiny part of them missing when everything, at last, came together—particularly after the heartbreak of 2003. "It was obviously devastating being traded. There's no question about that. But I was happy for them winning the World Series," Garciaparra told reporters, including NESN, at Fenway Park in 2014. "My teammates made me feel a part of it, which was great, and that's what I was grateful for. When they were going through the playoffs, I was getting calls from them when they were on the bus, and they were like, 'Hey, did you see that? You see what we're doing?' I'm like, 'Yeah.' And they would say, 'Hey, we're thinking about you.' I'm like, 'I'm watching.'"

A foil for Derek Jeter and part of a trio of great young shortstops who ascended in the 1990s along with Alex Rodriguez, Garciaparra won consecutive batting titles in his time in Boston. He had a .323 lifetime average when the Sox traded him to the Chicago Cubs in a four-way deal. Nomar fever caught on fast. Like the guy who traded him, Theo Epstein, Nomar need only be referred to by his first name. "The first two or three years he had on the scene, the Red Sox were looking for that," said Lou Merloni, one of Garciaparra's former teammates and closest friends. "They were looking for a draft pick, drafting another superstar. When he went out, he had such a distinct look that everybody recognized him, no matter where we went. And it was just the way his career started: Rookie of the Year [in 1997], MVP candidate years. The Nomar/Jeter, Red Sox/Yankee thing was at an all-time high, the debate about these two players. With every single year, it became more public and national, and people would just recognize him no matter where he went."

Pedro Martinez and David Ortiz are the only players whose star power compares to Garciaparra's since his departure. Not everyone had cell phones or high speed Internet in the Nomar era, so life more universally revolved around the TV—including to watch, say, *Saturday Night Live*. When Garciaparra hosted in 2000, he played himself in a recurring skit called "The Boston Kids," an exaggerated portrayal of Red Sox fans and their R-less accent, featuring Sully (Jimmy Fallon) and Denise (Rachel Dratch). Nomar went on a date with another guest on that show, actress Kate Hudson. "Sully, don't look directly at him!" Dratch yelled at Fallon when Garciaparra walked in the room to pick up Hudson for a date.

Garciaparra's celebrity was only increased because of a relationship and eventual marriage to soccer star Mia Hamm. Through it all, he and Merloni remained close. "Our families were so similar. I came from a big family; he came from a big Mexican family," Merloni said. "He was really all about family: his parents and his sister and his brother. To me that was what it was really always about. He always treated my family great, and I always loved hanging out with his family. So that was really the bond that we had. It was weird because he would hang out with buddies of mine, and you would never know it was Nomar, Rookie of the Year, MVP. He really was down to earth, and I think a lot of the last couple of years he spent in Boston, I think people really got a different impression with him with the way things were handled and the way things were done publicly."

On the field, Garciaparra had Hall-of-Fame hitting ability but just not enough sustained success as he battled injuries. In 2000 he batted an incredible .372, the highest average for any right-handed hitter in a

Red Sox shortstop Nomar Garciaparra hits a solo home run during the fourth inning of Game 4 of the 1998 American League Division Series. The six-time All-Star hit .323 that season.

qualified season from 1940 on. There have been 11 players to hit .370 or higher from 1940 on. In the group, there's just one other righty, Andres Galarraga. The other lefties were Tony Gwynn, Ted Williams, Ichiro Suzuki, Barry Bonds, Todd Helton, Larry Walker, George Brett, Rod Carew, and Stan Musial. Visually, Garciaparra's at-bats were mesmerizing because of an obsessive need to tighten his batting gloves. He remained in constant motion, tapping both feet before going into a bat wiggle.

Garciaparra was in the final year of his contract in 2004, and things had turned sour. The Sox had very publicly tried to land a different shortstop, A-Rod, in a trade prior to the year, and Garciaparra still didn't have a contract worked out. A trade to benefit both the clubhouse and defense—Jed Hoyer, assistant to the general manager in '04, called the deal one of the first sabermetric-based trades made—became inevitable. "[It was] about as thought out and pre-examined as any move we ever made," former Sox president Larry Lucchino said in 2017. "We talked to Nomar numerous times, tried to. I flew to Los Angeles. Tom Werner and I met with him early in the year, talking about how we didn't want to get into a free-agent year without getting a sense of whether we could sign him to a long-term agreement. We tried pretty hard, and even in July, when the issue came up of what are we going to do, facing the July 31 deadline, we insisted that we sit down and talk to Nomar and his agent face to face and make sure that things hadn't changed...that we were at least current on his feelings and his intentions. It's the prudent and the right baseball decision. And, of course, we were talking long term as well as short term. And it proved to be so in the short term, as we improved our defense and made some changes in the clubhouse chemistry. That worked out beautifully."

When Garciaparra turned down a four-year, $60 million offer in 2003, "that was the beginning of the end for him in Boston," Merloni said. Garciaparra liked the deal but wanted an $8 million signing bonus to more closely resemble Jeter's contract. "A day later the [Sox] came back and said the offer's off the table. Let's talk at the end of the year but let's not bring up the fact we talked about it," Merloni recalled. "The next day the paper, in *The Globe*, was Nomar turned down 4/60...That was the beginning of the end."

Merloni said Garciaparra felt his hands were tied: if he publicly criticized management, it wouldn't help him get a deal done. Some fans were upset that he hadn't just accepted what the Sox offered him. "He kind of took things too personal," Merloni said. "He kind of listened to that loud minority there can be in this town and started feeling like people were against him and didn't understand it. And most of the information was incorrect. He couldn't understand why people didn't get it or anybody ever thought he didn't want to be here. I think he took things very personal, and that was a problem, and it just snowballed after that."

The Red Sox got two former Gold Glove winners, first baseman Doug Mientkiewicz and shortstop Orlando Cabrera, when they sent away Garciaparra. Mientkiewicz caught the final out of the World Series, and the clubhouse dynamic did improve. From a baseball perspective, defense was the real focus. "Some of the contract negotiation stuff had certainly driven a wedge," Hoyer said. "When he came back that year from the foot injury, he wasn't playing defensively as he had in the past. He had been a really good defender, and we just, we looked up, like why, why is this team struggling? We're 10 over .500 in April. I think we were a .500 team for three months. It was a completely win-now team. We had Pedro, [Jason] Varitek, [Derek] Lowe, and Nomar [as] free agents. Better win now, or we're in trouble."

Garciaparra went on to play for the Los Angeles Dodgers and the Oakland A's after the Cubs. He did the old sign-a-ceremonial-one-day-contract move in 2010, retiring, appropriately, with the Red Sox.

29

TITO

No one will have a better first year as manager of the Red Sox than Terry Francona.

Skip started off on a surreal high in 2004. He was the leader of a curse-breaking group that balanced lawlessness—they were doing shots before games—with the unity and the mettle to rally in the American League Championship Series after trailing three games to none. Players' managers—and Tito is precisely that—are more or less the only managers these days. But back when Theo Epstein hired Francona, old-school disciplinarians and gruff military types were still more common. Even sought. After eight seasons and a second title with the Sox in 2007, Francona departed Boston at a complicated low. But for the most part, the breakup is buried deep in the past.

When Tito visits the Hub these days, the reception is warm and fuzzy. There's a-night-before-Thanksgiving-at-your-hometown-bar vibe. "It actually amazes me," Francona said in 2017, when he was honored at the Boston Baseball Writers Dinner. "Maybe people realize I'm kind of a normal person. I made more than my share of mistakes but still show up and try my best to do everything I can for my team. And I think in this town, especially, if people know you're trying, they appreciate that."

Francona has grown into the lone lion among current managers—with perhaps a couple foils in the National League in Bruce Bochy and Joe Maddon. Helming the Cleveland Indians since 2013, Tito would probably win American League Manager of the Year every year if the voting were conducted strictly as a popularity contest. His affect is hard to find anywhere else. He remains charming and disarming. He can calm players and woo the media. He's simultaneously self-deprecating and supportive, fiercely protective and hilarious.

There is a Cult of Tito, and it's a compliment to his charisma. "It's almost like he's a player," Kevin Millar said in 2012. "He has quirky things. We're a bunch of kids when the doors are closed. It's a little bit like Joe Maddon...This man allows you to be who you are. We're all different. Keith Foulke's different. He's a little more introverted. Millar's the idiot that's loud. Pedro's the fun-loving guy. Everyone's got a different personality in a different place. But let that person be who they are, and that's when good things happen. I think Terry did a good job of allowing that. Grady Little did a great job of allowing that also. That was a lot of the same group that Grady had, to give him credit. He was a very similar manager, more of a country dog."

Indeed, the respect Francona commands from players is near endless. But they also love his goofiness. "Behind the scenes, he is the most revolting, gross human being you've ever met," Curt Schilling said lovingly in a 2017 interview. "Tito was Pig-Pen. Some of the shit he does, you can't really repeat it. He'd call you into his office in Boston and he'd be sitting on the shitter with the door wide open. He'd be like 'Yeah, yeah, yeah, come over here. I need to talk to you,' that kind of dirty. And it was—I'm not trying to embarrass him—it was a funny story. He never stopped being a player from a goof-off perspective, which I thought was kind of funny."

Schilling started his Boston career in 2004, the same year Francona did. But Schilling has a unique perspective on Tito because they were together for nearly every game of Francona's first stint as manager. His first crack running the show came with the Philadelphia Phillies in 1997 and concluded with a gruesome 285–363 record. In the final season of 2000, Schilling was traded, and the Phils finished with 65 wins and a .401 win percentage. "In Philadelphia he was different," Schilling said. "He grew up. He had a lot of growing up to do and a lot of learning to do, as every manager does."

Heading into '04, the Red Sox were ready to move on from manager Grady Little regardless of Pedro Martinez's eighth inning in Game 7 of the 2003 American League Championship Series.

Like his late father, Terry Francona was a big league outfielder. His dad was Tito, and the name stuck with Tito's son. Terry played 10 years between five teams, and five of those years were in Montreal with the Expos. He was a lifetime .274 hitter, but his body was beat up. Francona flirted with going into real estate before becoming a coach and then manager in the Chicago White Sox system. He was famous well before Philadelphia or Boston because he was the lucky dog to oversee Michael Jordan's attempt at baseball in 1994. Tito was the manager of the Double A Birmingham Barons, the team that hosted Jordan and an absurd amount of publicity for a minor league team. Jordan hit .202 with three home runs, but there's worse prep for Boston than that kind of hoopla. "I do think, for whatever reason, that place is a little crazy," Francona said of Boston in 2017.

Just a tad.

But he won over Epstein and the young Sox front office heading into 2004. "He was awesome to interview," former assistant to the general manager Jed Hoyer said. "It's funny looking back on it now. It's a great life lesson because [the results were] really disappointing in Philly with these horrible bullpens. We spent a ton of time studying his time in Philly. What we really concluded in the end is: John McGraw couldn't have won with that team. Their bullpens were so bad. And then in the interview, he was like—I asked him about throwing Schilling 130 pitches. He's like, 'Here's who I had to bring in.'...He was really good, great personality. We felt like it was the right mix for our guys. Joe Maddon interviewed. We had a really good interview, but we felt like that was not the right fit at that moment. Tito had done it. He played in the big leagues."

The group he had to manage wasn't easy. Nomar Garciaparra was traded in the middle of 2004. Manny Ramirez was there—or somewhere in his own world. The fires sparked throughout the years. The payoff was worth it right away in 2004. "I got to enjoy our victory celebration for about a half-hour," Francona said in the eponymous book about his time in Boston written with *The Boston Globe* columnist Dan Shaughnessy. "All of a sudden, my phone's blowing up, and I'm getting messages about Millar talking about guys drinking Jack Daniels. I called Millar and said, 'What the fuck's wrong with you? We win the World Series, and I can't even enjoy it. Clean it up and keep me the fuck out of it.' And he said, 'Well, that's where we have a little problem because I told everybody you were right in the middle of it.' Then I hear from Johnny Damon, and he says, 'Hey, Tito, I'm going on Letterman tonight. I'll fix it.' I was thinking I'd be the only guy to win a World Series, then get fired during the offseason."

The relationships grew over the years. He treated Jon Lester and Dustin Pedroia like sons as he did so many of his players. One of his guys on the 2007 championship team was current manager Alex Cora. "In '05 Tito came up to me and he said, 'Alex, you're going to be a big league manager,'" Cora said during his introductory press conference. "I'm like, 'Nah, I don't know about that. I don't know if I want to do it.' He was, 'Well, you will be.'"

Though he could seemingly see the future, there's always a downfall. For Francona the 2011 season and a September collapse proved his undoing (as well as Epstein's). *The Globe* story from Bob Hohler, the infamous chicken and beer account, said team sources were concerned Francona was abusing pain meds. Francona had undergone myriad surgeries, including a knee replacement. He survived pulmonary embolisms. Tito had stockpiled Percocets, which concerned his daughter, per the book the manager wrote with Shaughnessy. Once MLB was alerted, Francona started a pain management program. In his book he denied having a drug problem. If he hadn't lost control of himself, he and everyone else lost control of the season.

What remains a point of contention—perhaps never to be fully understood—are the intents and sequence of events on the day Francona was fired. Or did he resign? That's the question. He went into a meeting with Epstein and ownership, and whether ownership's mind was already made up has been debated. "I talked to them after you left," Epstein told him, per the book with Shaughnessy. "It's pretty clear that the decision has been made."

Ownership denied Epstein's account in the book. In some ways it's irrelevant: it was time to move on, no matter how they arrived at that point. "He probably felt like he was surprised that we didn't extend his contract," Red Sox chairman Tom Werner said in a 2017 interview when asked about Francona's departure. "But we felt that it was time for a change. That's part of baseball. And I don't think that he was very happy that we decided to move in a different direction, but we felt that that was the right thing for the club."

Former Sox CEO Larry Lucchino said in 2017 he still had not read Francona's book because of what he heard to be an incomplete and adversarial approach toward ownership. But he spoke highly of Tito. No matter how poorly things end in Boston sometimes, the night-before-Thanksgiving moments do usually follow. "A very good manager, who deserves an enormous amount of credit for the way he worked with players, the way he worked with a fairly provocative kind of front office that had its own highfalutin concepts and ideas, and an ownership group that very much wanted to win," Lucchino said of Francona's legacy, "he had the personal gifts to overcome all of those potential problems and did a sensational job until the end. There's a cycle on everybody's career. Maybe that was the right end. That was a long cycle for a manager in Boston. That was a very long cycle. And there's proof in his inherent ability by being successful elsewhere."

And he has been successful with Cleveland. And the Boston fanbase still treats Francona with warmth even after his Indians swept the Red Sox in the 2017 American League Division Series.

30

DEWEY

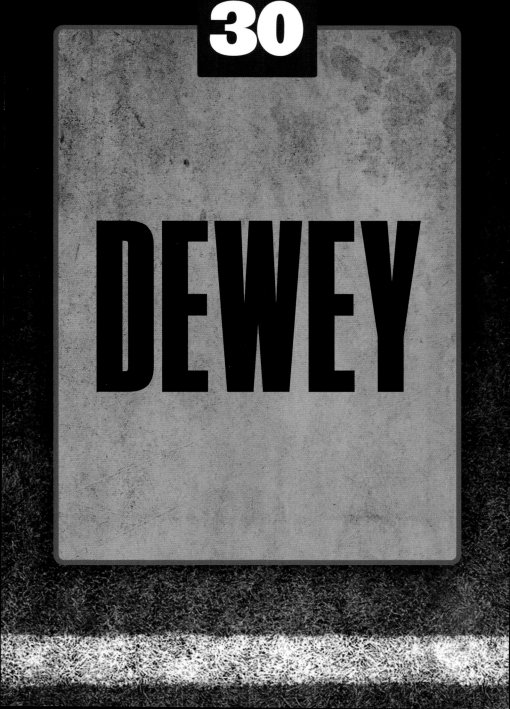

In December 2012, 40 years after Dewey's rookie season, former Red Sox general manager Ben Cherington was asked about his plans for right field in the offseason. "Dwight Evans, I'd take him," joked Cherington, less than two weeks before signing Shane Victorino. "The ability to cover the ground out there is pretty important."

There are two choices when discussing Evans and the similar studs who exist in a perceived purgatory between very good and greatness. You can: A, lament the fact Evans is not in the Hall of Fame or B, celebrate the reasons his absence has spawned an ongoing conversation in the first place. "What stands out with me with Evans is he could do everything: hit, run, field, throw, hit for power," former Red Sox manager Joe Morgan said. "So, he's a candidate for the Hall of Fame in my book because of all those things. How many guys do that? Not many. People didn't think he could run, but if you ever saw him run out a triple, you'd change your mind. He had these long strides and he was eating up the ground."

The accolades that have thus far been repelled by Cooperstown's padlock include a .272 average, .370 on-base percentage, .470 slugging percentage, and 385 home runs. All but one year of an even 20 in the majors were spent with the Red Sox. His final season in 1991 was with the Baltimore Orioles.

Born in Santa Monica, California, Dewey was always known for his defense, particularly in the first half of his career. Another in the long line of amazing outfielders to come through the Sox system, he won eight Gold Gloves. He was a fifth-round pick in 1969 and became close friends with Carl Yastrzemski. "Dewey did so many great things as far as when I was his teammate in Boston," Wade Boggs said, "an extremely hard worker and wanted to get the most out of his craft. And I think he did."

Rice, Fred Lynn, and Evans made up the most famous Red Sox outfield in club history. In Game 6 of the 1975 World Series, an inning before Carlton Fisk's wave-it-fair home run, Evans saved the night with his most indelible contribution. With a runner on first base and one out in the 11th inning at Fenway Park, the Cincinnati Reds' Joe Morgan hit a deep drive to right field. On his proverbial horse, Dewey ran it down with a leaping step to the warning track and had the presence of mind to fire it back to double off the runner, Ken Griffey Sr. The lead was preserved until Fisk led off the bottom of the 12th inning. "The catch was nice," Evans told *Sports Illustrated* for a 1985 feature. "But the thing I was proudest of in that series was in Game 3 when I hit a two-run homer off Rawly Eastwick that tied the game in the ninth. No one remembers it. What people remember about that game was that we lost when Ed Armbrister interfered with Fisk in the 10th. That's pretty much the way my career's gone."

He greatly improved over time. Evans was a career .262 hitter through his first nine seasons. But then in the strike-shortened 1981 season, he led the American League in home runs. In his first nine years, from 1972 to 1980, Evans had an on-base plus slugging percentage (OPS) of .792. From 1981 to 1989, the next nine years, he had an .886 OPS. He also patrolled the outfield in a way that earned him all those Gold Gloves. "He was a force in right field," reliever Calvin Schiraldi said. "You can go back to the ALCS [in 1986], and they didn't send a runner—even think about sending a runner—on a fly ball to right field that could've tied the game or won the game for them. He was a power hitter, home run, pull guy. But later in his career, he hit to all fields. Walt Hriniak helped him with that. He hit to all fields, lots of doubles...He was just a frickin' really good, great, all-around player."

He was a veteran presence as well, even for pitchers. Schiraldi remembered dinners with Dewey and Don Baylor in 1986—fine dining packaged with lessons on how to be a big leaguer. "It's just a game we get paid quite a bit of money for," Evans told the *Times*. "I feel fortunate and blessed in my family and my career. I'm grateful I've played the game this long in this town. When I see guys packing up and moving, I think of how we've been in the same house since 1976. To play this long is a privilege and an honor. We are New Englanders.

I grew up in Hawaii and was raised in L.A., but what I see out there is nice weather for New England. I like it here. This is home."

The do-it-all nature of Evans' game is consistently praised. But he nonetheless may not have been properly assessed when he was a Hall of Fame candidate in the 1990s. "His lifetime wins above replacement (WAR) of 67.2 ranks ahead of nine Hall of Fame right fielders, including contemporary Dave Winfield, and only slightly behind first-ballot inductee Tony Gwynn. Tim Raines, everyone's favorite cause this past vote, finished at 69.1," WEEI columnist John Tomase wrote in 2017. "Evans' Hall of Fame teammate, Jim Rice, finished his career at only 47.4. The skills that made Evans so valuable—on-base percentage, defense, extra-base ability—weren't fully appreciated during his playing days, and they meant practically nothing once he hit the Hall of Fame ballot, thanks to the exploits of two men."

Those men, Tomase contended, were Sammy Sosa and Mark McGwire and before that Jose Canseco. They were the stars of the performance-enhancing drug era, which is precisely when Evans was on the ballot. "I'm glad I wasn't in that era," Evans told Tomase. "I'm not saying I wouldn't have [used PEDs]. The temptation, the money, and it wasn't illegal early on. People say I'm crying [about the Hall]. I'm not crying. Am I bitter? I'm not. I think it's a sense of accomplishment when you get in. I see that with Jimmy [Rice]. All that hard work, and he got in. It was a job well done."

31

DAVE ROBERTS' STEAL

Henri Stanley never made the majors, so you shouldn't feel bad if you lack any recollection of his name, which is pronounced Ahn-ree. But if by some chance you do remember why he matters to Red Sox Nation, congratulations on that big, spacious brain you're carrying. We hope you play trivia in Allston.

Stanley, who went undrafted out of Clemson, had the minor league numbers—including a career .857 on-base plus slugging percentage (OPS)—as well as the skillset to get at least a cup of coffee in the bigs. He had a good batting eye, some pop. He could run too. Stanley got as far as Triple A for multiple clubs, including the Red Sox. He probably would have gotten a call-up in today's game, where there's a greater appreciation for statistics. Today, he's helping others make their way, working as a player agent.

But occasionally—every once in a blue moon—someone will remember that other thing Stanley was involved with. He is the guy the Red Sox traded to the Los Angeles Dodgers for outfielder Dave Roberts at the 2004 trade deadline. And Roberts proved the catalyst to the greatest postseason comeback in baseball history.

But Stanley's not asked about that connection to Red Sox history as often as you might think. "To my knowledge, unless it happened right after the trade, I can't recall anybody else [in the media] ever reaching out," Stanley said. "Sometimes people up there would make the connection and say thank you or hand me a newspaper clipping, or something of that nature. But nothing—no, nothing to the extent of reaching out on a phone call or anything."

A lot, and we mean a lot, had to go right after Roberts stole second base in the ninth inning of Game 4 of the 2004 American League Championship Series. But that narrowly secured stolen bag against the New York Yankees is remembered as the turning point of a series the Sox trailed three games to none.

Roberts was used as a pinch-runner at first base. The Sox were down 4–3 and were three outs away from being swept out of the ALCS at the hands of the Yankees. A year earlier against New York in the ALCS, the Sox at least had some fight, taking the series to seven games. Up to the point Roberts pinch ran, the '04 group had been bulldozed. The Boston-New York rivalry was at its modern peak. Mariano Rivera, the best closer in history, was on the mound. Catcher Jorge Posada was behind the plate. The play was so close at second base when Roberts ran, and the moment was so tense with the Sox three outs from being swept, that Roberts became the symbol of the tide turning. After his steal the Sox became the first and only team to win a best-of-seven series after trailing three games to none.

Kids these days might not even know Roberts outside of managing the Dodgers—never mind remembering Stanley. "They don't even know what their favorite ice cream is," Stanley joked, "much less a manager or a former baseball player these days...I'll use it obviously just in a joking way, when I'm out on the recruiting trail [as an agent]. I'll always kind of laugh with people and say, 'Hey, I'm probably the trivia answer to a question on a Monday night in South Boston.' At some Irish pub on a Monday night, they probably say, 'Who remembers who got traded for Dave Roberts?' That's probably my claim to fame certainly career-wise: getting traded for the guy who helped break The Curse."

Roberts himself has come to realize the individual moments of the Red Sox's 2004 playoff run are no longer emblazoned inside the memory of every baseball fan or big leaguer. Enough time has passed. During the 2017 playoffs on the day of the 13th anniversary of his famous stolen base, Roberts was asked if the moment ever comes up as a teaching point for his players. "Funny story," Roberts said. "Yu Darvish about two weeks ago, I guess, was surfing the Internet, and there was an aha moment. He ran across the stolen base and kind of put two and two together and didn't realize that was his manager. So he proceeded to kind of awkwardly approach me about it and talked about my goatee and how I could steal a base. He just couldn't believe that was my manager. So that was kind of funny. But I don't bring it up ever. But I think a message [exists there] that I do bring up in the sense of just being prepared for a particular moment and I was in 2004. Each guy on our ballclub, I think, can relate to that."

Before Roberts went on to manage the Dodgers, he was a 10-year outfielder in the majors—and a Dodgers player for two-plus seasons. Los Angeles dealt him to the Red Sox on July 31, 2004, in a one-for-one swap. The bigger news of the day in Boston was Nomar Garciaparra's departure in a wacky four-team trade, ending an era.

Come October 17, 2004, Roberts was everything. Kevin Millar worked a walk off Rivera, the typically infallible Yankees closer, to begin the ninth inning at Fenway Park. (If you want to argue the comeback actually began there, you'd have a point.) Pinch running for Millar, Roberts outraced catcher Jorge Posada's throw on Rivera's first pitch despite a suboptimal jump. Posada's toss was a touch too far to the shortstop side of second base and could have been a bit lower. With a headfirst dive, Roberts' left hand reached the bag before Derek Jeter's left hand lowered the tag. Bill Mueller, the batter at the time of the steal, singled Roberts home to tie the game at 4. Then in the 12th inning, David Ortiz ended it with a home run—as he would so many more times in his career.

Most baseball fans are reared with a belief, or at least a general understanding, that when a base runner steals a bag, they've stolen on the catcher. A strong arm behind the plate, like Ivan Rodriguez's, can deter theft. A poor arm, like Mike Piazza's, will invite steals. But as baseball has become more scientific, and both fan and media interest in the nitty gritty of every moment has expanded, we've gained a wider understanding of the importance of the pitcher in the chain of stolen-base prevention. Assuming a general competency among catchers, the determining factor is often how quickly the pitcher delivers the ball to the plate from the stretch. Does the pitcher employ a slide-step? Does he vary up his delivery times and looks to the plate, such that a runner is not able to get a great jump? Some can. And then some runners can override the whole system.

In Roberts' case he had to. He needed every bit of closing speed that led him to swipe 38 bags in 41 tries during the '04 regular season because there was no element of surprise. The whole building knew he'd be running. In a 2016 interview with *The New York Times*, Roberts gave credit to Maury Wills, one of his instructors from his playing days with the Dodgers. Wills stole 104 bases in 1962 (and 586 in his career) and prepped Roberts for exactly the scenario he faced in '04. "I said, 'Dave, one day you're going to be on first base and get the steal sign, and there's not going to be the element of surprise,'" Wills told *The Times*. "Everybody in the ballpark knows you're going to run, the whole country is going to be watching on TV, and that pitcher is going to be on his best with pickoffs, but you've still got to go."

Wills added, "That is when you're a real base stealer."

The funny part is when Roberts was traded to the Red Sox, he didn't want to go. He was a California guy playing in California and he was in tears. "It was a shock," Roberts said in an ESPN story. "I wanted to stay with the Dodgers. I didn't want to go to the East Coast. I loved what we were doing. You feel that your world is turning upside down. But in retrospect—I wouldn't change a thing."

Stanley, the guy Roberts was traded for, hadn't met Roberts as of November 2017. He was hoping to change that at baseball's annual winter meetings. "I got to try to shake his hand on a job well done," Stanley said.

32

2007

The 2004 Red Sox were darlings. They were easily adopted by outsiders, they were noble fighters for the common man, and they were Idiots. Three years later, screw 'em. Once the Sox won again in 2007, it became fair game for the outside world to start to hate the Sox, to jump off the bandwagon. Two titles in four years kills the underdog appeal. The slayers of the Evil Empire were turning into a nascent kind of Evil Empire themselves.

For through-and-through Sox fans on the other hand, it was time to brag. Nobody was doing it better. Theo Epstein and Co. were posterizing the rest of the sport. Joe Torre and the New York Yankees broke up after the Yanks were knocked out in the first round of the '07 playoffs—four years removed from their last World Series appearance and seven from their last win—while the Sox were making their own mini-dynasty. "We didn't feel like we were better than everybody else," Epstein said. "We just felt like a lot of the people and processes we had put into place were clicking on a lot of cylinders, so we were enjoying the results and looking forward to a bright future."

After a 96–66 regular season, the Sox swept the Los Angeles Angels of Anaheim in the first round. The only playoff games the Sox lost were in the American League Championship Series, when they staged another impressive comeback. This time they came back from three games to one against the Cleveland Indians. The poor Colorado Rockies were swept away in the World Series, which began with a Dustin Pedroia leadoff home run off Jeff Francis. "The second [title], I'm very

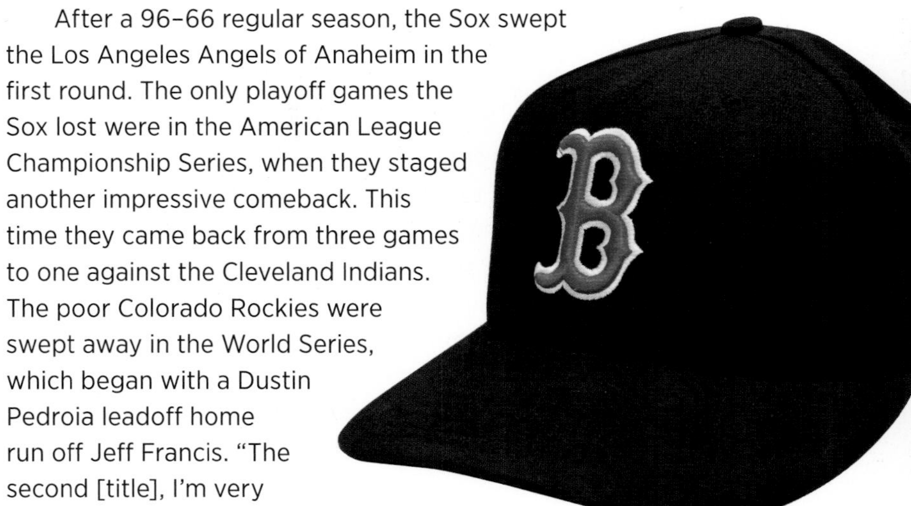

proud of," Red Sox chairman Tom Werner said. "Anybody can sort of do something once. The fact that we were able to accomplish it so soon after the first was very meaningful."

When a new regime is installed and wins quickly, there's always some amount of credit owed to the previous administration. (Hello, Dan Duquette.) Winning twice in four years as the Sox did under Epstein also reflects superior roster building, a superior blueprint. Sustainable winning requires a good farm system primarily because of economics. There's romanticism tied to players who come up through the system, lifelong players in one city if the stars align. But cheap, young talent wins—particularly these days.

A 2005 first-round pick, Jacoby Ellsbury, hit .353 in 33 games in the regular season and hit .438 (7-for-16) in the World Series. Pedroia, the Rookie of the Year and a second rounder in 2004, hit .317 in 139 games. (He made his debut in 2006.) "I thought our team actually started playing better baseball when the young kids got more involved," manager Terry Francona said in 2007. "Our defense was better. Our baserunning was better. We seemed to have more energy. It seemed like the veterans got a little bit more energized with those guys around. It was a good mix...Our owners give us a lot of money to go out and spend and get good players, but having guys come through your system is a great way to do it. And when they're able to come and contribute—and not just contribute but be pivotal players... it's a huge source of pride."

In his third season, crazy-eyed Jonathan Papelbon had 37 saves and a 1.85 ERA, striking out 13 batters per nine innings. He was a fourth rounder in 2003, the year of Epstein and Co.'s first draft. "All of a sudden you've got Ellsbury and Pedroia hitting on top of the lineup, getting on base seemingly every time up in that World Series," Epstein said. "You had [Jon] Lester starting the final game. You have Papelbon closing the door. It just stood in stark contrast to '04 where we had one homegrown player on the entire roster in Trot Nixon. All of a sudden, we had a dozen homegrown players on the roster. So it felt more like a full organization triumph, where everyone contributed—scouting and player development. Throughout the baseball operations department, there was a ton of pride in the years that led up to that moment. We felt like it was something we could sustain."

Epstein didn't win a title again until he left Boston, though that doesn't mean his sentiment was at all misplaced. The playoffs-as-kind-of-a-crapshoot reality sets in. Some would argue the 2008 team was actually better than 2007's. (Kevin Youkilis believes opening the '08 season in Japan after such a late October run in '07 is what did the Sox in over a long season.)

Along with the youth movement, hired hands were huge as well in '07. Japanese star Daisuke Matsuzaka's ballyhooed first year was in '07 and he threw a team-high 204⅔ innings with a 4.40 ERA. He was a better pitcher the following year. Nonetheless, for a guy who never quite lived up to the hype, he was a significant contributor to a title-winning season. Former Sox president Larry Lucchino compared the 2007 season to "a middle child" that can be overlooked. "But it was a sensational year," Lucchino said, "and in many ways very satisfying because we had to earn it with a different team. There were some bold moves at the end of '05 and early '06, including [trading for] Josh Beckett and Mike Lowell. One becomes the World Series MVP, and the other becomes the most significant pitching reason why we got to the World Series. So there was a lot of personal satisfaction in that one."

Beckett, the ace righty, and Lowell, the third baseman, were picked up in the same November 2005 trade, which sent out top prospect Hanley Ramirez 10 years before Ramirez would return as a free agent. Beckett went 20–7 in 2007, finishing second in the Cy Young voting to CC Sabathia, who threw more than 40 more innings with a tick lower ERA (3.21 vs. Beckett's 3.27). Sabathia, then with the Indians, went 19–7.

From the 13th game of the season on, the Sox were in first place. That was at the end of play April 18. At the end of day on May 20, the lead was 10½ games. No shot for anybody else. A wire-to-wire run can leave a season devoid of craziness, but there were a handful of memorable games. On Mother's Day the Sox put together a six-run ninth inning for a walk-off against the Baltimore Orioles. They started the inning down 5–0 and didn't score a run until there was one out. On September 1 Clay Buchholz threw a no-hitter in just his second career

After saving Game 4, closer Jonathan Papelbon celebrates the 2007 World Series sweep of the Colorado Rockies.

start. (Another homegrown stud, Buchholz was the 42nd overall pick in 2005.)

Throughout the year, the David and Manny show was still in full effect. A season after belting a career-high 54 home runs, David Ortiz went deep just 35 times in '07. But he also led the American League in on-base percentage at .445. His OPS+, which measures on-base plus slugging percentage (OPS) relative to the rest of the league, was 171. (You're average at 100, and at 150 you're 50 percent better than average.)

During the ALCS, when the Sox had to win the final three straight to take the series, Ortiz talked to the team ahead of Game 5. Speeches are always better remembered if they worked, and this one did. It didn't hurt that Ortiz hit .370 with a 1.204 OPS that postseason.

In his prime at age 27, Beckett had two wins in the series and was named the ALCS MVP. "Whether it be Chien-Ming Wang or CC Sabathia [going for the other team], nobody wants it more than me," Beckett said. "When I'm out there, I feel like the guys are all behind me and I just feel like we're better than everybody else."

The World Series left no doubt as to that. Pedroia hit the homer off Francis to begin the scoring deluge. Before another game at Coors Field, a security guard asked the diminutive Pedroia for his ID. The second baseman then told the guard that Francis would be aware of his identity. "I don't know if the 2007 season was overlooked," Pedroia said in 2013. "Anytime you win a championship, it's extremely hard to do. So I hope it's not overlooked."

What should never be overlooked is that the clinching game's starter, Jon Lester, had overcome a cancer diagnosis from the year before, the most meaningful story of all in a feel-good season.

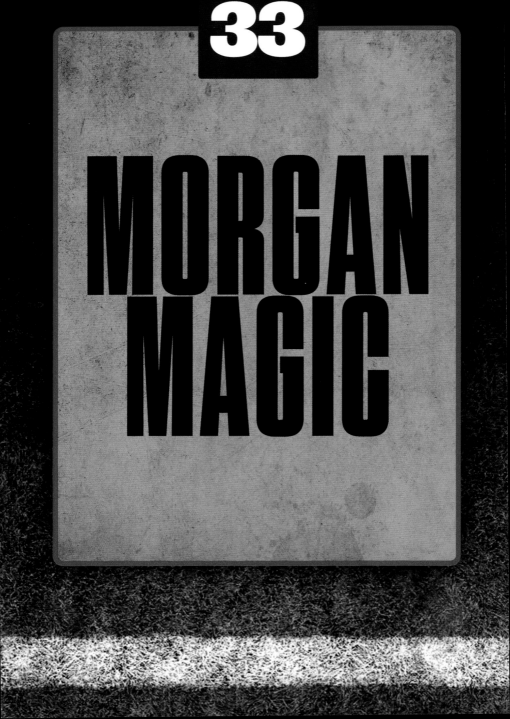

33

MORGAN MAGIC

He has an entire season of Red Sox baseball named after him—or at least half a season. But former Red Sox manager Joe Morgan downplayed the name "Morgan Magic" when asked about it during a 2017 interview, nearly 30 years after his takeover of the 1988 Sox led the team from mediocrity to the playoffs. "I really didn't pay attention to the Morgan Magic name, you know?" Morgan said. "Things were happening, and they were all good. We were winning, and everybody was happy and making money and all that business. So, I really didn't take a lot of stock in Morgan Magic."

The city certainly did. A Walpole, Massachusetts, native and Boston College alum, Morgan was the third-base coach for John McNamara, the manager who led the Red Sox oh-so-close to a title in 1986. Morgan's parents were both born in County Clare, Ireland, and, as Morgan put it, his father was "as Irish as the day was long."

McNamara was ousted after the '88 All-Star break. That gave Morgan—a salt-of-the-earth, baseball lifer—the opportunity he long hoped for. After 16 years managing in the minors, Morgan told the press when he was hired that he doubted such a day would ever come.

Morgan played 88 games in the big leagues as an infielder from 1959 to 1964 with five different teams before beginning a coaching career. But being a local boy running the Sox was its own nutty undertaking. People mailed various items to his home: framed pictures, "all kinds of junk," Morgan joked. "Oh yeah, it was a real whirlwind," Morgan said. "We had cars going by my house all the time, saying, 'There's where he lives' and stuff like that. Oh my God, it was unbelievable. The high school came down, and they brought the band down here and stood out on my front lawn and played songs for me. It was hectic. You couldn't go anywhere...it took forever to go get a bottle of milk or a loaf of bread. I had one guy that ran a store, I bought a hammer there one day."

Well, Morgan said he tried to, anyway. "He says, 'Don't pay, Joe. You don't have to pay.' For a hammer! You believe it?"

Still a coach on the day of the first game of the second half, Morgan was sitting at his locker at Fenway Park. The Sox were 43–42, nine games out in the American League East, and in fourth place out of seven teams. Based on the number of runs the Sox scored and allowed in the first half, they had underperformed record-wise—and maybe therefore were due for a lift.

The bosses went into McNamara's office. "And just then I looked up, and [general manager] Lou Gorman was coming in toward the front door of his office. And he stopped at my locker and he said, 'Well, we're going to make a managerial change,'" Morgan said. "'You're going to be the manager until we can find a manager.' I said, 'Don't look too far. You already got a manager.' That was it."

Apparently, that's all the Sox needed. Not to be confused with the Hall of Fame second baseman of the same name, Morgan rattled off 19 wins in 20 contests from the day he took over and 12 straight from the get-go. (People did confuse him with the Hall of Fame second baseman, though. "I just got a letter from a kid the other day," the Sox's Morgan told *The New York Times* in 1988. "He said: 'I'm not sure I sent the right bubble gum cards, but they came back signed. I want you to be honest. Did you sign them?' I had to be honest so I wrote back and told him I signed them. I've signed a ton of his cards. I got his signature down pretty good.")

There was no lack of talent for Morgan to work with. Third baseman Wade Boggs finished that season with a .476 on-base percentage, the highest mark of Boggs' career and an absurd clip for anyone. "I didn't make many changes, but I did insert [shortstop] Jody Reed in there," Morgan said. "He turned out to be really good...He hadn't been playing much at all before that. He thought I was gonna send him down to Pawtucket when I called him in the office that day. I used [first baseman Todd] Benzinger a little bit. I liked him as a player, got him playing time...I liked all those guys. They all paid off. Other than that all the other guys were there and playing."

Benzinger was a second-year player who was only with the Sox from 1987 to 1988. He made 61 starts in the second half vs. 39 in the first and performed considerably better down the stretch with a .264 average and .453 slugging percentage in the second half.

The first 11 games (and wins) Morgan managed were all at home. The second and the seventh victories were both walk-offs, impressing the Red Sox brass. "I think they had the feeling that I wouldn't be able to handle the Boston press and things of that nature," Morgan said. "But they were dead wrong."

But the seventh consecutive W is the one many remember because it brought a rather famous (or infamous) declaration. Before the game Gorman took away the interim tag. During the game Morgan didn't let anyone forget it.

The Sox led the Minnesota Twins 5–4 in the bottom of the eighth inning, when leadoff man Ellis Burks drew a walk. The No. 6 hitter, Hall of Famer Jim Rice, already had a hit in the game. Not only that, but Rice had a .455 average during the win streak: 10-for-22 with four walks and just two strikeouts. Spike Owen, a shortstop who finished his career with a .246 average, was sent up to pinch hit. Morgan wanted to bunt. Rice, 35 years old and in his second-to-last season, had not been credited with a sacrifice bunt since 1980, a span of more than a thousand games. (A bunt would not be called for today because giving up outs voluntarily is now understood to almost always be the wrong call—particularly when you're taking the bat away from a run producer like Rice.)

Rice shouted at Morgan and physically grabbed him during an argument in the tunnel that leads to the clubhouse. No punches were thrown, but Rice was suspended by the team for three games. When Morgan returned to the bench right after the skirmish, he told his players in no uncertain terms: "I'm the manager of this nine!" The Sox didn't score in the inning, and the Twins tied it in the ninth, but Boston won in 10 innings.

The Sox went 46–31 under Morgan, giving them an 89–73 record and first place in the AL East. The magic, though, didn't translate to the postseason. Boston was pitted against a far superior team in the Oakland A's in the best-of-seven American League Championship Series for the right to move on to the World Series. Oakland (104–58) had the likes of Mark McGwire and Jose Canseco with Dave Stewart leading the rotation and Dennis Eckersley in the bullpen. Oakland swept the Red Sox before losing to the Los Angeles Dodgers in the World Series. "It's very simple. They had a better team than us—hands down," Morgan said. "And if we couldn't win the first game, then the odds are the leaf wouldn't turn. But I thought maybe if we could win the first game...They were really good. They had everything."

Morgan came in second in Manager of the Year voting in 1988. He stuck around, managing the next three years in full and finishing above .500 every year. His Sox made the playoffs again in 1990, only to again be swept by the A's. The recognition never really left—at least, not around Walpole. They call him Walpole Joe for a reason. "I notice one thing though: the further you get away from Walpole, the fewer people recognize you," Morgan said in 2017. "Everybody around here does in Norwood and so forth. But if you go to Pittsfield or maybe some parts like that, not as many people recognize you."

34

EL TIANTE

Quirky motions and exaggerated stances have gone by the wayside. Kids today are taught cookie-cutter movements for the benefit of biomechanical efficiency—or something. But we know the truth: individuality is more enjoyable to watch. We want more guys like Luis Tiant. The game is better off with a pitcher who completely turns his back to the plate and stares into the center-field bleachers before delivering the ball.

That was just a sliver of what made Cuba native El Tiante such a draw in his eight years with the Red Sox, when—on a World Series-bound team in 1975 with the likes of Carl Yastrzemski—chants of "Loo-ie" could be heard the loudest. "He'd spin around, and I could see his face," said Sox outfielder Fred Lynn. "And then he turns around and flips one to the plate. Kind of an ultimate competitor, he would not come out of a game. If it was an important game, we wanted Luis on the mound. He knew how to win. He had really good stuff, by the way. And he threw really, really hard when he was with Cleveland [from 1971 to 1978]. And he actually could still throw the ball by guys when he got to us in Boston."

Tiant went 229–172 with a 3.30 ERA in 19 seasons while playing for six teams in the big leagues. He took to the signature, perplexing windup as a survival tactic, looking for something to revive him after a velocity drop owed in part to a broken clavicle. With an excellent career as validation, he said he would not discourage a youngster today from trying the same motion. "You can do it. You have to practice, which I did," Tiant said. "When I did it, I just came out and did it. Nobody told me anything: do this, do that. I just came and [thought] about *let me throw like this*. I go out and try, look in center field, look at the sky, and throw the ball."

The goofy choreography provided more than amusement. Tiant would throw a fastball, slider, curve, and change-up from three different positions: sidearm, three quarters, and overhead. "And the guy, the hitter, he don't know what to do," Tiant said. "Eyes open big... the ball was right in the middle of the plate, strike three."

Batters would ask catcher Carlton Fisk what they were watching, but Tiant said the unorthodox delivery helped him. "I got a better point of release for my control," Tiant said. "I won 172 games after that. You know, it helped me, but you have to try different things. I never was afraid...When you figure it out, I got 12 pitches. You throw three different pitches or four different pitches in different areas."

Tiant had an ERA of 2.84 and struck out 7.8 per nine innings in his first six big league seasons with the Indians from 1964 to 1969. He posted an American League best 1.60 ERA in '68, trailing only Bob Gibson of the Cardinals. That season was the last before MLB lowered the mounds in an attempt to give hitters a better chance, and it worked. Tiant struck out 5.5 per nine with a 3.36 ERA in his time with the Red Sox from 1971 to 1978. But that ERA relative to the rest of the league was basically just as good as it was in his time with the Indians.

Tiant's father, Luis Tiant Sr., may actually have been a better pitcher than his son. Tiant Sr. never had the chance to play in the big leagues, though, making his name in the Negro Leagues and in winter ball. Born in Marianao, Cuba, the younger Tiant didn't think he'd make the big leagues himself—never mind become a star.

Success had its cost. Tiant was playing in Mexico City in 1961, a year before the Cuban Missile Crisis. Normally, Tiant would return to Cuba for winter ball after the summer. "But the political embarrassment and potential economic hardship of massive Cuban emigration led Fidel Castro's government to ban all outside travel," wrote the Society of American Baseball Research's Mark Armour. "Accordingly, upon the advice of his father, Luis did not return home to Cuba in 1961, not knowing when or if he would see his parents again."

He, though, would someday see his parents again at Fenway Park in one of the most famous moments of his career. During the magical '75 season, U.S. politicians helped convince Fidel Castro to allow Tiant's parents to visit him in Boston. In August they embraced at the airport, and the elder Tiant, then 69, threw out the first pitch—twice. (He wasn't satisfied with the first.) The younger Tiant pitched in front of his parents for the first time as a big leaguer in late August, but it wasn't his best outing performance-wise. "Fourteen, 15 years, I don't see them," Tiant said. "They're coming back. That's the first time they see me pitch and that was a great time for me and maybe the most important thing in my baseball career...It was the best thing that happened to me."

One more great honor could be coming. Tiant doesn't lack for perspective and he's willing to share his feelings. Speaking in 2017, Tiant, an avid cigar smoker, sounded annoyed that the various Hall of Fame voters have overlooked him. "I don't give a damn about it. Whatever happens, happens," Tiant said. "These people do whatever they want to do...that's a crazy thing they be doing. I don't want to be sitting down and worrying about it anymore. I just sit here. I'm still alive. If they put me in before I'm dead, fine. If not, what are you going to do?"

But Tiant also seems to carry a reasoned sense of both his baseball experience and the big picture. He said multiple times that he achieved more than he ever could have expected. In a game where you could drown in statistics and attempts to compare performance across eras, Tiant's Hall of Fame candidacy rests more on context.

The difficult journey for players of color, or for those speaking English as a second language, didn't end once Jackie Robinson broke the color barrier. Tiant's journey is even more unique as one of the game's ambassadors from Cuba. "I get the worst sides of life, Cuban and black," Tiant said. "And then coming here and not speaking the language makes it worse...and then the towns you play or the state where you play...they're not liking us. They're screaming at us, they treated us like a dog. We can't do anything, we can't stay in the same hotels where the players stay. We can't eat in the same restaurant they eat, and when we go on the road, the players have to bring you the food. The white players bring you the food to the bus. That's the only way we can eat. They stay in the hotel, and we have to stay in the black section. At some peoples' house, they rent it for us. And that's the way it was—the people, the fans, they call you names, all game... You don't want people to call you names, telling you they're going to hang you, send you back to Africa.

Tiant noted that for his father, it was worse.

Unsurprisingly, difficult moments never fazed Tiant. He was the starting pitcher for the Sox in the Game 6 victory of the 1975 World Series—the game when Fisk waved a home run fair down the left-field line in the 12th inning—despite a performance from Tiant that wasn't up to his usual big-game standard. Throwing 163 pitches in a Game 4 probably took a lot out of him.

(Don't get Tiant started on the subject of inning limits today. "The system is the one that's killing the game," Tiant said. "And it's bad... look what happened in the World Series [to the Los Angeles Dodgers in 2017]. You got a starting pitcher pitching two innings. He throws a shutout for two innings, three innings, and they're giving up a base hit or walking somebody, you take him out. That's crazy.")

Tiant threw a two-hit shutout vs. the Toronto Blue Jays in Game No. 162 in 1978—an outing that forced a one-game playoff with the New York Yankees, who lost their final game of the regular season. The Sox lost Game No. 163 at the hands of one Bucky Dent.

Since retirement from the game, Tiant has been back to Cuba twice after what he thought may have been a permanent exile in 1961. Both trips have come in the new millennium. Still, today, he doesn't see enough caring for what really matters. "You have a beautiful car, $200,000 car. You get a heart attack. The car stays right there," Tiant said. "And you may be dead inside of your car. Because if nobody comes and help you, it doesn't matter...*Hate*. That word should never be used. They should take that word out of the dictionary."

35

FRED LYNN

Outfielder Fred Lynn, who had a lifetime .347 batting average at Fenway Park, readies to hit during his seven-year career with the Red Sox.

a broken left hand near the end of the season. "We hung out. We started to play golf together, we learned how to play golf together, which was very comical back then," Lynn said. "We spent some time off the field together and we're very close. I mean, I've known Jimmy since he was 20 years old and I'm 21. So we go back a long way, and every time we see each other, it's just like going back in a time machine. So it's very cool. I'm very proud of him, to be honest with you...He's from South Carolina, quiet kid, and he kind of let his bat do the talking. Fortunately for Jimmy and I, our first year, we had lots of personalities on our club, and when they stuck microphones in our face, we would answer a question, but we had lots of guys that wanted to talk. So it was great for us because we could just sit back and listen to the veterans spiel to the press. Jimmy, like I said, very quiet, very shy—and so was I back then."

The nickname for the duo came from the great Peter Gammons and even made *Merriam-Webster's*, which defined the Gold Dust Twins as "a pair of inseparable and indefatigable workers." If you seek the etymology, once upon a time, the packaging of a trademarked soap powder called Gold Dust depicted a pair of twin boys. Rice spent his whole career with the Sox and eventually made the Hall of Fame. The outfielders formed a trio with Dwight Evans as well.

There's something of a what-if game to play with Lynn. What if he stays? And what if he stays healthy? His seven years with the Sox produced a .308 average, .383 on-base percentage, and .520 slugging percentage. Naturally, production that good just had to be traded away because there was a contract dispute over some technical language. Hey, it's Boston.

The Sox dealt Lynn to the California Angels ahead of the 1981 season, taking Lynn away from Fenway Park. We can wax poetic about the Green Monster, but that place was really a haven if not heaven for Lynn. He hit .347 lifetime with a .601 slugging percentage at Fenway. He was batting .350 there at the time of the swap. There was another trade possibility. The Associated Press reported at the time that Lynn would be sent to the New York Yankees for Ron Guidry. But the Sox ended up trading Lynn to the Angels, and pitcher Frank Tanana was the primary chip the Sox got back for Lynn, who signed a four-year, $5.25 million deal with the Halos, making him the game's second highest paid player behind Dave Winfield.

Injuries cropped up during Lynn's time in Boston and became a greater issue going forward. His production in a single year never matched his 1979 output for the Sox, when he led the majors in wins above replacement at 8.8 while hitting for an AL-best .333 average and big-league best .423 on-base percentage and .637 slugging percentage. With 39 home runs to boot, his numbers made him worlds more productive than Don Baylor, the guy who actually won the AL MVP that year.

Nonetheless, '75 stands as Lynn's season most remembered. "[1975] was so special for New England," Lynn said. "Certainly the people that lived in that area think of me when they think of 1975 and my teammates."

36

ECCENTRIC CHARACTERS: A SPACEMAN AND AN OIL CAN

"Peter Gammons called me a walking non-sequitur," Bill Lee said. "And I said, I really take exception to the word 'walking.'" A 15-minute phone call with Lee more than proves Gammons' point. Here's a smattering of the topics we crossed in an interview that started off very broadly, which, I suppose, was just an invitation for non-sequiturs.

- **Red Sox pitching.** Lee said he can fix it. "They have to come to me if they want to win again."
- **Author Tom Wolfe.** Lee's book, *The Wrong Stuff*, played off Wolfe's title, *The Right Stuff*. The first chapter begins with these words: "God, it's dark. I am sitting in the lotus position on the floor of the office of Montreal Expo president and general manager John McHale. There is not another soul around."
- **Colin Kaepernick.** Lee supported social movements in his day. "I was the Colin Kaepernick way before Colin Kaepernick," Lee said.
- **His cool nickname.** He notes, "I've always signed my name since '73, I've always signed it, 'Earth, Bill Lee.' I've always been an Earth person and not an around and around and around and around. It's all a bunch of lunacy." He's quoting a song at this point. "Harry Nilsson, 'Space Man,' that song, embraces me more...than anything else." Some lyrics from that song that he does not cite: "But now that I am a spaceman, I'd rather be back on the pad/ Hey, Mother Earth, won't cha bring me back down safely to the sea."

Lee is wholly fascinating and, in some cases, may be on to something. We shouldn't call him crazy because making light of those who do suffer from mental illness isn't amusing. No, with Lee we can settle on more apt terms: *colorful, eccentric, out there, a different cat*. "They just don't get it," Lee said of a general *they*. "They don't know me. That's the whole thing. Everybody thinks they know me, but no one really does." What I do know is that he's 80 times more interesting to have a discussion with than most baseball players you'll encounter and, ultimately, he's smarter than most all of them, too.

Lee went to the University of Southern California and was in his formative 20s during the formative '60s. And, of course, he's a lefty. He pitched 14 years in the majors, including 10 with the Sox from 1969 to 1978 and the rest with the Expos. He had a 3.62 ERA overall. He hasn't stopped pitching yet either. He stays active in amateur ball.

He openly documents his drug experimentation in *The Wrong Stuff*. "Marijuana never hammered me like a good Camel," Lee wrote. "I believe the thing about marijuana that causes a stoner for people is that the majority of people are right-handed. This means they think with the left side of the brain...But left-handers, such as yours truly, are used to using the right side of the brain, the correct side. The smoke puts us totally in sync with nature."

Recreational drugs have never been foreign to baseball. There was another Red Sox pitcher, a righty, who has had a decades-long battle with addiction to hard drugs, someone who also marched to the beat of his own drum and kept pitching well beyond 50 years of age. Dennis Ray "Oil Can" Boyd was one of several solid pitching prospects the Sox developed in the early to mid-1980s, along with Bob Ojeda, John Tudor, Bruce Hurst, and Roger Clemens. And Boyd's story comes with some levity but also great austerity. In his memoir—*They Call Me Oil Can: Baseball, Drugs, and Life on the Edge*, written with Mike Shalin—Boyd said that his nickname was given to him in 1977 when he was 17. He and his best friend, Pap, found some liquor that they shouldn't have had their hands on. A local drunk in the neighborhood saw the boys and told on them—and said that he found the boys drinking whiskey from oil cans. Pap called Boyd "Oil Can" the next day. "I wrote 'Oil Can' under the bill of my cap," Boyd wrote. "Then my high school shortstop, Ricky Irby, picked up my ball glove and cap one day during spring practice and he saw the nickname in my cap...That's how the name got from the streets to the baseball diamond."

A black man from Mississippi, Oil Can grew up in the segregated South and was called every awful name in the book. "My brother Mike was the inspiration that got me to the major leagues," Boyd wrote. "His story also helped me get kicked out of the major leagues. I was always so bitter about Mike's career, knowing that Mike would probably have been one of the best fucking baseball players who ever lived...He was drafted by the Dodgers in '73, but he ended up not receiving a contract. And why? Because he got a white girl pregnant."

The Sox were in a spell of mediocrity when Oil Can arrived in 1982. Fred Lynn was gone, so too was Carlton Fisk, and Clemens was a couple years away, debuting in '84. Oil Can created some instant excitement in his starts. He was demonstrative on the mound and would pump his fist with more or less every strikeout. Opponents weren't exactly thrilled. Only in recent years has such expressiveness started to garner widespread approval.

It was nonetheless entertainment in those days. When the Red Sox had a fog delay in Cleveland, Oil Can said, "That's what you get for building a ballpark on the ocean." Fenway Park loved him, and he had good stuff to match his persona, a huge arsenal of pitches. He had heat plus longevity. From 1984 to 1986, Boyd threw 33 complete games, an impressive feat for a guy with a frame of about 155 pounds. "I love Oil Can," pitcher Calvin Schiraldi said. "He was his own bird. He did things his way and he didn't care...But when it came time to show up and do his job, he wanted the ball. That's all you can ask, I mean, is give me the frickin' ball. That's what he wanted, that's what he wanted. He didn't care what anybody else thought. He was going to do what he wanted to do. And that's cool."

It wasn't always cool for everyone. Oil Can could be quite brash with bold predictions. That confidence turned into outrage when he was not selected as an All-Star for a second straight year and he quit the team. He was suspended for 21 days. He eventually returned in August. But while he was suspended for deserting the club, he was physically hurt and felt he was never the same.

Boyd said he went to go buy cocaine during his suspension but was warned cops were on to him. When he got home, he had an incident with the police, who tried to wrench his arm behind his back. "Every other day my arm wouldn't feel good," Boyd wrote. "I was stretching it and everything, but all the while I'm saying to myself, *These guys really did hurt my arm*."

A belief from manager John McNamara that Boyd was under the influence of something—booze or drugs—kept him out of Game 7 of the World Series. Boyd in his memoir said he was neither drunk nor high. Injuries, though, started to take their toll. Like Spaceman Lee, Boyd went from Boston to Montreal. He loved his time with his Expos, where he played from 1990 to 1991: "Someone once asked me which guys were cool in the Expos clubhouse. My answer: 'All of them.'"

37

THE 2011 COLLAPSE

What's amazing about the 2011 collapse is the residual trauma felt in its wake. Any time a contending Red Sox team drops a couple games in September, the cries of: "It's 2011 all over again" automatically follow. That's true for some in the media as well. Come on, folks. If we're being reasonable, it's hard to replicate that kind of heartbreak. You probably don't want to relive it.

Contrary to popular belief, not every venerated Red Sox figure leaves miserable. Nonetheless, many do leave under unfavorable conditions, and the stunning failure of '11 paved the exit for two of the most famous Red Sox never to play for them: general manager Theo Epstein and manager Terry Francona. "Disappointment," Epstein said in the visiting clubhouse at Camden Yards in the early morning hours of September 29, 2011, right after the Red Sox were eliminated from the postseason. "We got off to a bad start, 2–10. It was 81–42 [after that], and then September happened: 7–20. It's impossible to explain, huge disappointment. We have no one to blame but ourselves. We did this to ourselves."

There were some tremendous individual performances that season. In March the *Boston Herald* famously put out a paper with the headline, "BEST TEAM EVER!" Not quite. The Sox had loaded up over the winter, trading for Adrian Gonzalez and then giving him a $154 million contract. Free-agent bust Carl Crawford got $142 million. For a while the Sox did look like an excellent team. In his only full season with the Sox, Gonzalez hit .338. He, Jacoby Ellsbury, and David Ortiz all had on-base plus slugging percentages (OPS) above .900. Josh Beckett's ERA was 2.89. Yet, as it was later reported, Beckett was part of a group of veteran pitchers who lost focus as the season spiraled out of control.

At the beginning of the final month of the regular season, the Sox were in the hunt for a division title. Simply locking up a playoff spot seemed an afterthought. Of course they'd make it.

Consider that on September 4, the Red Sox (84–54) held a nine-game lead in the American League wild-card race over the Tampa Bay Rays (75–63). But by the final day of the season on September 28, the nine-game lead was gone, and the Rays and Sox were tied for the wild-card at 90–71. The Sox were on the road against the Baltimore Orioles; the Rays were at home against the New York Yankees.

What followed is a day of baseball that sits in the conversation for the most insane day in regular-season history. The National League wild-card was in a tie as well—the St. Louis Cardinals edged out the Atlanta Braves—and home-field advantage was undecided elsewhere.

Early on, the Rays seemed willing to make the path easy for the Sox. The Yanks went up big early and led Tampa Bay 7–0 as late as the bottom of the eighth inning. But the Rays scored six in that frame, a comeback visible for all to see at Camden Yards. The Sox and O's were in a rain delay, and the video board showed a portion of the other game. With the Rays down to their final strike in the ninth, the otherwise unremarkable Dan Johnson, a pinch hitter, roped a liner just high enough to the right-field corner, tying the game at 7. The Rays went to extras with momentum on their side.

The Red Sox needed a win to at least ensure a one-game playoff with the Rays for the wild-card. But the final game for Boston was just a microcosm of the month. They choked.

The Sox were up 3–2 in the ninth when closer Jonathan Papelbon faltered. The winning run scored on Robert Andino's single to left field on a ball that was nearly an out. Crawford slid feet first with his right hand extended, but while sliding on the grass, the lip of his glove couldn't quite get under the ball. The disappointment of the play embodied Crawford's introductory season in Boston.

Then the Sox were forced to wait, watching as the Yanks-Rays game went to 12 innings. Evan Longoria's home run to the left-field corner, a low liner just like Johnson's shot in the ninth, sent the Rays to October and sent the Sox home. What went wrong? The Sox's pitching for one. Sox starters had a 7.08 ERA in September with 13 losses tagged to them.

Then there was the menu—chicken and beer. Far worse has entered a major league clubhouse. But the look was brutal. John

Tomase, then at the *Boston Herald*, was the first to report about an affinity for beer in the clubhouse. Then came the comprehensive autopsy. "Boston's three elite starters went soft, their pitching as anemic as their work ethic," *The Boston Globe*'s Bob Hohler wrote in October. "The indifference of Beckett, Lester, and Lackey in a time of crisis can be seen in what team sources say became their habit of drinking beer, eating fast-food fried chicken, and playing video games in the clubhouse during games while their teammates tried to salvage a once-promising season."

In his eighth season, Francona no longer had the same clubhouse influence. He was also participating in MLB's drug program to address his abuse of pain medication, a condition Hohler reported. Eating fried chicken and some boozing weren't the biggest problems. They were merely symptoms of something larger. "It was more disturbing for me to think that they would not protect each other, or one guy wouldn't tell another guy to knock it off," Francona said in his eponymous book written with the *Globe*'s Dan Shaughnessy. "I wanted them to protect each other ferociously."

The storyline about the 2011 collapse became one centered mostly on psychology. Talented and loaded with star players, the Sox were a combustible group that didn't mesh. A bit of nuance may be appropriate. All that can be true, but the Sox also may have been due for a fall. Tom Tippett, an analyst who started to do work for the Red Sox in 2003 before he left in 2016, felt the Sox were enjoying a particularly high level of luck early in the year. "I said to myself—and I might have said to some of my colleagues [in 2011]—I hope we remember how well things are going later on when this normalizes," Tippett said in 2016 at Saber Seminar, an annual conference for charity in Boston. "A lot of things were going well early."

And there was worry, if only latent worry. Regression spares very few. Tippett remembered a May conversation from 2011 at a time he said the Red Sox had a high batting average on balls put in play, suggesting luck. "I don't know what the narrative of this season should be," Tippett said, "whether it should all be focused on September and all the interpretations people made about why that happened, or whether a more measured analysis of that year would say, 'Hey, we caught a lot of breaks for a while, and then nothing went right for a while.'"

Epstein, in the visiting clubhouse at Camden Yards the night it all ended, couldn't exactly take a nuanced approach. "We can't deny that this month happened just because it was preceded by four months of being the best team in baseball," Epstein said. "We'll have to take a very close look at everything that's not right we have to fix, and that includes the whole organization."

He didn't wind up fixing it, though. Epstein left for the Chicago Cubs, where he had complete control as a team president. Tito took a year off from managing. "It's time for a new voice here," Francona said at his farewell press conference. "Don't everyone forget: a month ago we were on pace to win about 100 games. When things start to go, I wanted desperately for our guys to care about each other on the field. I think I referenced that a few times. I wasn't seeing that as much as I wanted to. When I thought I tried to help make that better, and the coaches also, I just wasn't ever comfortable. You've heard me say all the time about going in one direction and getting through challenges and meeting them together. I just didn't think we were doing that. That's my responsibility to get them to do that. It just wasn't happening to my satisfaction."

And onto the scene came Bobby Valentine. Collapse precipitated disaster.

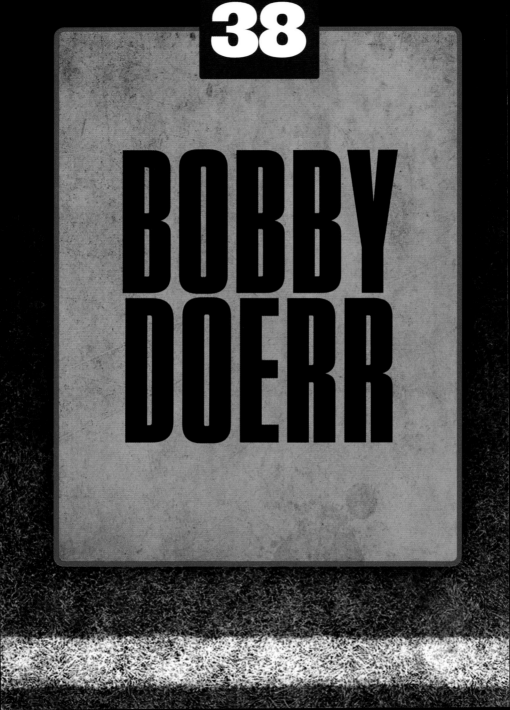

38

BOBBY DOERR

Just before he died at 99 years old in 2017, Bobby Doerr was the oldest living member of the National Hall of Fame. He was also the only remaining major leaguer who played in the 1930s. For any second baseman in Boston—from Dustin Pedroia, to whoever directly succeeds Pedroia, to the super hyped Yoan Moncada-level prospect 50 years from now—the position's standard-bearer will always be Doerr.

A right-handed hitter from Los Angeles, Doerr batted .409 (9-for-22) in the 1946 World Series, a seven-game loss to the St. Louis Cardinals. He hit .288 lifetime with 223 home runs, a mark that stood at the time of his retirement as the third highest total amassed by a second baseman. He posted double-digit long balls in 12 straight seasons squarely interrupted by 1945, when he didn't play at all as an enlisted Army man during World War II.

Doerr is remembered as an equally stellar defender. "I never saw him misplay a ball, and he had the best backhand of any second baseman I ever saw," Johnny Pesky had said.

A Pacific Northwest resident with the attitude to match, Doerr was a revered coach, as well. Even as a player, his demeanor provided a contrast to the greatest hitter who ever lived, his great friend Ted Williams. Dwight Evans was not a contemporary of Doerr, but he nonetheless felt his impact. "He was nothing but a role model on how to act and how to carry yourself," Evans said. "Everyone I knew, who knew him, absolutely adored him. When I was around him, he was just gentle and

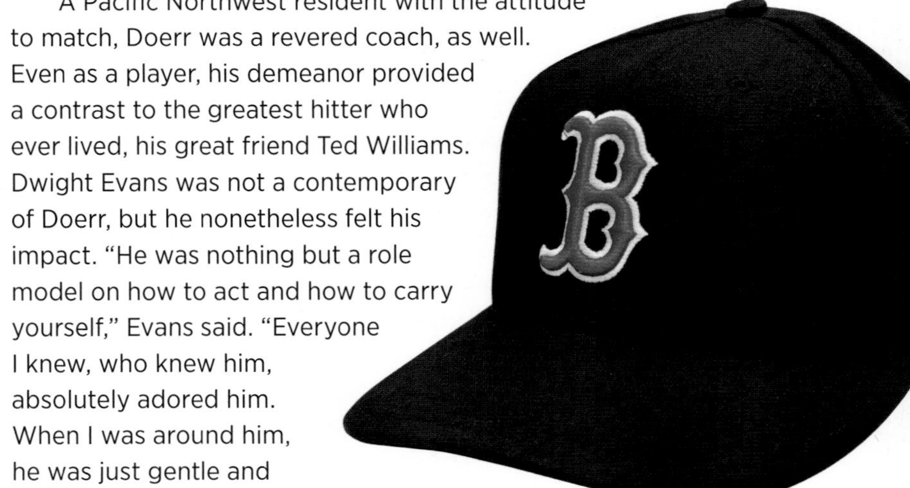

a beautiful human being. We'd talk about fishing. I love to fish. He was a guide and had that boat on a river in Oregon. And he talked about hitting in simple terms, not too mechanical, but little things that would help players. The way he coached was almost like a father, not berating or anything. He was special."

Doerr is a beloved symbol of a bygone era. All 14 seasons he spent in the big leagues were in Boston, and his career was long paired with Williams' career. Doerr got to the big leagues in '37 at only 19 years old, and Teddy Ballgame joined forces two years later in '39, when Williams was just 21. The only time they were apart in Doerr's big league career was owed to both men's time in the service. The two grew close as teenagers in the Pacific Coast League because of their shared love of hunting and fishing. They went to Western movies together.

Hall of Fame second baseman Eddie Collins (who never played for the Sox) was the team's general manager from 1933 to 1947. Collins took a trip to see Doerr and shortstop George Myatt in the PCL in 1936. "While he was here, he saw Ted and became interested," Doerr said in Leigh Montville's book, *Ted Williams*. "He signed me and he wanted to sign Ted."

Williams was too young to be plucked at the same time, but Collins made sure that when the time came for bidding on Williams that he was front and center. "We never had a captain, but he was the silent captain of the team," Williams famously said of Doerr.

Yet, they flowed most differently inside the game. In *Summer of '49*, David Halberstam wrote that Williams would grow frustrated when Doerr would not remember precisely what pitch he hit. Williams was the exacting scientist. Doerr was calmer, perhaps a little more willing to accept the fate of an at-bat as just that, but was nonetheless a savant. "Doerr was as comfortable with himself as Williams was not," Halberstam wrote. "He knew he was talented...But he did not push himself obsessively, as did Williams. The difference on occasion drove Williams crazy."

Only three Sox players have more All-Star selections than Doerr, who had nine: David Ortiz (10), Williams (18), and Carl Yastrzemski (18). "I met him my first spring training with the Red Sox in 1959. Just a very low key, nice guy," Yastrzemski said upon Doerr's passing. "He was the guy that helped me the most in 1967. I started off slow, and he was the one that got me to raise my hands up higher, told me to get them up a little higher because I was going to go straight away. And he told me, 'No, you have a lot of power, use it.' He was really a big help to me and he was close to everybody. Everybody loved him. There wasn't a thing about him that you could dislike. As classy as they come."

World War II touched all corners of life, including box scores. The Red Sox roster was reshaped more than any other. Per Richard Johnson's *Red Sox Century*, 22 players put in a total of 53 years in the service from 1942 to 1945. Doerr remained stateside—for a time. According to Bill Nowlin's biography at SABR, Doerr was exempt from the draft because he and his wife Monica had a young son and because he had a perforated eardrum. But as the war effort mounted, so too did the need for more help. Doerr left late in the 1944 season, playing his final game before 1946 on September 3, 1944. The Sox were two and a half games out in the middle of a pennant race they would not win. Doerr reported to the Army, finishing out his time in the service at Camp Roberts in California. In his first year back with the Sox, the team was a juggernaut that just fell short.

Doerr's career was cut short because of back problems, but he finished with six seasons of 100 RBIs. After his last in 1950, it took 26 years for another second baseman (the Cincinnati Reds' Joe Morgan) to drive in 100. As of 2017 Doerr was the only Red Sox player to have hit for the cycle twice.

Doerr was just 33 when he retired, but he didn't leave the game for good. He was the first-base and hitting coach on the 1967 Impossible Dream team. "He worked extensively with Yaz," Johnson said. "Yaz, the man of a thousand stances and the guy who was always sort of changing what he was doing at the plate, did not get off to a good start that year...And Bobby Doerr worked tirelessly with him. And Yaz asked for the help, too. Yaz's work ethic that year was extraordinary, and, of course, it paid off, but Bobby Doerr was his hitting guru and worked very close with him. Ted Williams was certainly available in spring training, but Ted was such an intimidating presence. Basically he was on such a higher plane than everybody. It's hard for him to communicate, whereas Bobby Doerr was much more of a soft spoken, gentle sort of a fatherly presence, whereas Ted was like George S. Patton. And so I think his mentorship of Yaz during the '67 season—much like pitching coach Sal Maglie's mentorship of Jim Lonborg—really contributed much to the success of those players and of that season. So I think Doerr gets a nod for the role he played that year with Yastrzemski."

Relationships are at the heart of Doerr's memory. Doerr, Williams, Pesky, and Dom DiMaggio were the inspiration for Halberstam's book *The Teammates: A Portrait of a Friendship*. "Bobby never swore or used cuss words," said Dick Flavin, the Red Sox's public-address announcer and poet laureate, when Doerr died. "He wasn't sanctimonious about it. He just didn't join in when the talk got a little earthy. When we were visiting Ted on the trip made famous by David Halberstam's book, *The Teammates*, Dom said at one point, 'Gee, I wish Bobby was here.' Johnny said, 'Yeah, but we couldn't talk this way if he was.' When I was growing up, he was the favorite player of the vast majority of kids. Almost everyone had a Bobby Doerr model glove. None of us could identify with Ted with his outsized talent, personality, and flaws, but we could all identify with Bobby. He was the man our parents wanted us to become. That might explain why he was Ted's favorite player, too. For older guys of my generation, his passing marks the loss of the last vestige of our boyhood. Life will go on for us, but it will never be the same."

39

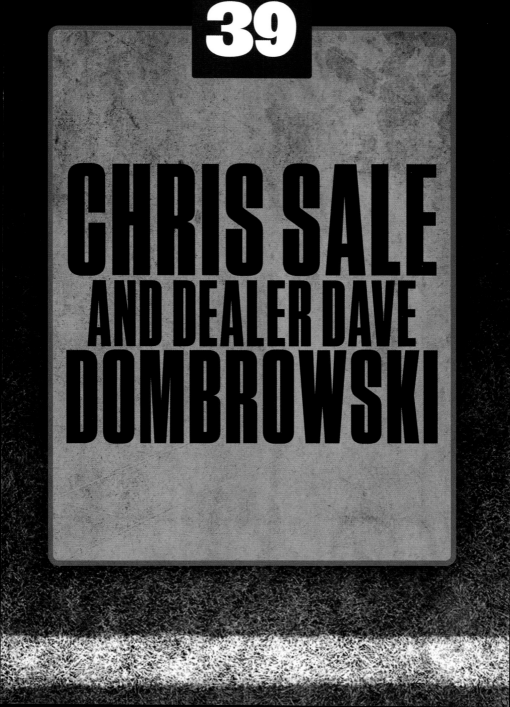

CHRIS SALE AND DEALER DAVE DOMBROWSKI

On the day the Red Sox introduced Dave Dombrowski in 2015, he telegraphed the blockbusters he would eventually pull off: a 2015 deal with the San Diego Padres for closer Craig Kimbrel, the $217 million contract for David Price the same offseason, and then a year later, a mammoth trade for the American League's preeminent strikeout artist, Chris Sale.

Dealer Dave doesn't mess around. From the get-go in Boston, Dombrowski knew he wanted arms. Big, established, 95 mph-and-up arms. "We need to find some better pitching," Dombrowski said on August 19, 2015, at his first press conference. "How we go about it will still have to be determined...But we need to improve the starting pitching and also probably the bullpen over time. A lot of times you can go into the offseason with particular goals, and those players aren't available...People look at an organization. They say, 'Why don't you go get that type of player?' Well, the reality is he doesn't exist. But if you told me, 'What would I love?' I would love to have power pitching. I love power pitching overall."

Oh, those power pitchers sure do exist, and it didn't take long for Dombrowski to collect them like Pokemon. Very expensive Pokemon. Sale was the biggest prize of all.

Dombrowski's title of president of baseball operations was technically a first for the Red Sox when he came on board. But the gig came with the same basic job description as the general managers who preceded him, but there was one notable difference. Dombo was supposed to be operating with more autonomy than his predecessors. Larry Lucchino outranked general managers Theo Epstein and Ben Cherington, and Lucchino was no longer in power when Dombrowski arrived.

Dombo's resume is long, and his reputation is bold. After starting his hike up the ranks in the Chicago White Sox front office in 1978, he's surpassed 40 years working in Major League Baseball. In the

One of Dave Dombrowksi's marquee acquisitions, Chris Sale throws a pitch during Game 1 of the 2017 American League Division Series.

job Dombrowski held before coming to Boston, he couldn't get the Detroit Tigers over the hump. He built the 2002–15 Tigers, which saw two World Series defeats and another two American League Championship Series losses. (One of the ALCS losses was delivered by the 2013 Red Sox.) Dombrowski did build and sustain competitive teams in those years—albeit at great cost. He spent a ton of late Tigers owner Mike Ilitch's money with a mandate from Ilitch to keep pushing.

In 2015 the Red Sox were less than two full seasons removed from the '13 World Series run engineered by Cherington. But major league success quickly dissipated, and the team was headed for last place for a second straight year. Big signings like Hanley Ramirez, Rusney Castillo, and Pablo Sandoval were disappointments. In his first season with the Red Sox, Rick Porcello was having a rough year, too.

So when Ilitch and Dombrowski divorced in the summer of 2015, Red Sox owner John Henry was ready for a reunion. Henry and Dombrowski were previously together in 1997, when Dombrowski won a World Series as the GM of Henry's Florida Marlins. The Red Sox farm system Dombrowski inherited was in full bloom, and Dombrowski immediately dipped into it, trading top prospect Manuel Margot in a package for Kimbrel. He also signed Price, a pitcher he acquired via trade in his Detroit days.

But in Dombrowski's two 93-win seasons with the Red Sox, no move stands out like the Sale trade. The stage was the 2016 winter meetings outside of Washington, D.C., where all of the baseball world was gathered. David Ortiz was gone, and the Red Sox needed to replace his production. They decided they could do so by bolstering their pitching rather than their lineup. Dombrowski, as he's wont to do, set his sights on the absolute best pitcher available. The cost was steep. Cuban infielder Yoan Moncada, who had briefly played in the big leagues, was the consensus No. 1 prospect in baseball at the time. The Red Sox also traded a kid who can throw 100 mph, Michael Kopech, in a four-player package to land Sale from the White Sox.

Farm system? What farm system?

We exaggerate, mostly. Bold doesn't always pay off. Dombrowski's efficiency with resources—prospects and dollars—is fair to question. At the same time, the spectacle of a blockbuster gone right can be pretty awesome. Through Year One, no one could argue the results either.

In Sale's first April in Boston, he was terrific. "Would I say I'm surprised? Yeah," Sale said in the midst of an excellent May. "But at the same time, I wouldn't say I am. I'm having fun. I know that. It's a very result-oriented game, but results can be very skewed because two guys can work the same, do the same things on the same day at the same time, and get two totally different results in this game. So while people like to look at the results, sometimes they can be skewed...I look more in my preparation than I do in the results."

In spring training a lot of the talk around Sale tied back to the minefield playing in Boston can prove to be. Adjusting to the pressure, the stage, the scrutiny, Price struggled with it. Porcello didn't do well in Year No. 1. Very few have.

Sale punched that narrative in the face while punching out everyone. Tall and lanky with a crossfire delivery that releases the ball unusually far to the first-base side, Sale's 308 strikeouts in 2017 were the second most in Red Sox history in a single season. Had the Red Sox not skipped Sale's final start of the regular season to keep him fresh for the playoffs, he likely would have broken Pedro Martinez's record of 313 strikeouts from 1999.

In the big data era, where scouting reports and spin rates can dictate game plans, Sale is the rare bird that doesn't need to study much. He actively avoids learning about the opposition, in fact. He virtually never shakes off his catcher, and if he does, it might just be an attempt to throw off the opponent. All three of his pitches—fastball, change-up, slider—can melt hitters.

Sale's catcher in 2017, Sandy Leon, discussed the opposing hitters with Red Sox coaches. But Sale's goal was zen. His stuff is so good, his ability so superlative, that he can afford to think less while pitching. "You could look at it like that," Sale said. "I look at it for me as just clearing my mind. When I'm out there, I'm not worried about what this guy's hitting over the last X amount of at-bats because if I read on a scouting report that he's hitting .450 on fastballs in, I'm still going to throw a fastball in. And if I know that going in, I could be timid throwing that. You don't ever want to throw a pitch in the big leagues, hoping, praying, defensively. That takes all that away from me."

With a lithe frame, Sale dedicates the time he would otherwise spend prepping hitters to his body. He's in fantastic shape even if he looks almost scrawny. His motion is unorthodox, and repetition is therefore difficult. His Achilles heel has been fatigue, and it appeared to show up again at the end of the 2017 season, but he's always been driven to stay in excellent condition. "He's got a lot of really good physical qualities already," Red Sox assistant strength coach Mike Roose said. "He's very flexible naturally just by his genetics. His endurance is extremely high. He works on that [doing cardio]. You can tell. We knew right from the first week of spring training [that] endurance is something he works on. He might squat more than all our starters, believe it or not. I was surprised."

Sale's poor postseason debut was a surprise to many. He allowed seven earned runs and three home runs in Game 1 of the American League Division Series, though he was facing the eventual world champion Houston Astros. Nonetheless, in a Cy Young-worthy campaign that finished with a 2.90 ERA, he proved to be the most exciting starting pitcher to call Fenway home since Pedro, making his boss' blockbuster look good in the process.

40

HARRY AGGANIS

When Harry Agganis died in 1955, the Greek Orthodox Church suggested to some 400 pastors throughout the United States and Canada that services be held in his honor. The church said it had never taken such a step for an athlete before, and Agganis had played just 157 games in the big leagues. "All priests should devote the sermon of the day to Harry Agganis, his personality, devotion to God and country, and contribution to America," read Archbishop Michael's circular.

Why all the attention for a Red Sox first baseman who was only in his second season? Because for nearly a decade, Agganis had already been known as perhaps Boston's most indomitable athlete. Nicknamed the "Golden Greek," Agganis was a standout at Lynn Classical High School before becoming a two-way force for Boston University. The burgeoning pride of both a city and a region, he was just 26 years old when he died of a pulmonary embolism—a blood clot in the lungs—at a Cambridge, Massachusetts, hospital. He was initially admitted because of a persistent cough and eventually diagnosed with pneumonia.

There are still folks who say Agganis is the greatest athlete they've ever seen. Others believe he's the greatest the Boston area has ever produced period. "You talk to people of that generation, and his death is a marker in their lives much the way that [John F.] Kennedy's was," said historian Richard Johnson, the curator of The Sports Museum. "It was one of those things you didn't forget where you were when you heard the news. It was like, *Wow, how could that happen?*"

Many thought Agganis should have pursued pro football, and he was open to the idea had baseball not worked out. A lefty, Agganis was just starting to come into his own with the Sox, batting .313 in his final season. He was ascending on a preordained path to stardom. But in a region where town lines burst with pride, Agganis even transcended local stardom.

As a 17-year-old in 1946, he was selected to a national showcase game at Wrigley Field on a team managed by Honus Wagner. That same year he led Lynn Classical to a win against a school from Virginia in a North-South championship football game played in front of more than 18,000 at the Orange Bowl in Miami. His 20-yard touchdown pass to open the fourth quarter was the difference. He was a quadruple threat on the gridiron: he punted, ran, played defense, and, of course, played quarterback. Clipper Smith was the coach of the Boston Yanks football team in 1947. "There's a kid," Smith told *The New York Times*, "who can play regularly on my team right now. And I wouldn't be surprised if he could make every other team in the league."

Agganis stayed in town for college, choosing Boston University so he could take care of his widowed mother, Georgia. He was the seventh of seven children and stood 6'2". Some speculated Agganis had more at stake in his matriculation. Indeed, he could have gone most anywhere he wanted. "The grapevine insists that the Boston Red Sox had spotted him long before anyone else and that they had paid his way through college," *The Times* speculated posthumously about Agganis' choice. "So they picked one close to home where they could keep an eye on him and where they could watch his progress."

As a first-generation American, Agganis' story is the most classic of All-American threads. He was the son of Greek immigrants, devoted to his family, and committed to ensuring his mother benefit from the limitless opportunity she helped provide him. "When he was in high school, a couple of his football games were on TV," Johnson said. "Can you imagine that in 1947? They were all on the radio...Agganis was already a star. He was already front-page news before he even went to college. There are not many high school athletes that achieve that sort of notoriety. When he turned down the Cleveland Browns to join the Red Sox, it was another pretty dramatic thing. The choices he made: he could have gone to Notre Dame on a scholarship, he was recruited by any number of big time collegiate football programs."

In 1949 the first game legendary Dodgers voice Vin Scully ever did play-by-play for was at Fenway Park. He was not assigned a baseball game but a Boston University football game. Agganis was under center.

In November of 1950, Agganis, the pride of BU, was on the cover of *Sport* magazine. He briefly left school to join the Marines before returning so he could continue to support his mother. Agganis decided in November 1952 he would start his pro baseball career the following year. "Of course, I hate to give up football and I appreciate all the nice things everyone said about my playing," Agganis told the Associated Press after his farewell performance in the Senior Bowl in January 1953. "But I realized I couldn't do both. I made my choice when I decided to play baseball with the Red Sox and I'm going to concentrate on trying to make good with Boston." It couldn't have hurt that the Red Sox hired Agganis' high school baseball coach to run a farm team that was based in Lynn, Massachusetts (though Agganis did not play for that team, heading instead to a farm team in Louisville, Kentucky).

His football prowess wasn't forgotten as he transitioned to baseball full time. The day Agganis made his first big league start and notched his first big league hit was a frigid April 15, 1954. "The Red Sox should furnish Harry Agganis with football atmosphere all season at Fenway Park," read the first sentence of *The Globe*'s story on Agganis' 2-for-3 day.

The final numbers of Agganis' big league career: 11 home runs (all in '54), a .261 average, 67 RBIs, a .331 on-base percentage, and .404 slugging percentage. But everything was trending upward in his second season with a .313/.383/.458 line.

On the football side, the Browns traded the rights to Agganis to the Baltimore Colts (in a 15-player deal). The Red Sox, who weren't the most impressive franchise in the '50s, could have reached a point where they allowed Agganis to go to the Colts' training camp. There, he may have competed with Hall of Famer Johnny Unitas. "That would have been interesting to see how history might have changed," Johnson said. "He clearly was certainly a better collegiate quarterback than Johnny Unitas."

Agganis' deterioration was sudden. A bout with pneumonia first hospitalized him in May of 1955 and then again in June. The governor of Massachusetts and various mayors were among the attendees at his funeral services. Hundreds and perhaps as many as 2,000 people reportedly crowded into St. George's Church and an auxiliary building. Manager Mike Higgins left the Red Sox team to attend the funeral, as did pitcher Frank Sullivan. "God has taken him at this time to bring home to young people everywhere how high they can go from nothing if they work hard and live good lives," Georgia said at her son's funeral.

The Red Sox were playing the Washington Senators in D.C. on the day of the funeral in a game that Boston general manager Joe Cronin wanted postponed. The teams moved forward with the game when it turned into a benefit for the Red Cross. Its start was delayed an hour, and a memorial was held at the stadium in Washington. An estimated 20,000 flocked to Fenway for a tribute as well. A foundation was established in Agganis' name to provide scholarships for student-athletes, and Boston University's main indoor sports venue is still called Agganis Arena. A wire story reported in Lynn noted two days after Agganis' death: "The local Western Union office indicated yesterday's volume of messages was its largest single day in 20 years."

41

DICE-K

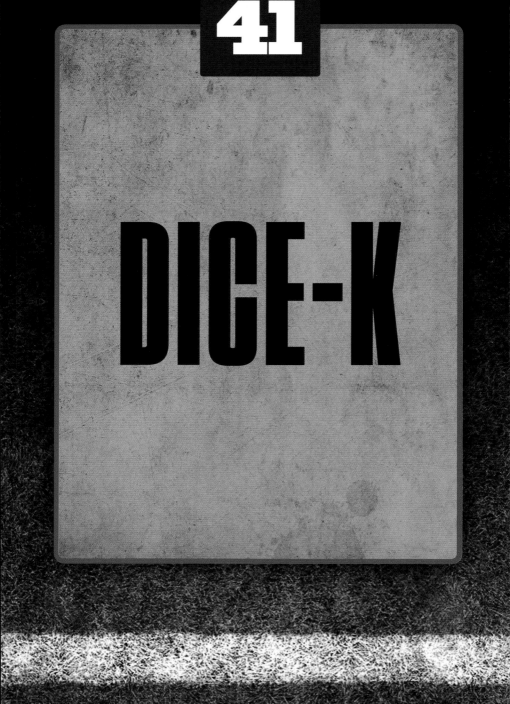

The mania outshined the man. Well, the pitcher, at least. The experience was still pretty cool. Daisuke Matsuzaka was billed as a mythical sensation from a faraway land. In reality, Dice-K was a very good pitcher who got hurt and had to forever fight the aforementioned depiction. And our preconceived notions about the righty—unlike something you've ever seen before!—were indeed rooted in a faraway land, allowing them to grow unchecked like wildfire.

He was neither a bust nor a boom. But if we have to choose, he was closer to the former—only because the hoopla stirred unrealistic expectations. Dice-K's first season (15–12, 4.40 ERA) with the Red Sox in 2007 wasn't exactly a bad time in club history. His second year (18–3, 2.90 ERA) was his best individually. He went 33–15 with a 3.72 ERA in the regular season combined through Years One and Two. "We won the World Series that year, that first year," former assistant general manager Jed Hoyer said. "He won some big playoff games for us. In some ways you could spin a story however you want to spin it. He wasn't the second coming everyone was hoping for. But the early years were fairly good. I've always been so fascinated by it because I feel like there were some games early on where he showed the glimpses of what he had been in Japan just like big strikeout games, games he was unhittable."

So much happened before then. There was a tremendous build-up to Dice-K's signing in December 2006. He was a new kind of expensive. The right-hander came to the Sox at a price tag of $103.1 million—unheard of for an international player. There was $52 million committed to the pitcher himself on a six-year deal, plus $51.11 million paid as a posting fee—what it cost to pry him loose from the Seibu Lions of Japan's top rung, Nippon Professional Baseball. (Note that's vastly less money than Shohei Ohtani commanded when the Los Angeles Angels inked him prior to the 2018 season because MLB's rules changed. Just in terms of fuss, Ohtani is probably a good comparison to the interest in Dice-K.)

Sox owner John Henry chose that $51.11 number out of a bit of superstition, according to the *Boston Herald*. When Henry first got involved with the attempt to buy the Red Sox, Henry was known simply as Investor 11. His group's bid won out, so he wanted to keep that mojo going with Dice-K. The Sox also felt another team might be willing to bid as much as $50 million, which was not the case. The runner-up was the New York Mets at around $40 million.

Aside from the usual benefits of good pitching, the Sox believed Matsuzaka's presence would bring increased financial gain: more Japanese fans. "You need to try and do what you can to connect the players to the fanbase and create things," Red Sox president Sam Kennedy explained. "But at the end of the day, the best marketing vehicle is a competitive and winning baseball team. And in 2007 [Dice-K had 15 wins]. But he was part of a rotation that delivered a World Series championship. That's what matters. Every time someone asks me, 'Oh, what about this potential free agent, or this trade?' At the end of the day, we need to do what we can to win 90, 95 games, win a division, go on, and play deep into the postseason. You can't fabricate fan interest around marketing one or two players. It's gotta be: you have to show that you're in it to be competitive in October."

When Dice-K first arrived, though, there was some fabrication to sort through. Confusion, really. There was a media saga about a pitch, the gyroball, he didn't even throw. The gyroball is best understood as a slider that doesn't break—a backup slider in U.S. parlance. It's a pitch that can be confusing to a hitter because it looks like it should break and then doesn't. But it's also an offering that can be positively murdered because—wait for it—it does not break. Turns out the confusion about the gyroball was a result of a translation error.

Matsuzaka was 26 years old when he debuted with the Red Sox, but he had been in the spotlight for a decade already. Lore, legend, and Gyroball-like talk had buzzed around him for a while. Former Red Sox outfielder Reggie Jefferson was a teammate of Matsuzaka's on the Seibu Lions. Longtime RedSox.com beat writer Ian Browne spoke to Jefferson for the book *Dice-K: The First Season of the Red Sox $100 Million Man*. "What struck Jefferson most was just how big Matsuzaka was," Browne wrote. "Not physically big, but big in the minds of the people of Japan."

"It was like nothing else I had ever seen," Jefferson told Browne. "I played with Pedro [Martinez], Roger Clemens, Randy Johnson, but this guy was just more famous than any of those guys...When we traveled we came out of the hotel, there would be 200 screaming fans just waiting to see him everywhere he went. I tell people he was like a rock star like Elvis. It was so unique."

Matsuzaka's star rose early. Before his eight-year career with the Lions for whom he went 108–60 with a 2.95 ERA and recorded two ERA titles, he dominated Koshien, Japan's national high school championship that draws immense attention. About 50,000 fans watch teenagers in a tournament where every game is a single-elimination contest among 49 teams that were already regional champions. Matsuzaka threw 250 pitches in one game, spanning 17 innings. (Youth coaches, please don't do this.) Twenty-four hours later, he threw another inning. In the final game, he capped it all off with a no-hitter.

The magic of youth isn't always sustained, you may have heard, especially when one has had that kind of strain and workload early in one's career. Dice-K's eight major league seasons in the U.S. concluded with a 4.45 ERA. He spent six seasons with the Sox and another two with the Mets. He topped 200 innings once (his first season) and finished with fewer than 100 innings in five of his eight seasons. He underwent Tommy John surgery in 2011. "I didn't expect the six years to end the way it did end," Matsuzaka said at the end of the 2012 season with the Sox. "It was really hard on me mentally for a while now. But there were some great memories. The first year, winning the World Series was great. But I wasn't able to perform to my expectations after the first two years, so I'm really disappointed and I'm really apologetic that I wasn't able to perform to my expectations. I didn't see coming back from Tommy John to be this tough. It's just been really hard and tough being able to maintain my body to be able to pitch. I know I need to get better and I'm just really grateful for the doctors and trainers that have been with me throughout the rehab process from the bottom of my heart."

Dice-K was still an active player in 2017, pitching in the Puerto Rican Winter League. But his shoulder was ailing him, and in November he parted ways with the Japanese team, the Fukuoka SoftBank Hawks, he joined from 2015 to 2017. He left the Hawks the day after they won a title without him. "I'm sorry that I wasn't able to meet everyone's expectations during the three years [with Fukuoka]," Matsuzaka said in a statement released in November 2017, per *The Japan Times*. "I wanted to celebrate with my teammates proudly if that were possible. I have no words to express how thankful I am...I believe that I will join my fans and my teammates on the field one day and continue to look forward."

42

THE GREEK GOD OF WALKS

At last, Kevin Youkilis has found a way to monetize the "Greek God of Walks." You can buy a shirt now that says "Greek God of Hops" on it from the brewery Youkilis runs in California called Loma Brew.

You'd be correct to point out that Youkilis had already, in fact, monetized his incredible batting eye that led to the nickname. In his eight-plus seasons with the Red Sox from 2004 to 2012, the burly, bald, and beloved corner infielder from Cincinnati had a .388 on-base percentage. His 20/11 vision helped with his incredible ability to discern balls and strikes and led to roughly $56 million in salary in the entirety of his 10-year major league career.

But that Greek God nickname is not something Youkilis loves through and through. Billy Beane of the Oakland A's came up with the moniker, as chronicled in *Moneyball*—the most famous book about baseball this century and perhaps the most important baseball book of all time. Youkilis, in turn, became the symbol of an era: a player who was better appreciated than he would have been probably even five years earlier. He didn't look the part of a ballplayer, but he outplayed so many.

At the turn of the century, many front offices and scouts did not know how to precisely quantify truly valuable production. Pure athleticism was always easy to identify for scouts and the like, but the rest was undersold, more ambiguous. Sure, this guy has an outstanding batter's eye, but should that put him ahead of a potential five-tool kid who fits well into his uniform? In some cases, absolutely.

Youkilis was the Sox's eighth-round selection in 2001. He hit .366 in his career at the University of Cincinnati with a school-record .499 on-base percentage. Literally half the time, the guy avoided making an out. He'd be a first rounder if he put up those numbers today. But on-base percentage wasn't widely talked about back then.

Beane, then carrying the title general manager for the A's, knew what gold the Sox found. But the Red Sox wouldn't deal him, as author Michael Lewis chronicled in *Moneyball*. The book was released in 2004, the same year Youkilis made his major league debut. The attention was definitely fun at times for Youk, but being a poster boy can wear you out. "It's just one of those things that got old," Youkilis said. "Like when you hear people say, 'Hey get a walk!' And you're like, 'What the hell? I'm trying to hit.' You know? It wasn't horrible. But it's just funny...Every time I had to explain to somebody, I'm not Greek. I'm sorry. They're like, 'what?'...I need a self-explanatory nickname. 'Youk' is easy. People all know Youk. Name change!"

He laughed as he explained this. Youkilis was known to be surly with the media in his playing days, but he's really an entertaining character. Youkilis is not Greek, but he is Jewish. His family's name changed long ago from Weiner, as his family fled oppression. The Greek God of Walks nickname brought more than just inquiries of origin, however.

It brought hype. The book created buzz and ultimately expectations for him in the public's eye. He was able to meet those expectations, but there was this public perception created that he was supposed to be excellent, that he was a preternatural talent preordained to hit.

He was, indeed, very gifted. But to keep his big-boned body functioning at a high level was a ton of work. Fielding, particularly at third base, didn't come to him as easily as hitting.

Yet, Youkilis felt how hard he worked never really infiltrated the popular narrative. He was the *Moneyball* dude born to draw walks. He was supposed to be this good. "So part of that book was the best thing that ever happened, and part of it was, 'Oh, wow, this guy's in this book, so he's got to be this legit prospect and all that,'" Youkilis said. "Only the people like Theo [Epstein] and people like that saw what I did. Even Kevin Millar came up to me. I remember one year he was like, 'Man, I didn't think you were going to be this good of a ballplayer.' And he's like, 'Don't take that the wrong way.' He goes, 'That's credit to you, what you've done.' I was always just trying to get better. My weight and all that, it's just 'cause of my body type. People just look at your body type, and they judge you. Now, they do it less.

From his very unique batting stance, Kevin Youkilis readies for a pitch in 2012, his final year with the Red Sox.

I was 230 pounds. I had to work hard. My biggest thing was I had to work hard to get my body to where it needed to be."

Youkilis is part of Tom Brady's family, and Brady is a part of the Youkilis family. Youkilis married Brady's sister Julie. Youkilis is not on the TB12 diet plan, but he does closely watch what he eats even in his post-playing days, maybe more closely. (He's a fan of the 80/20 rule, where you can indulge 20 percent of the time.)

Youk wondered what he would have looked like had he simply cut out bread in his playing days. But clubhouse culture typically means you eat what all the other guys are chowing on. Add in the travel schedule, and a different diet from peers is uncommon. "I would look at other guys—we're all in the same room together," Youkilis said. "Certain guys, you got to watch what you eat. Know your metabolism and know your body. Other guys would eat stuff so I would eat stuff. So I wasn't probably where I should have been in a lot of ways. But I tried my best to eat all the right things."

Youkilis' best years were his earliest, when he was able to stay on the field the most. He didn't have full playing time in 2004, learning from a ton of veterans. In the next championship season in 2007, he hit .288 with a .390 on-base percentage and .453 slugging percentage while playing 145 games. He hit 16 home runs with more power to come. He ripped a career-high 29 homers in 2008, when he finished third in the American League MVP voting. Teammate Dustin Pedroia won the award.

From 2007 to 2010, Youkilis hit .303 with a .400 on-base percentage. But his body was already working against him by the final season of that stretch. He was down to 102 games.

Youkilis had a strange batting stance as a right-hander with his hands held high, and the bat pointed toward left-center field. His hands were constantly moving, like he was churning butter in the sky. His feet were close together, and his knees bent considerably before a leg kick.

He went off in the 2007 American League Championship Series, batting .500 in a seven-game series (14-for-28) that saw the Sox climb back from a 3–1 deficit to win. He went deep three times.

The 2011–12 debacles for the Sox as a whole coincided with the end to Youkilis' Red Sox career. The chicken-and-beer scandal of September 2011 left a lot of people hurt. Red Sox players, reeling from a terrible final month of the season, wanted to know who aired dirty laundry in public. Some teammates believed it was Youkilis. He swears it wasn't. "That was the most unbelievable thing that I'd ever dealt with in my life," Youkilis said.

Youkilis and Bobby Valentine didn't get off on the right foot, and the Sox had a prospect they wanted to get playing time for in Will Middlebrooks. So the veteran was traded to the Chicago White Sox. Pulled during a July game at Fenway Park when the trade was done, Youkilis got a hearty ovation on his way out.

43

EARLY HALL OF FAMERS

A century makes almost every memory dusty. Making it to Cooperstown, earning a spot on a wall in upstate New York brings some form of permanence. But it doesn't really guarantee a fanbase's continued remembrance. Eventually, if you've been out of sight for long enough, you're mostly out of mind.

How you count the number of Red Sox Hall of Famers is subjective. Many luminaries who at one point or another played for the Sox, like Rickey Henderson, have been inducted into Cooperstown but did not do their finest work in Boston. One way to consider the Sox's representation: there are 22 players and executives/owners in the Red Sox Hall of Fame, which is run by the team, who are also in the National Baseball Hall of Fame. Good luck naming them all.

The best of the bunch may have been Tris Speaker, a center fielder from Texas, who was with the Sox from 1907 to 1915. He won an American League MVP award in 1912, the year Fenway Park opened. They won a World Series that season and again in 1915, his final year with the team. Speaker was a foil to Ty Cobb, the Detroit Tigers' center fielder and fellow Hall of Famer. Cobb was a better pure hitter. But Speaker was more well-rounded, a double-play threat even from the outfield.

A left-handed hitter, Speaker's 792 doubles are most in major league history, ahead of Pete Rose's 746. "If you could hypothetically choose from every Red Sox player, and they were all like 26 years old in the prime of their career, I think Tris Speaker is the best all-around player in Red Sox history," said Richard Johnson, curator of The Sports Museum in Boston. "I think it's clear. Now, Ted Williams, over a period of a career, yeah, I mean, he's one of probably one of the two or three or four greatest hitters of all time. Ted, Josh Gibson, Babe Ruth, and Ty Cobb would form the top four, I think. But Speaker's defense, he made unassisted double plays in center field. That alone was worth the price of admission to watch him play. He's the all-time leader in doubles.

Because he played most of his career in the deadball era, 80 percent of it, a lot of those doubles would have been home runs with the live ball. And unlike Ted, not that this was Ted's fault, he was a champion, too. I think Speaker is a player that gets lost in the shuffle often."

Speaker was part of what Society for American Baseball Research (SABR) author Don Jensen called one of the best fielding outfields in history. Harry Hooper (another Hall of Famer) played right, and Duffy Lewis (a Red Sox Hall of Famer, but not in Cooperstown) flanked them in left. But playing as a unit didn't exactly beget kinship. Jensen wrote that Speaker and Lewis were often not on speaking terms. Lewis was an Irish Catholic. "Religious differences had created cliques on the club with Speaker siding with other Protestants, including Joe Wood and Larry Gardner," Jensen wrote.

Cy Young is the great exception amongst Sox players from more than a century ago. He's a name we really can't forget, barring the zombie apocalypse or a drastic reimagining of baseball's awards. Outside of Babe Ruth, no other Hall of Famer from the early 20th century—and in Young's case, the late 19th century—is mentioned more often than Young. There's a benefit to having your name become synonymous with pitching excellence. Outpitch the league? Win the Cy Young award, two per year these days.

Of Young's 511 wins, 196 were in Boston. He spent eight years with the Sox, who were known for all but Young's final season in Boston as the Boston Americans. The only team he spent more time with was the Cleveland Spiders, his first big league franchise. Per Johnson's book *Red Sox Century*, Young signed with the Red Sox for $3,500 prior to the 1901 season. He brought a personal catcher, Lou Criger, along with him.

Young, who was already 36 years old then, won three games in the 1903 World Series, the first ever Fall Classic, and was also the first man to throw a pitch in the World Series. He went 2–1 against Honus Wagner's Pittsburgh Pirates in what was then a best-of-nine series, not best of seven. "If a right-hander crowded my plate," said Young after retiring as a player, via Bill Nowlin and David Southwick's SABR biography, "I sidearmed him with a curve, and then, when he stepped back, I'd throw an overhand fastball low and outside. I was fortunate in having good speed from overhand, three-quarter, or sidearm. I had a variety of curves—threw a so-called screwball or indrop, too—and I used whatever delivery seemed best. And I never had but one sore arm."

Young, it seems, believed in giving back. He once missed the first few weeks of spring training to tutor the pitching staff at Harvard, per *Red Sox Century.*

A name whose recognition falls somewhere in between Speaker and Young is Jimmie Foxx. He spent most of his career at first base and with another team, the Philadelphia Athletics. But his Sox career was still fearsome: a .320 average with a .605 slugging percentage and 222 home runs from 1936 to early 1942. Foxx finished his career with 534 home runs. "Jimmie Foxx was still mashing the ball pretty well after he became a Boston player and won his third MVP in 1938," said Matt Rothenberg, manager of the National Hall of Fame's research center. "Here's a guy who's probably one of the more underrated Hall of Famers in my personal opinion. Even though he has the hits and he's got a lot of good power numbers, he just doesn't get the recognition I think sometimes that guys like Ruth or Mays or Aaron, guys like that tend to get, Mantle. When he was with the Athletics for all those years is where he really started to get to his status, his back-to-back MVP seasons in '32 and '33. He hit over 40 home runs in those two straight seasons and won a Triple Crown in '33."

One of Foxx's A's teammates, Lefty Grove, joined Foxx in Boston. Grove pitched for only two teams—the A's for nine years and the Sox for eight, with the Sox taking the back half.

Johnson wrote that Grove's fastball was the best in baseball—"the near-equal of Walter Johnson's or Joe Wood's." He also had a short fuse, one of the early examples of a temperamental but magnificent pitcher.

But by the time Grove, who won 300 games in his career, joined the Sox, that fastball was on its way out. "Going on the downward end when he was with the Red Sox in the 1930s," Rothenberg said. "Still a good pitcher...He had a really good curveball, and that was really what led him to a lot of his success."

As learned in SABR's biography by Jim Kaplan, Grove thought he just threw too hard to learn how to throw a great breaking ball early in his career. "I actually was too fast to curve the ball while with Baltimore and Philadelphia," Grove said. "The ball didn't have enough time to break because I threw what passed for a curve as fast as I threw my fastball. I couldn't get enough twist on it...Now that I'm not so fast I can really break one off, and my fastball looks faster than it is because it's faster than the other stuff I throw. A pitcher has time enough to get smarter after he loses his speed."

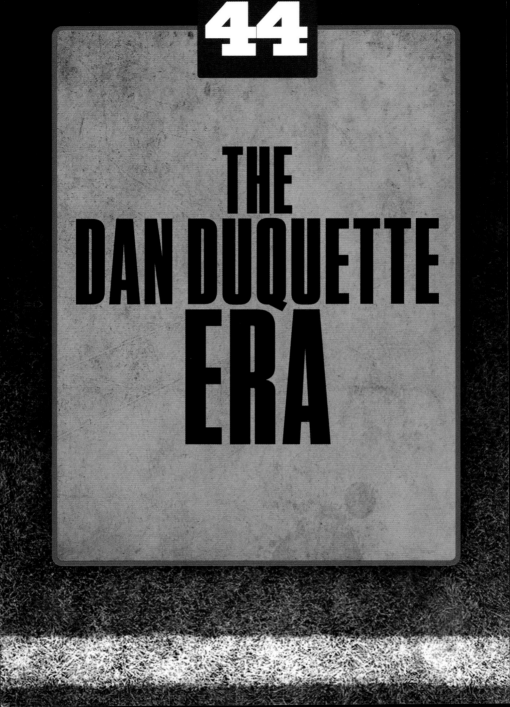

44

THE DAN DUQUETTE ERA

Nomar and Mo Vaughn. Troy O'Leary and John Valentin. Kevin Kennedy and Jimy Williams. Rocket and Jose Canseco. Five straight strikeouts from Pedro in the 1999 All-Star Game. General manager Dan Duquette did not win a World Series in Boston. He did not break The Curse, nor did he pluck David Ortiz out of free agency for a little more than $1 million. But the '90s were a rip-roaring time of their own at Fenway Park, and the groundwork Duquette laid in his eight seasons as general manager from 1994 to 2001 (he was fired in 2002, but before the season) should be remembered but not over-romanticized.

The plans were being drawn. Duquette and his .544 winning percentage (695–582) were, at the least, owed a holiday card once it all came together. "Theo and his group did a really good job putting the final touches on that group," Theo Epstein's right-hand man Jed Hoyer said. "[Kevin] Millar and [Bill] Mueller and [David] Ortiz and [Curt] Schilling. Yeah, listen, I think it's definitely shared credit. But there's no question that group, there was a lot of influence from people that Dan had brought in, for sure."

Pedro Martinez, Derek Lowe, Jason Varitek, Trot Nixon, Johnny Damon, and Manny Ramirez were already in Boston when Theo Epstein took over after the 2002 season. Tim Wakefield and Alan Embree and Doug Mirabelli, too. Kevin Youkilis was in the pipeline.

Duquette, who today is competing against the Red Sox as general manager of the Baltimore Orioles, has always been a little bit of an odd duck. A tad socially awkward. But he automatically had some street cred when he left the successful Montreal Expos to run the Sox ahead of the 1994 season. Like his eventual successor, Epstein, Duquette is a local kid. (Prior to Epstein, there was one season, '02, where Mike Port was interim GM.)

Duquette was born in Dalton, Massachusetts, and went to Amherst College. In 1999 he hired another Amherst alum who would one day run the Red Sox, Ben Cherington. Duquette also opened an eponymous sports academy in Hinsdale, where he spent his years between GM gigs with the Sox and the Orioles, who hired him in 2011.

Heading into the strike-shortened '94 season, the Sox gave Duquette a five-year deal. Far from verbose, Duquette could appear cold and calculated and, particularly in his time with the Sox, he could spar with the media. "Over the next couple of years, we're going to renew the roster with new life," Duquette said at the time of his hiring, via *The Boston Globe*'s Nick Cafardo. "We're going to bring in younger ballplayers, more players in their prime years between the ages of 27 and 32. We have a number of players on the downside of the curve. We have to bring in more players from our farm system."

In his first draft running the Red Sox, the first selection the Sox made was Nomar Garciaparra. One of the more notable things Duquette said at the time of hiring: "One of the traps of a major market team is the thought you have to have name players to drive your revenues."

In addition to drafting a name player, Duquette inherited one. First baseman Vaughn, the left-handed slugger whose earrings always stood out, hit 230 homers in his Sox career from 1991 to 1998. That's practically double the runner-up, John Valentin and his 118, on the list of Sox long balls from the 1990s.

Vaughn, nicknamed the Hit Dog, was a Northeast guy with a permanent Northeast winter gut. He was born in Connecticut and went to Seton Hall in New Jersey (the same school as Valentin). Ask a script writer to come up with the image of a middle-of-the-order hitter, and Vaughn is your guy. His top-heavy body craned over the top of the plate, a warning sign before an upper cut so powerful that his body often fell slightly backward. He won the 1995 American League MVP.

Because it wouldn't be a Red Sox story without some sense of acrimony between management and player, Vaughn and Duquette wound up butting heads, and Vaughn left as a free agent. "The feud became public in 1996," Paul Doyle wrote in the *Hartford Courant* in 1998. "Vaughn was continually critical of management, while Duquette took subtle swipes at Vaughn. Under the surface the sniping was intense. Vaughn refused to participate in team-sponsored appearances, instead focusing on his own charity work. And despite a weight clause in his contract, Vaughn was uncooperative and rarely allowed the team to weigh him. The team was hearing rumors about carousing, Vaughn was hearing rumors about management spies monitoring his moves."

In his final year with the Sox in 1998, Vaughn hit a walk-off grand slam at the home opener. That was April 10. On April 1, on Opening Day against the A's in Oakland, Duquette's signature trade acquisition made his Red Sox debut with seven shutout innings of three-hit ball and 11 strikeouts.

The Pedro Martinez era had begun.

Ramirez's signing before the 2001 season was worth every penny. But trading for Martinez was franchise altering on a transcendent plane. Martinez was untouchable. Duquette pulled off the deal for him in November 1997 with a package of top pitching prospect Carl Pavano and Tony Armas Jr. "We had an interest in Pedro Martinez, of course, for a long time," Duquette said after the trade. "And we were looking for some sign from the Expos in regards to what direction they were going to take with their ballclub and we got that shortly after the end of the season. We met with them in Florida at the World Series... Carl Pavano's name came up during those discussions in Florida at the World Series. Carl Pavano is an excellent young pitching prospect. He's got a chance to be a real fine pitcher. The good news is that we're in a position with our farm system where we have a couple of good pitchers, and we're going to utilize our farm system to acquire an ace for our major league staff. And that's why we made the trade."

This was actually the second time Duquette traded for Pedro. He brought him to the Expos, where he first became a star, in a deal with the Los Angeles Dodgers.

But Duquette made some other suave swaps as well. A 1997 deal with the Seattle Mariners was beyond lopsided. The Sox landed Varitek and Lowe in the same July 31 deal for Heathcliff Slocumb, a reliever who wasn't even having a good season. "I was scared to death," Varitek said in 2014 via NESN. "Things had just started to get better for me over [in the Seattle organization] as a player. I started to see some light at the end of the tunnel defensively, started to settle in a little bit offensively, having a good year, and then you're traded. So once you get your feet on the ground, you're somewhere else."

Varitek eventually became a captain.

Duquette had his share of missteps. Maybe more than his share. He didn't support manager Jimy Williams after Williams had a confrontation with outfielder Carl Everett. Duquette let Roger Clemens walk away as a free agent. Vaughn, too.

When John Henry's purchase of the Red Sox was finalized in 2002, Duquette was let go immediately. "Duquette's emphasis on statistics over character left the clubhouse in constant turmoil and tormented fans who didn't share his actuarial approach," the Associated Press wrote at the time of his dismissal. "It may be true, as Duquette said more than once, that the Red Sox spent more days in first place than the Yankees last season, but that meant little for fans who have been starving for a championship since their grandfathers were born."

As *Boston Herald* columnist Steve Buckley put it, "The more-days-in-first-place thing was a disaster." Duquette noted that pseudo-accomplishment following an 82-win, second-place finish in a turmoil filled '01 and is still occasionally mocked today for misunderstanding what fans wanted to hear. Duquette did have one first-place finish to his name in Boston, which occurred in 1995. The Sox went to the postseason for back-to-back years in 1998 and 1999, the first time that had happened since 1915–16.

It didn't help Duquette that he was up against the burgeoning New York Yankees dynasty. The two squared off in the 1999 American League Championship Series, and the Sox won just one game in the best of seven. The Yanks won the World Series. "I wish we beat the Yankees in '99," Duquette said when asked about his regrets. "That was a series I always dreamed about, growing up."

The dream came true eventually. But he had to watch from afar.

45

1946

The war ended, two of the greats were rumored to be on the verge of changing places, and one of the most famous home runs in Fenway Park history was belted to right field.

Plus, there was the usual disappointment. There's some sardonic amusement to remembering that all four times the Red Sox went to the World Series between the 1918 and 2004 titles, they lost in seven games. The 1946 World Series played against the St. Louis Cardinals was the first in that quartet of heartbreak, but the year was loaded with storylines beyond the just-miss. There was even a requisite World Series scapegoat.

Ted Williams, Bobby Doerr, and Johnny Pesky were among those to return from World War II for the 1946 season, creating a Red Sox team that was reloaded and ready to thrive, a flush parallel to the rest of the victorious country. "I was in Australia in the Navy during the war," center fielder Dom DiMaggio said in Leigh Montville's *Ted Williams*. "I'd been doing a lot of thinking. I decided I was a free agent. I even might have written a letter to the Red Sox, saying I didn't belong to them anymore. I didn't think I did. I didn't think I belonged to anyone. Well, [manager] Joe Cronin came out to see me in San Francisco. He was really mad. The veins were popping out of his head. He said the Red Sox owned me and he was there to sign me up for $11,000. This was not the figure I had in mind."

Free agency was a long way off. DiMaggio anticipated that attendance was about to boom, and it was. The Sox drew 1,416,944 in '46 up from roughly 800,000 in 1945, per Baseball-Reference.com. "Williams, Doerr, DiMaggio, and Pesky all were into their best baseball years. Tex Hughson, Mickey Harris, and Joe Dobson were returning frontline pitchers," Monvtille wrote. "Added to the cast were veteran slugger Rudy York obtained from the Tigers and pitcher Dave 'Boo' Ferris."

There wasn't much of a pennant race to watch in the American League. The Sox won 41 of their first 50 games, and by mid-July their lead was in double-digits. It never dipped below 11½ games from August 3 on. (The team hit a little losing streak before closing out the pennant, and the champagne that had already been ordered became something of a punch line.)

On June 9 that year, Williams hit the red seat home run, an estimated 502-foot shot to right field off Detroit Tigers righty Fred Hutchison. Today it is commemorated with a red seat in a sea of green ones in the bleachers at Fenway Park. The ball landed on the straw hat of an Albany, New York, man named Joseph Boucher. (The bleachers in those days were indeed bleachers rather than individual seats. The red seat is No. 21 in Section 42, Row 37.)

Fenway Park hosted the All-Star Game in the midst of the Sox's success, and like the Pedro Martinez Show in 1999, the home team's star shone brightest at the Midsummer Classic.

Teddy Ballgame went 4-for-4. Rip Sewell of the Pittsburgh Pirates threw an Eephus pitch that Williams requested a demonstration of before the game, per *Red Sox Century*. Williams drilled one of the slow, loopy offerings he saw in the game for a home run en route to a 12–0 win. Williams said he never swung at a pitch as hard as he did that one.

As fearsome a club as the Sox were—Pesky hit .335, Williams hit .342, and DiMaggio hit .316—they ran into trouble at the worst time. An exhibition game intended to keep the Red Sox sharp as the National League pennant race concluded may have been the Sox's undoing. Williams was hit in the right elbow by a curveball that didn't curve thrown by Mickey Haefner of the Washington Senators. There were supposed to be two more exhibition games, but they were canceled.

Williams went 5-for-25 in the World Series with five walks and five strikeouts. He had no home runs, one RBI. Those seven games were the only ones the Splendid Splinter ever played in the postseason, which in his time consisted only of the World Series. Williams was asked more than 50 years later what he would change—if he could change anything in his life. "I'd have done better in the '46 World Series," Williams said in Montville's biography. "God, I would."

Williams faced a defensive shift—shading him to pull—in the World Series that year, but it wasn't as extreme as the shift he first faced from Lou Boudreau, the Cleveland Indians manager, earlier in the season. There were a standard two men on the left side of second base in the World Series, but the third baseman wheeled around closer to second than the shortstop was. In the regular season, Boudreau played just one fielder, the third baseman, on the left side, which is similar to the defensive tactic more commonly employed today. You've seen it against David Ortiz and plenty of other pull-happy left-handed hitters when the defense employs three men on the right side of the field and one on the left.

Williams felt that the shift didn't hurt him until 1947 and beyond. The outlook for the World Series hinged on a larger issue to Williams at least in hindsight. "Now comes the series with the Cardinals, and for me it was ill-fated from the start," Williams wrote with John Underwood in *My Turn At Bat: The Story of My Life*. "They were all gassed up after a tight race. They even had to play the Dodgers in a playoff to break a tie. We had won the pennant by 12 games and for the last month we just fiddled around. It had been the kind of season that positively breeds overconfidence."

It's a well-known tale that the New York Yankees and Red Sox spoke of swapping Joe DiMaggio for Ted Williams. The best remembered incarnation of that deal is believed to have been hatched in 1947 during a bar conversation (drunken negotiation?) between Sox owner Tom Yawkey and Yankees owner Dan Topping at celebrity go-to Toots Shor's in Manhattan.

But even before then, Williams walked into the '46 World Series with the specter of such a trade over his head. "Dave [Egan] of *The Boston Record*, claiming good authority, reported that after the World Series Williams would be dealt to Detroit for Hal Newhouser or to New York for Joe DiMaggio," wrote Jerome M. Mileur in *The Stars Are Back: The St. Louis Cardinals, the Boston Red Sox, and Player Unrest in 1946*. "The Tigers and Yankees denied any deal. The Red Sox said nothing."

Williams, who was basically at war with Egan, said in *My Turn At Bat* that "there was never any foundation to the story whatsoever, but there it was in the papers, and how do you think that made me feel?" The basic logic behind such a deal was that Williams would have done better in either the Yankees' or Tigers' home parks. But Williams never wanted to play in New York—it wasn't a conventional ballpark from either an offensive or defensive standpoint—despite enjoying the crowds.

Either way, the timing was unseemly. "While the Sox had the right to trade Williams, to allow the story to leak out on the eve of the club's first appearance in the World Series since 1918 was both inexcusable and one helluva way to run a ballclub," Glenn Stout and Richard Johnson wrote in *Red Sox Century.*

But the Red Sox still had their chances on the field in seven games. Whether Pesky, the shortstop, really cost them in one of those chances is up for debate. The Sox and Cards were tied at 3 in the eighth inning of the finale of the series played in the afternoon at St. Louis' Sportsman's Park. Enos Slaughter—now the reference point for a play known as Slaughter's Mad Dash—scored from first base on a double from Harry Walker to left center. There were two out. Leon Culberson, who was in center field in place of the injured Dom DiMaggio, didn't have a great arm. If you watch the grainy video of the play, Pesky appeared to hesitate slightly on the throw, which may or may not have been the problem so much as the seeming lack of mustard and accuracy on the throw. Many contended Pesky would not have had a chance at Slaughter with a perfect throw.

Just based on Slaughter's location—about a step beyond third base—when Pesky got the ball, a truly perfect throw might have done it. The shortstop made the toss from near the far edge of the infield dirt. Either way Slaughter deserves most of the credit for forcing a play. The Cardinals scored the decisive run in a 4–3 win. "I get the ball and I could hear everybody was screaming and hollering," Pesky told the Associated Press in 2004. "If I had a [Nomar] Garciaparra arm, I might have had him. I knew as soon as I got the ball I couldn't get him."

There was vindication for Pesky when the Sox swept the Cardinals, who bested the Sox in 1967 as well, in the 2004 World Series. But the play wasn't something he was keen to remember. "Pesky said softly, 'I don't want to talk about it,'" *The Boston Globe*'s Nick Cafardo wrote of the 2006 reunion for members of the 1946 team at Fenway Park. "But Doerr chimed in that the shortstop always 'got a bad rap on that.' And Pesky recalls Cronin telling him, 'I hope they don't break your heart,' concerning the fallout over the play."

46

BOGGS

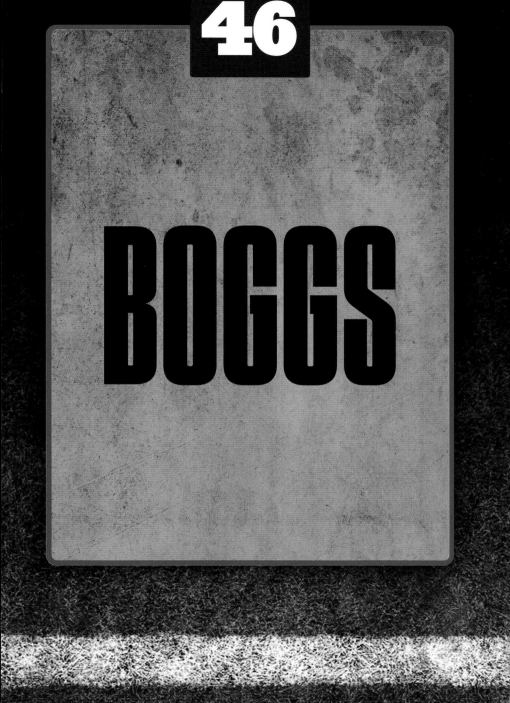

Wade Boggs' numbers were always gaudy, and some of them won't ever be repeated. The Hall of Famer hit .328 lifetime, including .338 with the Sox in the first 11 years of his career. He racked up five batting titles. Four years in a row in Boston from 1986 to 1989, Boggs had at least 200 hits and 100 walks. There have been four such seasons since, and the last occurred in 2003 courtesy of Todd Helton. "Those days are long gone," Boggs said. "That record will stand."

They don't make 'em like Boggs anymore, a true on-base machine who didn't seek out homers so much as he did solid contact and good pitches. His lifetime on-base percentage is .415 to rank No. 24 on baseball's all-time list. "I was Moneyball before Moneyball," Boggs said. "That was my job."

Marvelously mustachioed, Boggs is confident and incisive when it comes to explaining his craft. It feels greedy and reprehensible to wonder what could have been had Boggs had more years like one of those insane 200/100 seasons. In 1987, the year after one of the Sox's ill-fated World Series runs, Boggs hit 24 home runs. "Back then, I mean, we really didn't have a lot of video tape, and I never really looked at video tape either. I just looked at the flight of my ball," Boggs said. "And I was hitting a lot more high fly balls. Rather than deep line drives, I was hitting actual high, long fly balls. And some of the parks that you'd visit, if you'd hit a ball to left-center and got it up into a jet stream or something like this and you hit it high enough, the wind would actually aid the distance on the ball. It just snowballed and snowballed and snowballed."

The most homers Boggs compiled in any other season was 11 in 1994 with the New York Yankees. In his 18 years in the majors, '87 and '94 are the only seasons Boggs busted out double-digit dingers. But clearly he was capable of hitting for real power. This is not a criticism at all of one of the greatest pure hitters and third basemen of all time. It's merely a curiosity. What was different in '87, when he also had a .363 average, and could that power have carried over to other seasons? "You have to understand hitting philosophy," said Boggs, who batted from the left side and read Ted Williams' *The Science of Hitting* growing up. "When you play in a park such as Fenway Park for 81 games and my power was to left-center, I'm constantly driving the ball high off the wall. Had I played 11 years at Wrigley Field, I would have probably hit 350 home runs. I think the atmosphere sort of enabled me not to hit for home runs. I had a lot of doubles, and that was the consequence of hitting balls off the wall. And the majority of my power was right-center to left-center, and I play in the biggest part of the ballpark. Then when you go back and study film of '87 vs. other years, my hands were completely different in '87 and, consequently, hitting a lot more fly balls rather than line drives. So, when you've got a lot of lift—sort of like the way the guys are swinging nowadays, I mean, they're swinging straight up."

There was nothing that prompted the hand position that produced the pop in '87. Boggs said it just happened. When he hit 11 homers in the strike-shortened '94 season with the Yanks, he had a pulled ribcage muscle and was consciously trying to do something differently. Extending his arms was painful, so he tried to pull balls inside and use Yankee Stadium's short porch to his advantage. "I tried to duplicate the ['87] swing in spring training of '88, and it was a nightmare," Boggs said. "Through two weeks of spring training, I was hitting about a buck 25, struggling to hit line drives because I tried to duplicate that left-hand [position] way under the right hand, and I was just popping balls up to the infield. Then I got back into the groove of sort of paralleling my hand through the strike zone and getting back to that line-drive swing. So it wasn't a conscious effort—I would've loved to hit 500 home runs. It's not like I walked to the plate and said, 'God, I hope I hit a 27-hopper through the infield.'...When you hit the ball so deep in the strike zone as I do, you're not going to get the lift and elevation [like those] guys that hit the ball further out in front of the impact zone than I do. I waited so long on the ball to see spin, not to be fooled. Guys nowadays look like they're swinging with blindfolds on. They swing at balls in the dirt, balls over their head, and it's like

Legendary for his partying ways as much as his lofty batting average, Wade Boggs celebrates the Game 7 victory against the California Angels in the 1986 American League Championship Series.

they make up their mind to swing, and the guy could hold on to the ball and not throw it, and they would swing."

They called him the Chicken Man. Famously a follower of upwards of 100 superstitions, Boggs has become something of a pop culture figure throughout the years. Every day, he ate a chicken sandwich. He's appeared on *The Simpsons*, as well as *It's Always Sunny in Philadelphia*. "It's manifested itself," Boggs said. "They do TV shows about you. *Always Sunny*, and you're on *Cheers* and *Simpsons* and various things like this, but they're quirky, just certain things that happened. The chicken was part of the superstition that came to grow in itself, along with the other 80 superstitions that I had.

"But in the event of the other thing, I don't talk about it a lot. It's something that happened, and a lot of people want to talk more about it than I do."

The "other thing." Oh, you know, that thing. Rather than his consistent poultry consumption, Boggs is more well-known off the field for his legendary boozing capability. The legend began with the number of beers he could drink on a cross-country flight with different estimates in the 50 to 70 range. "But you know I don't promote it," Boggs said, laughing. "I don't go out there and publicly promote it or anything like that."

Then, Boggs told actor Charlie Day of *It's Always Sunny* that he actually drank 107 beers, and Day told that story on TV to Jimmy Fallon. So...is it true? Is the accurate number 107? "Yeah," Boggs said. "That's what I told Charlie Day, yeah."

There was one "other" thing in Boggs' life. He had a famous affair with a woman named Margo Adams, who later sued him, making national gossip columns.

But there hasn't been as talented a pure hitter on the Red Sox since Williams. What Boggs wishes people understood is that he really did want to stay in Boston and finish his career with the Sox just like the Splendid Splinter. Instead, he wound up leaving the Sox for the rival Yankees. Maybe "leaving" isn't the most accurate verb. "The misconception that everyone has is that I left Boston," Boggs said. "That's the misconception that people really don't know anything about and don't know about Mrs. [Jean] Yawkey offering me [a deal] at the end of the '91 season to stay in Boston to follow in the footsteps of Ted and Carl [Yastrzemski], and I told her, 'Where's the pen? I'll sign right now.' She [suffers a stroke in] January of '92, dies. I get to spring training, they take the offer off the table, negotiate through spring training. [The] best that they could come up with was a year and an option at very little money, didn't really negotiate through the season, had a horrendous season in '92. And then at the end of the season, they didn't offer me arbitration to come back, and I became a free agent. So the misconception of me leaving Boston to go to New York, I needed a job. And Mr. [George] Steinbrenner was gracious enough to offer me a three-year deal, and I don't think anybody in their right mind would have turned it down."

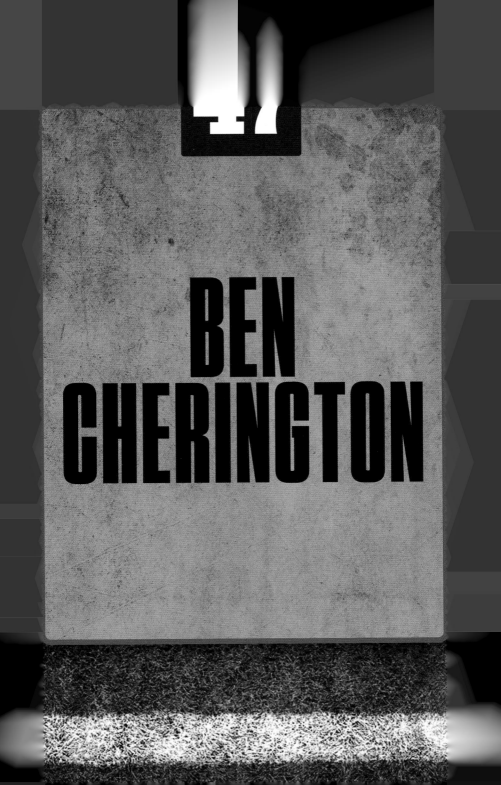

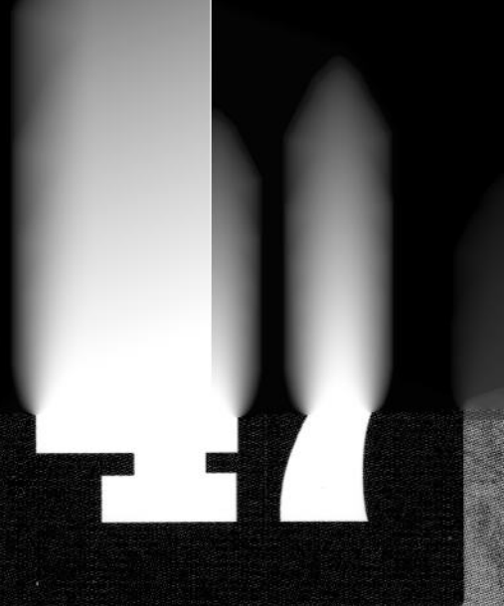

BEN CHERINGTON

Ben Cherington deserved better. The Red Sox general manager for less than four full seasons had a first two years on the job that were filled with both difficulty and overwhelming success. He navigated an abysmal season in 2012, a stunning trade with the Los Angeles Dodgers as bloodletting in August of that year, and then a World Series win for a city in need just the very next season. But after the '13 parade, Cherington lasted only one more full season, exiting in August 2015. It was a quick hook even for a town where win now is always the mind-set. "It will be one of the more sort of misunderstood eras in Red Sox history," Red Sox president and longtime Cherington colleague Sam Kennedy said, "because it was filled with stark contrast."

When Theo Epstein and Terry Francona left the Sox after the 2011 season, disarray is a kind way to put the state of the Red Sox organization. The huge investment in free-agent outfielder Carl Crawford ahead of '11 was already working out poorly. The clubhouse was in troubling shape after the chicken-and-beer stories suggested a lack of complete investment amongst some of the pitching staff, including 2007 fan favorite Josh Beckett. (For as wonderful as Epstein was, his final Sox moves were not close to his best.)

To make matters worse, the Sox were about to hire a manager, Bobby Valentine, who would only complicate an already spiraling dynamic. First, though, the Sox needed a GM. Cherington was entering his 14th season with the Sox. He was an area scout who predated Epstein in the organization, coming on in 1999. "Just going back to 2011, when the change happened and the Cubs asked permission for Theo right in the wake of Tito leaving, that was obviously a huge, huge change," Kennedy said. "I remember it was natural and obvious that Ben was the right person to succeed Theo. It was Larry's choice. It was Theo's choice. It was my choice. It felt like he was the right person. John [Henry] and Tom [Werner] ultimately approved that. At the time, the Anaheim Angels...[called me] and asked for permission to talk to Ben. I said, 'Sorry, he's about to become general manager of the Red Sox.' So there was lot of interest in Ben elsewhere and internally."

A highly thoughtful and forward-thinking person, Cherington didn't have quite the rock star persona as Epstein, but few do. He did have the necessary acumen. A big believer in collaboration, Cherington grew up in New Hampshire and played four years of baseball at Amherst College—the alma mater of Dan Duquette, who was in charge of the Sox when Cherington was first hired. "He's got a scouting background that enables him to use all approaches to evaluate a player," John Farrell, Cherington's second managerial hiring, said in 2013. "His personality is such that he includes others to have a voice...Ultimately, he's the one that's going to make it and be responsible for it, but his leadership style is one that is very even-handed. It's emotionally controlled to where there's not knee-jerk reactions. He doesn't have a need to grab the limelight. He's a diligent worker, a hard worker that is all about finding the best people available and surrounding himself with them. He's done a hell of a job in taking one situation and making changes to correct it as he sees fit."

Cherington was a co-GM when Epstein briefly left the organization in the 2005–06 offseason. Before that he was a farm director and later became assistant GM. His resume was loaded, and his career track pointed toward running the organization. When he was hired in October 2011, the managerial search was his first task, but hiring a manager later in the offseason is a disadvantage. Former New York Mets manager Bobby Valentine was Red Sox president Larry Lucchino's pick. (Like Cherington's time as GM, Lucchino's time as Sox president also ended in 2015.)

Cherington agreed and did what he could to support Valentine, but the Valentine era began to disintegrate in spring training. In retrospect, Cherington probably should have pushed back harder against Bobby's hiring. In the midst of a 69-win, last-place finish in 2012, Cherington organized an August trade with the Dodgers that scrubbed some open wounds for the Sox, sending out Crawford, Beckett, and Adrian Gonzalez in a nine-player megadeal that moved more than a quarter of a billion dollars in payroll obligation away.

Gonzalez, performing well, was a valuable piece the Sox had to give up to move the others. "It gave us an opportunity to kind of re-forecast what this year's team would look like," Cherington recalled in 2013, "and what teams multiple years down the road would look like...I liked them all personally. It wasn't about those guys. We were looking at a situation where, if we hadn't done it, we were going to be back scrambling again in the offseason to sort of try to fix things in the margins and not be able to really reshape things."

Then it was time to hire a manager again. The Sox wanted to bring back their old pitching coach, John Farrell, but he was managing the Blue Jays. So Cherington engineered a trade to get Farrell out of his contract, trading big league infielder Mike Aviles for the skipper. But the job that Cherington did in the 2012–13 offseason with free agency was what was most remarkable. He focused on depth, which was part of the 2011 team's undoing, and made a lot of smaller bets in terms of salary commitments that all paid off. Free agents like Mike Napoli, Koji Uehara, David Ross (setting a back-up catcher on his way to stardom), and Shane Victorino all were integral parts of the '13 World Series run. He was almost too good. The Sox's success with small bets made them reticent to later offer Jon Lester the larger kind of deal he deserved.

Cherington had some missteps in the following years. Pablo Sandoval was a terrible addition as a free agent, and heading into 2018, the Sox were still waiting for Cuban outfielder Rusney Castillo to blossom. Hanley Ramirez and Rick Porcello have been a mixed bag, but both players had excellent 2016 seasons.

One of the harder things to sometimes decipher about the Red Sox is who makes what player personnel decision—Lucchino or the GM, ownership or the GM, whatever it may be. The player moves, both good and bad, in Cherington's time were ultimately his. "He would say that those were," Kennedy said. "And by the way, the decision to protect and ferociously hold on to Mookie [Betts], Xander [Bogaerts], Jackie [Bradley Jr.], all of the deals that he didn't make or did make—look this guy was the general manager and won a World Series championship in '13. He was a critical, huge part of the '04 and

'07 championships. I think far too much credit and far too much blame goes to the one person."

Even with multiple mistakes, Cherington didn't hand out a contract as large as say, David Price's. He was indeed conservative when it came to dealing away top prospects, perhaps too conservative. But the fruits of that farm system paid off, naturally, in the years immediately following his departure. The sharp downturn of 2014 and 2015 led Sox ownership to seek out Dave Dombrowski to head up baseball operations. Cherington could have stayed under Dombrowski, but he chose to leave.

With pieces Dombrowski added, the Sox rebounded to have two straight 93-win seasons that are certainly owed in part to Cherington. "He was part of the organization for a long time," Werner said. "I look at Ben as being very critical to the development of some of the talent that obviously blossomed when they got to the major leagues. Ben, I think by his own admission, performed certain parts of the GM job better than other parts. And I think when we got to a point where we had finished last for a couple of years and we felt like the cupboard was somewhat bare in the minor leagues, I think we decided to bring in somebody else. Again, maybe the culture of baseball is that we all are sort of serving for a while."

Heading into 2018, Cherington was working for the Toronto Blue Jays and in position to someday become a GM again when the fit is right for him.

48

PEDROIA

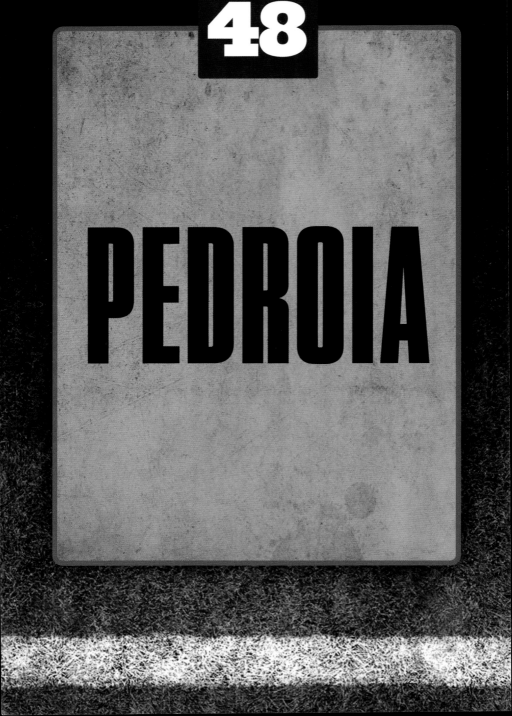

Dustin Pedroia's on-field accomplishments deserve a stand-alone vetting without his size being mentioned. If we're being realistic, that will never happen. His size has influenced his personality too much. "I better play hard because I'm not very big," Pedroia said in 2013. "I've just got to try to find other ways to help us win. That's what I do. I try to show up and do all I can to help the team win that day, and hopefully it turns out well."

Pedroia is usually dressed in full uniform well before his teammates. He plays through myriad injuries, possessing a pain threshold rare even in a sport where everyone is perpetually nursing something. He hobbled his way through the end of the 2017 season, helping the Red Sox finish off an American League East title before undergoing surgery on his left knee for a second straight winter. That procedure meant Pedroia likely would miss 2018's Opening Day. Had he been able to start, he would have tied Carl Yastrzemski's club record of 12 straight Opening Days started at one position. (Yaz did it in left field.) Half as a joke and half with sincere concern, Kevin Youkilis said he worries what Pedroia will do when he retires. Aside from family, baseball is really everything to Pedroia.

But his approach to the game can't be entirely tied back to his stature. Let's not assume Pedroia would have an entirely different work ethic were he a foot taller. He's a classic baseball rat, a tag that is not attached to every big leaguer or even every big league star. "He goes out there and plays 100 percent every single game," said Astros second baseman Jose

Altuve in October 2017. "He never takes it for granted. He dives, he slides, he does everything the right way...To play the same position that Dustin Pedroia, former MVP, World Series [champion], everything he has accomplished, I feel really proud."

Altuve skimmed the surface of Pedroia's CV. And why was Altuve asked to talk about Pedroia? Oh, you already know. They're both teeny second basemen that you just want to stuff in your pocket and carry home or something like that. Pedroia's Red Sox and Altuve's Houston Astros played against each other in the '17 American League Division Series. Pedroia is listed at 5'9"; Altuve is listed at 5'6". (The official readings, though, cannot always be trusted. Pedroia told *Boston Magazine* in 2009 that he's 5'8", 170 pounds. Altuve has admitted he, too, is an inch shorter than what's in print and is just 5'5".)

Naturally, Pedroia was long doubted because of his size. "Not really [by] coaches," Pedroia said in his rookie year in 2007. "Once I think I go out there and play and play hard, I think that coaches kind of like me. But you always hear that stuff from outsiders, fans, or it could be media or guys you play against. They always doubt you. But you've just got to keep going out there and proving them wrong."

Pedroia is short and bursting with energy, but he's not exactly a classic underdog.

Consider that he went to Arizona State, one of the premier baseball schools in the country. He wasn't a late or even mid-round draft pick either. On the contrary he was the Sox's second-round draft pick in 2004 at No. 65 overall and a finalist to win the Golden Spikes, the most prestigious award in college baseball, which is given annually to the best player.

Why did these things happen? Because Pedroia is one of the most gifted athletes any time he takes the field. He had a .493 slugging percentage in his second full season in the big leagues, when he won the American League MVP award in 2008. His 213 hits were tied for the most in the majors with Ichiro Suzuki. Pedroia's 54 doubles stood alone atop the majors, and he had 20 stolen bases, 17 home runs, and a .326 average mixed in.

As a rookie Pedroia began the 2007 World Series sweep of the Colorado Rockies with a leadoff home run against lefty Jeff Francis.

But Pedroia's never been one to need much tutelage on his swing. "He works at it," former Red Sox hitting coach Chili Davis said of Pedroia's hitting. "And he knows what he needs to work at. Rarely does he come in the cage, and I got to go to him and go, 'Hey, you need to do this.' He'll come in and he'll tell you, 'I need to get my top hand stronger, my stride's getting too long.'"

A Northern California native, Pedroia is antithetical to the region's laid-back stereotype. His hometown of Woodland, California, is in the Sacramento area. He was a San Francisco Giants fan, so he liked Barry Bonds, which is kind of amusing given their differing profiles. Pedroia said he tried to model himself on a former infielder, fellow Sacramento native Fernando Vina, who was also vertically challenged.

Pedroia has played second base for the Sox for so long that it's easy to take his defense for granted. When he was hurting in 2017, everyone was reminded of his next-level range and quick first step. "He played second base as well as anybody," Curt Schilling said during Pedroia's rookie year. "The thing that I remember hearing from Pat Murphy, who I know very well, his coach at ASU, a couple years ago after I had seen Dustin for the first time: when you meet Dustin for the first time, you kind of step back a little bit because he's not that usual minor league kid with a relaxed demeanor. He's somewhat, 'I'm going to kick your ass, and there's nothing you can do about it.' That's a little different. I enjoyed the fact that he and I were very much in tune when I pitched. I need my infielders to communicate and I need them to be on their toes and make adjustments on the fly and I talked to them in depth about it, about moving around based on pitch selection and not always having to turn around and move them myself. He was another guy who...defense was the priority."

Bearded with a hawkish nose and (these days) thinning hair, Pedroia sometimes will mouth off to media standing in the clubhouse. He may ask a younger reporter he doesn't recognize what the hell they're doing in there. It's all for fun, or at least, usually. He's a believer in Bigfoot, too. But nonsense appears to be at a minimum.

An impatience always seems to be boiling inside Pedroia, who can be a verbal boxer. (So he can be short verbally, as well.) "He's a very positive person," Davis said. "To some people that don't know him, they might take him the wrong way—like he's arrogant—but he's just positive. He's like any other player. When he's having his down times, it bothers him. Pedey is baseball. He is all baseball."

And he knows his audience. When David Ortiz was roasted for charity at House of Blues across the street from Fenway Park, Pedroia took to the podium and said it was a good thing the height of the microphone was adjustable. If he had to stand on his wallet, Pedroia said, he'd be up to the roof.

There's a chance he could have been richer had he let himself reach free agency. A contract extension Pedroia signed in 2013 not only promised him $110 million, but also gave him the chance to retire in the only major league uniform he's ever worn. He's under contract with the Sox through 2021. Long-term contracts are risky business, but Pedroia is a long-standing exception to most rules. "There's a lot of good players that have been really good into their 30s," former general manager Ben Cherington said the day Pedroia signed the deal. "With Dustin, yeah, you have to look at what's happened before and sort of look at history. And we do projections and we do the objective look at it because that's part of our job. But sometimes there comes along someone who is a little bit different, and Dustin is different. So if you're betting on someone to still be good and stay good deeper into the contract, you bet on someone like Dustin.

"From a performance standpoint, he does a lot of different things to help win a game because he's so good in so many different areas. His value to the team maybe is different than people would have looked at 20 years ago. He helps the team defensively, on the bases, with the bat. He gets on base. He doesn't strike out. He hits for good power for a second baseman. It's the sum of a lot of really good parts, never mind all the off-field stuff that makes him so unique. I just know that he's here, and there's nobody else that we'd want as our second baseman."

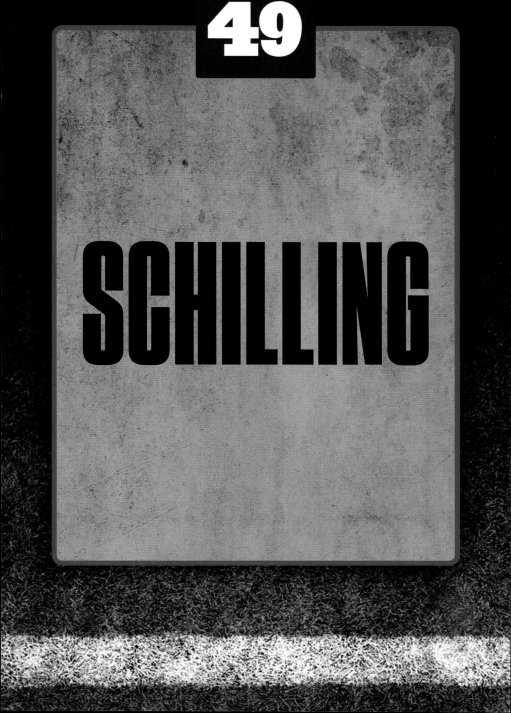

49

SCHILLING

Curt Schilling and his wife, Shonda, were talking in 1992 after Schilling's first full year in the majors. He was with the Philadelphia Phillies then, his third big league team in just five seasons, and his potential was starting to materialize. At age 25 the talkative, outgoing righty served up a 2.35 ERA over 226⅓ innings. "The two things I told her that night: I want to win the [Roberto] Clemente award because that was my dad's favorite player," Schilling said in 2017, referring to the award given annually to the player most dedicated to community and charitable efforts. "And then, I want—when I'm done—for all the guys I've suited up with, if they have one game to win and their life depended on it, that they'd want me to have the ball. And the guys on the other side wouldn't. And that was what I worked for."

Schilling won the Clemente award in 2001, the same year he and Randy Johnson formed one of the greatest pitching tandems of all time for the Arizona Diamondbacks, powering a seven-game World Series win against the New York Yankees. Schilling's 56 strikeouts set a postseason record. Schilling's D-backs provided the first hint the great Yankees dynasty could be slowed—if just barely. In '01 the Yanks had won four of the previous five titles and had played in five of six straight World Series.

Come the 2003 offseason—after the Yanks lost yet another World Series and the Sox lost yet another American League Championship Series—the Red Sox needed a push. They needed a pitcher they could pair with Pedro Martinez. Schilling's big-game prowess is his calling card and central to his Hall of Fame candidacy. A fastball/splitter pitcher with top velocity, Schilling finished his postseason career with a 2.23 ERA in 133⅓ innings plus an 11–2 record. (The record for wins is 19 held by Andy Pettitte.)

Luckily for the Sox, Schilling, who had a no-trade clause, was willing to waive it. When Sox bosses Theo Epstein and Jed Hoyer showed up for Thanksgiving at his Arizona home during a negotiating window to seal the deal, they found he wasn't fearful of the Bambino's ghosts. "All the hoopla around The Curse and all that other bullshit is bullshit," Schilling said of his mind-set. "This is going to work out, and that's eventually why I said, 'Listen, I'll basically put my money where my mouth is. We win a World Series, I get an extra $2 million.'"

There were more clauses involved, but the idea was simple: he would make a lot more money if he helped the Sox to their ultimate goal. Schilling didn't have a player agent and thinks that choice proved wise. The 37-year-old Schilling negotiated with the execs—who happened to be younger than him—on his own. "It was a lot more personal than I think a lot of people understand," Schilling said, "first of all because of Theo and Jed's personalities. We sat

Curt Schilling's blood-soaked sock—a result of a tendon injury stabilized by sutures—in Game 6 of the 2004 American League Championship Series will live on in Red Sox lore.

around Thanksgiving day and watched football. We didn't talk about any of the negotiating. It was like a break in the negotiation. I think their ability to make me comfortable—'cause now one of the things a lot of people don't know is I had the Yankees on the phone. They reached out to me during this whole thing, in violation of rules I'm assuming, to let me know that if I could hold out and not do anything until the [negotiating window] deadline that they would show up the day after and they would throw down a blank check. I kind of had that going for me from a leverage perspective, but I never really used it because the barrier coming here was they made it very clear they could not pay me more than Pedro because there was a certain pride issue, I guess. I don't know what you call it, but that was never a factor in my negotiating. I never needed to be the highest paid guy. I just wanted to make what I make and I wanted to win a World Series."

Former Sox president Larry Lucchino was a part of the negotiations for a day, too. "It was getting to an impasse very quickly," Schilling said. "And he was sitting in one chair, and Theo was sitting in another to his right, and in between them was the 2001 World Series trophy. And I said, 'Look guys, listen,' I said, 'We're going to come up with a number that I agree with or this isn't going to work.' But I said, 'The fact of the matter is this: you need me to come win one of those for you guys because you can't do it yourselves.'"

Schilling's post-playing life hasn't been the quietest. An outspoken political conservative, he lost a job at one of the most prominent media outlets, ESPN. He was involved in a video game venture that went bankrupt and involved a lot of taxpayer money in Rhode Island. In part because of his celebrity, it became a highly publicized matter. Schilling thinks his character has been misunderstood by some. "I don't have a yes/no answer to questions," Schilling said. "If you're asking me a question, I'm passionate about the answer. I'm going to answer it. So the print media, I learned it too late, but it's probably not my best venue. I don't think there's anything that really came out—other than the people that still want to believe the sock was fake."

As the Red Sox made their incredible comeback during the 2004 ALCS, Schilling had the ball in Game 6. The Sox had already won two in a row to send the series back to New York.

The son of an army man, Schilling's physical state wasn't a guarantee. He had trouble pushing off the mound because of a right ankle injury involving the tendons, which were stabilized with sutures. As with the contract, creativity came into play—this time from the Sox medical staff, including Dr. George Theodore and Dr. Bill Morgan.

With blood in the white sock visible for all to see on the national telecast, Schilling threw seven innings of one-run ball, allowing just four hits. A three-run homer from Mark Bellhorn gave him room to breathe for a 4–2 win. "I couldn't wear the hightops because they were putting too much pressure on the stitches around the sutured area," Schilling said after Game 6. "There's a little bit of blood on my sock, but that's just from the area. Yeah, we will do it again if we can find a way to pull this out tomorrow. We'll do it again for the World Series."

At the time the Sox still needed to win Game 7. And they did, becoming the first team down 3–0 in a postseason series to come all the way back. "I laugh now, when I look back at what people were saying and how much people were talking shit," Schilling said, "because I remember the clubhouse. We never—I don't ever remember thinking it was over. I mean, I was worried as hell. We're down 3–0, you know? And baseball, it's not like basketball. I don't get to get out on the floor and push the ball up the court. I got to sit up there and rah-rah until I pitch again."

Schilling had three years left in him, winning one more World Series with the Sox in '07. He was out all of 2008 with a shoulder injury and retired the next year. His legacy will always be tied to 2004 for providing the mind-set that the Yankees could be beaten. He knew, having already done it just three years earlier. "Just like in 2001," Schilling said, "I was a part of something that will never ever, ever be forgotten in baseball."

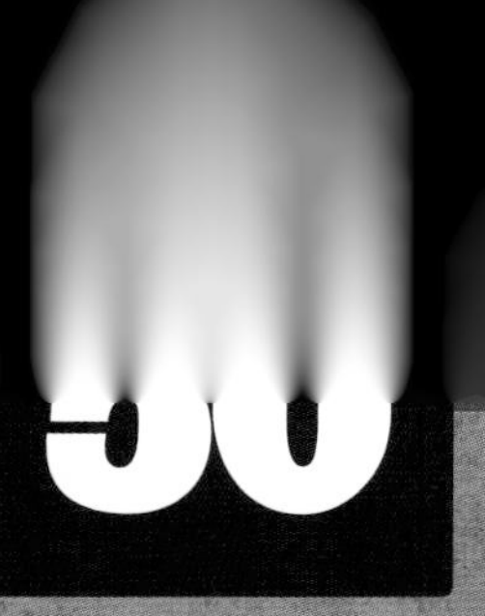

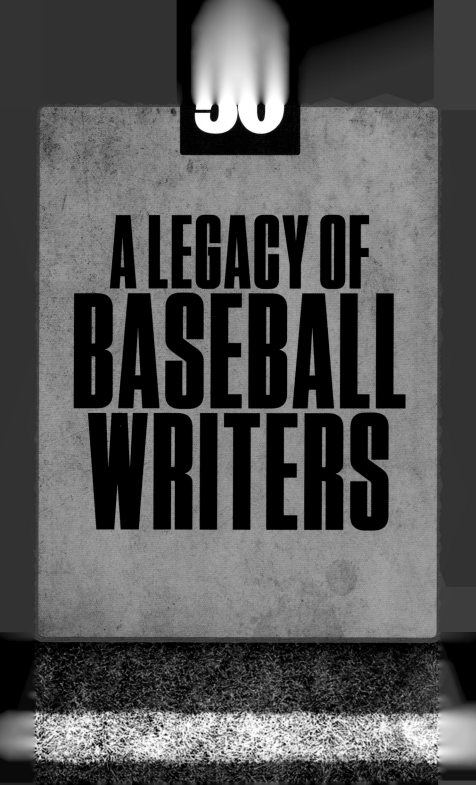

A LEGACY OF BASEBALL WRITERS

As a child Theo Epstein began his day with his typical routine. "*Globe* sports section every day with breakfast," Epstein said. "My brother [Paul] and I would fight over it. I'd usually win." (Of course. We get it. You win a lot.) "That's not what I meant!" Epstein said, laughing. "He had other interests as well. I didn't.

"So [Peter] Gammons, Bob Ryan, Jackie MacMullan, Michael Madden, yeah, I remember reading all the Red Sox stuff always, of course. There was a lot of good stuff in there: Kevin Paul Dupont on the Bruins, Jackie MacMullan on the Celtics, Ron Borges on the Patriots. It was a pretty darn good sports section. And Gammons, of course, the Sunday notes all through."

(Epstein felt bad after the fact he forgot to mention Leigh Montville.)

Those Sunday notes, which Gammons popularized, may be what people most associate with Boston baseball writing. The Sunday notes more closely resemble what baseball writing has become on a day-to-day basis: fewer basics about the game you already watched or followed on Twitter and more about everything else you couldn't know. It was an enterprising mind-set. "It's a whole page, devoted to one sport," *Boston Herald* columnist Steve Buckley said in a 2017 interview. "When I was a beat writer, you check into your hotel on Thursday and you spend all Thursday afternoon calling. Everyone had their own notes network."

Buckley wrote Sunday notes in his time as a beat writer as well. He was in touch with other writers

DUELING NEWSPAPERS

On December 8, 2017, the *Boston Herald* announced it was filing for bankruptcy, jeopardizing one of the great reporting races in American media—sports, or otherwise. "This was a newspaper mecca," said Michael Holley, a former columnist for *The Boston Globe* on WEEI that day, as calls about a suspension for Rob Gronkowski and trades for Giancarlo Stanton shifted to the media landscape.

Even as newspapers went through drastic change and cutbacks in the first decade of The Aughts, the *Herald* and *The Globe* held steady when it came to baseball coverage. As it was told to me in my time at the *Herald*, sports would be the last thing to go if the paper ever bowed out. Boston's heartbeat is some combination of sports and corruption scandals. (The same day the *Herald* announced bankruptcy and its pending sale to a larger newspaper chain, a former state legislator was arrested on charges of taking kickbacks, including hundreds of pounds of Dunkin Donuts coffee.)

Costs certainly were trimmed at *The Globe* and *Herald*, but Red Sox games were still staffed in a way that could only compare to one other major league city, New York.

Both newspapers in 2017 were still sending not one, but two reporters to every Red Sox road game. Consider, on the flip side, that there are some cities where only one newspaper exists, and some road games may pass without a reporter from that paper on hand. Yet the Boston papers—one broadsheet and one tabloid—were still combining for four bodies.

A combination of mutual respect and dislike amongst *The Globe* and *Herald* reporters has long come with the territory. Such competitiveness sometimes gives way to something closer to enmity. But there's also a symbiotic relationship at play: the urge to beat the other paper to a story makes for better details in both papers because reporters are driven to put out the best product. "Every edition of every newspaper has a story you won't find in the competing newspaper," *Herald* columnist Steve Buckley wrote for the paper the day following the bankruptcy news. "It might be a major scoop, or a daring editorial, or an off-the-wall take by a columnist that'll boil one reader's blood while making another reader laugh out loud. That's what the *Herald* does. It's also what *The Globe* does. It's one of the first things I learned about this business: each newspaper makes every other newspaper stronger, hungrier...better."

and people throughout the game, and the collection of anecdotes created a tapestry of national perspectives once a week. "What's your best quote of the week?" Buckley said, recalling the discussions he'd have while writing for *The News Tribune* in Tacoma, Washington. "And something wacky would happen with the Mariners: Dick Williams would juggle baseballs and wear a clown nose."

Sunday notes were all the details and color and things you had no idea you'd be interested in. They were the opportunity for a reporter to think outside the box and separate themselves from everyone else. *The Boston Globe* and *Boston Herald* both still run them as do many papers and some web-only outlets.

Gammons is the reason that type of baseball reporting exists. "I believe he was the best every day baseball writer that ever lived," said *The Boston Globe* columnist Dan Shaughnessy, whose own career was helped and influenced by Gammons, "'cause of the time that he worked in and the changes that were coming over the industry at the time and the teams he had to cover. And the readership that he had to service. I just thought it was kind of a perfect storm of all those things, and that it brought out the best in everybody, kind of culminating in '75, when I was graduating from college, and they had that team and that World Series and people were so into it, and there was so much love for the team, and it was unqualified. It wasn't the edge or the nastiness or the subculture of negativity that we have now. It was kind of very innocent and baseball centric, and perhaps that was just me thinking it was that, but that's how I saw it at the time."

Gammons, who's from Groton, Massachusetts, joined *The Globe* in 1969. In 2004 he was named the J.G. Taylor Spink Award winner, a lifetime achievement award given annually at the Hall of Fame ceremonies in Cooperstown. (Writers technically are honored at the Hall of Fame but are not inducted into it.) "And all of a sudden the ball was there, like the Mystic River Bridge, suspended out in the black of the morning" began Gammons' story from Game 6 of the 1975 World Series in *The Globe*. "When it finally crashed off the mesh attached to the left-field foul pole, one step after another the reaction unfurled: from Carlton Fisk's convulsive leap to John Kiley's booming of the 'Hallelujah Chorus' to the wearing off of the numbness to the outcry that echoed across the cold New England morning." (I am deeply sorry that the prose of this book reads nothing like that.)

The sports media landscape in every city is evolving, but it's always going to be competitive in Boston. The fight for information is a product of the hunger to consume all things Red Sox from the most rabid fanbase in the country. As long as that fire exists, so too should a large amount of media. The coverage's quality should match the fans' fervor. The enjoyment of baseball in Boston has long been enhanced for many by the excellence in writing provided over the years by its papers and other outlets. "It was a big deal for me in high school to get *The Globe*, [which] started to expand its circulation into central Massachusetts, which is where I was," Shaughnessy said. "And all of a sudden it was the Bible coming out our way."

Radio may now be the dominant format in Boston when it comes to influencing the fanbase. Two thriving stations, WEEI and 98.5 The Sports Hub, play off the papers and other outlets but also set the agenda themselves. A combination of debate, speculation, perspective, anger, and humor make the medium a funhouse, if not always the most factual funhouse. Nonetheless, the romanticism of the papers hasn't disappeared. Epstein has his breakfast table. Buckley remembers the ink on his hands after delivering the *Herald* as a kid. Baseball and nostalgia are bedfellows, particularly in Boston. Newspapers have always wrapped both in a perfect package.

[Acknowledgments]

I'm not quite sure how this book came to be. Please allow me to review my enablers.

Kevin Youkilis' willingness to write the foreword provided great encouragement for a clueless first-time author. His insights were articulate, outdone only by the brilliance of the beers he crafted and shared with me at his restaurant in California, Loma Brew.

This venture would have been near impossible were it not for those willing to lend me their time and memories. Interviews made all the difference. In alphabetical order, a huge thank you to: Wade Boggs, Steve Buckley, Billy Conigliaro, Theo Epstein, Jed Hoyer, Richard Johnson, Sam Kennedy, Bill Lee, Larry Lucchino, Fred Lynn, Lou Merloni, Joe Morgan, Jim Rice, Matt Rothenberg, Curt Schilling, Calvin Schiraldi, Dan Shaughnessy, Henri Stanley, Luis Tiant, and Tom Werner.

Jeff Fedotin, my editor at Triumph, was an incredibly patient and understanding guide. Stacey Glick of Dystel, Goderich & Bourret the same. Thanks to Josh Williams for reaching out in the first place.

My former *Boston Herald* colleagues Michael Silverman and Steve Buckley made an effort to help me, which was greatly needed and appreciated.

Pam Kenn of the Red Sox was very generous in helping to arrange some of the above interviews. Zineb Curran, Leo Foussekis, Diana Lee, Natalie Lynn, and Steve Alexander also helped connect me to some of the above.

Kevin Gregg, Kevin Doyle, Justin Long, Jon Shestakofsky (now of the Hall of Fame), Abby Murphy, and Daveson Perez have made covering the Red Sox easier for years. You too, Chris Gilligan and Kyle Montemagno.

Ian Browne has been a wonderful mentor since the day I arrived in Boston. (You too, Amy "Skipper" Browne.) Rob Bradford is annoying, but I appreciate him anyway. Alex Speier and Silverman have always looked after me. Tim Britton, Jason Mastrodonato, and Jen McCaffrey—you guys are okay. John Tomase, Chad Jennings, Nick Cafardo, Sean McAdam, Gordon Edes, Scott Lauber, Brian "Little Mac" MacPherson, Chris Mason, Steve Hewitt, Ron Chimelis, Dan Barbarisi, and Amalie Benjamin are among the other Red Sox writers past and present I count as talented influences as well as friends.

Shi Davidi and Mark Feinsand, fellow Triumph authors, were needed advisors. Thanks to Harry Weber for letting me turn the couch into an office and to all the friends who put up with me while writing.

Art Martone, Kevin Miller, and Princell Hair at NBC Sports Boston were generous in both hiring me and helping me find time to write. Dan Quinn, Bill Messina, Glenn Gleason, Dave Sherrym, and Sam Gaddes were among those who made life easier at Fenway every day and night in 2017.

A career is cumulative. I owe a ton to the editors of my past: Sean Lishansky, Mark Macyk, Andrew Egan, Matt Zeidel, Matt Chayes, Al Vieira, the late Charlie Jaworski, Jon Star, Hank Winnicki, the great Bill Hill, Kristen Zimmerman, Ed Kubosiak, Reid Laymance, Nick Mathews, Mark Murphy, and Sean Leahy.

Donovan Hohn believed in my writing and in turn gave me something to believe in.

Anne, Sharon, Marvin, and Helen, I miss you.

My father, Steve, brought me to Fenway for the first time nearly two decades ago. Tim Wakefield pitched. We sat in center field. To Steve, to Grandma Mary, and to my mother, Linda, thank you and I love you.

[Bibliography]

Books

Boyd, Dennis; Shalin, Mike. *They Call Me Oil Can: Baseball, Drugs, and Life on the Edge.* Triumph Books (2012).

Browne, Ian. *Dice-K: The First Season of the Red Sox $100 Million Man.* Lyons Press (2008).

Browne, Ian. *Idiots Revisited.* Tilbury House Publishers (2014).

Castiglione, Joe; Lyons, Douglas B. *Can You Believe It? 30 Years of Insider Stories with the Boston Red Sox*. Triumph Books (2012).

Halberstam, David. *Summer of '49.* William Morrow & Company (1991).

Lee, Bill; Lally, Richard. *The Wrong Stuff.* Three Rivers Press (2007).

Madden, Bill. *Steinbrenner: The Last Lion of Baseball.* HarperCollins (2010).

Montville, Leigh. *Ted Williams: The Biography of an American Hero.* Random House (2004).

Ortiz, David; Holley, Michael. *Papi: My Story.* Houghton Mifflin Harcourt (2017).

Francona, Terry; Shaughnessy, Dan. *Francona*. Houghton Mifflin Harcourt (2013).

Shaughnessy, Dan. *The Curse of the Bambino.* Dutton (1990).

Martinez, Pedro; Silverman, Michael. *Pedro.* Houghton Mifflin Harcourt (2015).

Stoutt, Glenn; Johnson, Richard A. *Red Sox Century: The Definitive History of Baseball's Most Storied Franchise* (2000).

Williams, Ted; Underwood, John. *My Turn at Bat: The Story of My Life.* Pocket Books (1970).

Yastrzemski, Carl; Eskenazi, Gerald. *Yaz: Baseball, the Wall, and Me.* Warner Books (1990).

Websites

asapsports.com
baseballhall.org
baseball-reference.com
deadspin.com
ESPN.com
FOXSports.com
MassLive.com
MLB.com
NBCSportsBoston.com
newspapers.com
sabr.org/bioproject
WEEI.com

Periodicals and Wire Services

Boston Herald
Hartford Courant
Sports Illustrated
The Boston Globe
Burlington Free Press
The New York Times
The Fitchburg Sentinel
The Daily Item
Newspaper Enterprise Association
The Associated Press

Television

The Tonight Show Starring Jimmy Fallon